The Aşvan area seen from north of the River Murat (1972).

THE AŞVAN SITES SERIES
Keban Rescue Excavations, Eastern Anatolia.

British Institute of Archaeology at Ankara

Monograph No. 18

THE AŞVAN SITES 3
KEBAN RESCUE EXCAVATIONS, EASTERN ANATOLIA
DOĞU ANADOLU, KEBAN KURTARMA KAZILARI

THE EARLY BRONZE AGE
ERKEN BRONZ ÇAĞI

Antonio G. Sagona

with the assistance of
Claudia Sagona

Published by

THE BRITISH INSTITUTE OF ARCHAEOLOGY AT ANKARA

1994

British Institute of Archaeology at Ankara,
c/o British Academy, 20-21 Cornwall Terrace,
London NW1 4QP

This book is obtainable from Oxbow Books, Park End Place, Oxford OX1 1HN

ISBN 1 898249 02 4
ISSN 0969-9007

© British Institute of Archaeology at Ankara and the author, 1994

Photographs by David French

Typeset and printed by Rekmay, Ankara, Turkey
Tel : 90-312 231 09 26
Fax : 90-312 231 30 45

Contents

List of Figures

List of Plates

List of Tables

Pl. 1   Aşvan Kale seen from the north (1968).

Pl. 2   The Taşkun Mevkii and Taşkun Kale area seen from the south (1970). Taşkun Mevkii
is the low mound at the centre left, Taşkun Kale the high mound at the centre.

Preface

Our understanding of human settlement in the Turkish Euphrates basin has been illuminated rapidly over the past two decades due to a series of rescue excavations at archaeological sites threatened with destruction by the waters of several dam lakes. The Aşvan sites, excavated by the British Institute of Archaeology at Ankara between 1968 and 1974, under the overall directorship of David French, belong to the first round of operations which salvaged material situated within the reservoir area of the Keban dam (Figs 1 and 2).[1] More recent years have seen the completion of investigations at sites further downstream that fall within the areas of the Karakaya dam and the larger Atatürk dam, which are part of the continuing multipurpose and integrated development project for Southeastern Anatolia, the Güneydoğu Anadolu Projesi (GAP).[2]

Despite the constraints imposed by the pressures of rescue archaeology, the large scale salvage of clusters of contiguous sites has provided a detailed record of past human activity in the Turkish Euphrates region. This is the third volume of final reports on the British excavations at the Aşvan sites; the previous two, by Stephen Mitchell and Anthony McNicoll, deal with the Classical and Medieval remains at Aşvan Kale and Taşkun Kale.[3]

My examination of the Aşvan material came almost a decade after excavations were completed. In 1982, whilst completing my doctoral research on the Early Trans-Caucasian culture, both David French, Director of the British Institute of Archaeology at Ankara, and the late Alan Hall, then Honorary Secretary of the Institute, kindly invited me to work on the Early Bronze Age material from the Aşvan sites. A major study season ensued at Elazığ in the winter of 1983/84 (November-February), followed by a shorter season in 1986. My thanks are due to many, and in particular: David French and the late Alan Hall for their encouragement and support; the Turkish authorities for permission to study the Aşvan material held in Elazığ museum; Ferhan Memişoğlu, then director of Elazığ museum, and her staff for making my wife and me comfortable during our visits to the museum; Guillermo Algaze for providing me with the catalogue and other sections of the Kurban Höyük excavation report before its publication; Françoise Summers and the staff at Rekmay for their care and patience in formatting my manuscript into its final form; and finally, my wife, Claudia, for sharing the burden of drawing and inking the illustrations, and for her assistance in preparing the figures. I would like to express my gratitude to the following bodies for their financial assistance which helped to make this publication possible: British Institute of Archaeology at Ankara, Research Grant 1983/84; University of Melbourne, Faculty of Arts, Special Research Fund 1986; Australian Academy of Humanities, Travel Grant 1986/87.

NOTES
1. Whallon 1979.
2. Algaze 1989b; Özdoğan 1977; Serdaroğlu 1977.
3. Mitchell 1980; McNicoll 1983.

A.G. Sagona
Melbourne, 1990.

The photographic archive for Taşkun Kale and Taşkun Mevkii has suffered serious loss at some time in the years between the publication of Taşkun Kale and the present. Despite all efforts the missing negatives have not been found. It is regretable, therefore, that this report cannot be illustrated at the desired level.

D.H. French
Ankara, 16.12.1993.

Abbreviations

Abbreviations Used in Bibliography

Abbreviations follow the guidelines set out in *American Journal of Archaeology* 90 (1986): 384-394.

Additional Abbreviations

BIAA   British Institute of Archaeology at Ankara.
Keban 1   Acaroğlu, I (ed.) 1970. 1968 Yaz Çalışmaları. 1968 Summer Work. Ankara (Keban Project Publications Series 1, No. 1).
Keban 2   Pekman, S. (ed.) 1971. Keban Projesi 1969 Çalışmaları. Keban Project 1969 Activities. Ankara (Keban Project Publications Series 1, No. 2).
Keban 3   Pekman, S. (ed.) 1972. Keban Projesi 1970 Çalışmaları. Keban Project 1970 Activities. Ankara (Keban Project Publications Series 1, No. 3).
Keban 4   Pekman, S. (ed.) 1974. Keban Projesi 1971 Çalışmaları. Keban Project 1971 Activities. Ankara (Keban Project Publications Series 1, No. 4).
Keban 5   Pekman, S. (ed.) 1976. Keban Projesi 1972 Çalışmaları. Keban Project 1972 Activities. Ankara (Keban Project Publications Series 1, No. 5).
Keban 6   Pekman, S. (ed.) 1979. Keban Projesi 1973 Çalışmaları. Keban Project 1973 Activities. Ankara (Keban Project Publications Series 1, No. 6).
Keban 7   Pekman, S. (ed.) 1982. Keban Projesi 1974-75 Çalışmaları. Keban Project 1974-75 Activities. Ankara (Keban Project Publications Series 1, No. 7).
LAAA   Liverpool Annals of Archaeology and Anthropology.
METU   Middle East Technical University.
ODTÜ   Orta Doğu Teknik Üniversitesi.
TAD   Türk Arkeoloji Dergisi.

Bibliography

ABESADZE, Ts.N.
1969   *Proizvodstvo Metalla v Zakavkaz e V-III Tysiacheletii do n.e.* Tbilisi (Georgian with a Russian summary).

AKSÖY, B. and DIAMANT, S.
1973   Çayboyu 1970-71. In French, D.H. et al., Aşvan 1968-1972: An Interim Report, *AnatSt* 23: 97-108.

ALESSIO, M. et al
1983   C14 Dating of Arslantepe. In Frangipane, M. and Palmieri, A. (eds), Perspectives on Protourbanization in Eastern Anatolia: Arslantepe (Malatya). An Interim Report on 1975-1983 Campaigns. *Origini* 12: 575-80.

ALGAZE, G.
1986   Kurban Höyük and the Late Chalcolithic Period in the Northwest Mesopotamian Periphery: A Preliminary Assessment. In Finkbeiner, U. and Rollig, W. (eds), *Gamdat Nasr: Period or Regional Style?*: 274-315. Wiesbaden.
1989a   The Uruk Expansion: Cross-cultural Exchange in Early Mesopotamian Civilization. *Current Anthropology* 30: 571-591.
1989b   A New Frontier. First Results of the Tigris-Euphrates Archaeological Reconnaissance Project, 1988. *JNES* 48: 241-81.

ALGAZE, G. (ed.)
1990   *Town and Country in Southeastern Anatolia, Vol. II: The Stratigraphic Sequence at Kurban Höyük.* Chicago (OIP 110).

AMIET, P.
1963   La glyptique syrienne archaique. *Syria* 40: 57-83.

ARSEBÜK, G.
1979   Altınova'da (Elazığ) Koyu Yüzlü Açkili ve Karaz Türü Çanak Çömlek Arasındaki İlişkiler. *8. Türk Tarih Kongresi, Ankara 11-15 Ekim 1976. Kongreye sunulan Bildiriler I*: 81-92. Ankara.

BEHM-BLANCKE, M.R.
1987   Die Grabungen auf dem Hassek Höyük, 1978-1979. Hassek Höyük Kazıları, 1978-1979. In Göker, U. (ed.), *Aşağı Fırat Projesi 1978-1979 Çalışmaları. Lower Euphrates Project 1978-1979 Activities*: 131-148. Ankara.
1988   Periphere Ninive 5 - Keramik am Oberen Euphrat. *Mitteilungen der Deutschen Orientgesellschaft zu Berlin* 120: 159-72.

BEHM-BLANCKE, M.R. et al.
1981   Hassek Höyük. Vorläufiger Bericht über die Ausgrabungen der Jahre 1978-1980. *IstMitt* 31: 5-93.
1984   Hassek Höyük. Vorläufiger Bericht über die Ausgrabungen in der Jahren 1981-1983. *IstMitt* 34: 31-149.

BİLGİ, Ö.
1985   1984 Dönemi Malatya-Köskerbaba Höyük Kurtarma Kazıları. *7. Kazı Sonuçları Toplantısı*: 143-149. Ankara.

BRAIDWOOD, R.J. and BRAIDWOOD, L.S.
1960   Excavations in the Plain of Antioch I, the Earlier Assemblages phases A-J. Chicago (OIP 61).

BRANDT, R.W.
1978   The Chalcolithic Pottery (Chapter 3). The Other Chalcolithic finds (Chapter 4). In van Loon, M.N. (ed.), *Korucutepe. Final Report on the Excavations of the Universities of Chicago, California (Los Angeles) and Amsterdam in the Keban Reservoir, Eastern Anatolia 1968-1970, Vol. 2*: 57-60 (Chap. 3); 61-63 (Chap. 4). Amsterdam.

BRICE, W.C.
1966   *South-West Asia.* London (Systematic Regional Geographies 8).

BUCHANAN, B.
1966   *Catalogue of Ancient Near Eastern Seals in the Ashmolean Museum, Vol. I. Cylinder Seals.* Oxford.

BURNEY, C.A.
1958   Eastern Anatolia in the Chalcolithic and Early Bronze Age. *AnatSt* 8: 157-209.
1980   Aspects of the Excavations in the Altınova, Elazığ. *AnatSt* 30: 157-167.

BURNEY, C.A. and LANG, D.M.
1971 *The Peoples of the Hills: Ancient Ararat and Caucasus*. London.

CANEVA, I.
1973 Scavi nell'Area Sub-occidentale di Arslantepe: Note Sull'industria Litica di Arslantepe. *Origini* 7: 183-215.

CRIBB, R.
1991 *Nomads in Archaeology*. Cambridge.

DARGA, M.
1982 Şemsiyetepe Kazıları 1981 Yılı Çalışmaları. *4. Kazı Sonuçları Toplantısı*: 55-62. Ankara.
1983 Şemsiyetepe Kurtarma Kazıları 1982 Yılı Çalışmaları. *5. Kazı Sonuçları Toplantısı*: 91-96. Ankara
1985 Şemsiyetepe 1984 Yılı Kazı Çalışmaları. *7. Kazı Sonuçları Toplantısı*: 119-128. Ankara.

DEWDNEY, J.C.
1971 *Turkey*. London.

DURU, R.
1979 *Keban Projesi Değirmentepe Kazısı 1973. Keban Project Değirmentepe Excavations 1973*: 1-55 (Turkish), 59-115 (English). Ankara (METU Keban Project Publications, Series 3, No. 2).

DZHAVAKHISHVILI, A.I.
1973 *Stroitel'noe delo i Arkhitektura Poselenii Iuzhnogo Kavkaza V-III Tysiacheletii do n.e.* Tbilisi.

DZHAVAKHISHVILI, A.I. and GLONTI, L.I.
1962 *Urbnisi I: Arkheologicheskie Raskopi Provedennye v 1954-1961 gg. na Selishche KvatskhelEB I (Tvlenia-Kokhi)*. Tbilisi. (Georgian with a Russian summary).

ERTEM, H.
1974 Han İbrahim Şah Kazısı, 1971. Han İbrahim Şah Excavations, 1971. *Keban* 4: 59-63 (Turkish), 65-69 (English).

ESİN, U.
1970 Tepecik Kazısı 1968 Yılı Ön Raporu. Tepecik Excavation 1968 Campaign, Preliminary Report. *Keban* 1: 147-158 (Turkish), 159-172 (English).
1972 Tepecik Kazısı, 1970. Tepecik Excavations, 1970. *Keban* 3: 139-147 (Turkish), 149-158 (English).
1973 İstanbul Üniversitesi Prehistorya Kürüsü Tepecik Kazıları (Elazığ). *TAD* 20 no. 2: 39-62.
1976a Tepecik Kazısı, 1972. Tepecik Excavations, 1972. *Keban* 5: 101-108 (Turkish), 109-17 (English).
1976b Tülintepe Kazısı, 1972. Tülintepe Excavations, 1972. *Keban* 5: 119-33 (Turkish), 147-63 (English).
1982a Die Kulturellen Beziehungen Zwichen Östanatolien und Mesopotamien sowie Syrien Anhard Einiger Grabungs und Oberflaedienfunde aus dem Oberen Euphrattal im 4 Ht. v. Chr. In Nissen, H.J. and Renger, J. (eds), *Mesopotamien und seine Nachbarn. XXV Rencontre Assyriologique Internationale, Berlin, 1978, vol. 1*: 13-21. Berlin.
1982b Tepecik Kazısı, 1974. Tepecik Excavations, 1974. *Keban* 7: 71-93 (Turkish), 95-133 (English).
1987 Değirmentepe, 1986. *AnatSt* 37: 184-85.

ESIN, U. et al.
1979 Tepecik Kazısı, 1973. Tepecik Excavations, 1973. *Keban* 6: 79-96 (Turkish), 97-114 (English and German).

ESIN, U. and ARSEBÜK, G.
1982 Tülintepe Kazısı, 1974. Tülintepe Excavations, 1974. *Keban* 7: 119-25 (Turkish), 127-33 (English).

FRANGIPANE, M.
1985 Early Developments of Metallurgy in the Near East. In Liverani, M., Palmieri, A. and Peroni, A. (eds), *Studi di Paletnologia in Onore di Salvatore M. Puglisi*: 215-228. Rome.

FRANGIPANE, M. and PALMIERI, A.
1983a A Protourban Centre of the Late Uruk Period. In Frangipane, M. and Palmieri, A. (eds), Perspectives on Proto-urbanization in Eastern Anatolia: Arslantepe (Malatya). An Interim Report on 1975-1983 Campaigns. *Origini* 12: 287-448.
1983b Cultural Developments at Arslantepe at the Beginning of the Third Millennium: The Settlements of Period VIB. In Frangipane, M. and Palmieri, A. (eds), Perspectives on Protourbanization in Eastern Anatolia: Arslantepe (Malatya). An Interim Report on 1975-1983 Campaigns. *Origini* 12: 523-74.
1987 Urbanization in Perimesopotamian

Areas. The Case of Eastern Anatolia. In Manzanilla, L. (ed.), *Studies in the Neolithic and Urban Revolutions: The V. Gordon Childe Colloquium, Mexico, 1986*: 295-318. Oxford (BAR International Series 349).

FRANKFORT, H.
1939 *Cylinder Seals: A Documentary Essay on the Art and Religion of the Ancient Near East.* London.

FRENCH, D.H.
1971 Aşvan Kazısı, 1969. Aşvan Excavations, 1969. *Keban* 2: 31-33 (Turkish), 35-37 (English).
1973 Aşvan 1968-72: The Excavations. In French, D.H. et al. Aşvan 1968-1972: An Interim Report. *AnatSt* 23: 73-91

FRENCH, D.H. et al.
1972 Aşvan Kazıları, 1970. Aşvan Excavations, 1970. *Keban* 3: 45-53 (Turkish), 55-62 (English).
1974 Aşvan Kazıları, 1971. Aşvan Excavations, 1971. *Keban* 4: 25-41 (Turkish), 43-58 (English).
1979 Aşvan Kazıları, 1973. Aşvan Excavations, 1973. *Keban* 6: 1-5 (Turkish), 7-11 (English).

FRENCH, D.H. and HELMS, S.
1973 Aşvan Kale: The Third Millennium Pottery. In French, D.H. et al. Aşvan Kale 1968-1972: An Interim Report. *AnatSt* 23: 153-158.

FUKAI, S. et al.
1974 *Telul Eth-Thalathat. The Excavation of Tell V, the Fourth Season (1965), vol. 3* Tokyo (The Institute of Oriental Culture, University of Tokyo).

HAUPTMANN, H.
1972 Norşun Tepe Kazıları, 1970. Die Grabungen auf dem Norşun-Tepe, 1970. *Keban* 3: 87-101 (Turkish), 103-17 (German).
1974 Norşun Tepe Kazıları, 1971. Die Grabungen auf dem Norşun-Tepe, 1971. *Keban* 4: 71-82 (Turkish), 87-99 (German).
1979 Norşuntepe Kazıları, 1973. Die Grabungen auf dem Norşuntepe, 1973. *Keban* 6: 43-60 (Turkish), 61-78 (German).
1982 Norşuntepe Kazıları, 1974. Die Grabungen auf dem Norşuntepe, 1974.

Keban 7: 13-40 (Turkish), 41-70 (German).
1983 Lidar Höyük, 1982. *AnatSt* 33: 254-56.
1984 Lidar Höyük, 1983. *AnatSt* 34: 226-228.
1985 Lidar Höyük, 1984. *AnatSt* 35: 203-205.

HAUPTMANN, H. et al.
1976a Körtepe Kazıları, 1972. Die Ausgrabungen auf dem Körtepe, 1972. *Keban* 5: 25-31 (Turkish), 33-39 (German).
1976b Norşun Tepe Kazıları, 1972. Die Grabungen auf dem Norşun-Tepe, 1972. *Keban* 5: 41-69 (Turkish), 71-100 (German).

HELMS, S.
1971 Taşkun Mevkii. *AnatSt* 21: 8-10.
1972 Taşkun Mevkii. *AnatSt* 22: 15-17.
1973 Taşkun Mevkii 1970-71. In French, D.H. et al., Aşvan 1968-1972: An Interim Report. *AnatSt* 23: 109-120.

HILLMAN, G.
1973 Agricultural Resources and Settlement in the Aşvan Region. In French, D.H. et al., Aşvan 1968-1972: An Interim Report. *AnatSt* 23: 217-224.

HOH, M.R.
1981 Die Keramik von Hassek Höyük. In Behm-Blancke, M.R. (ed.), Hassek Höyük. *IstMitt* 31: 31-82.
1984 Die Keramik von Hassek Höyük. In Behm-Blancke, M.R. (ed.), Hassek Höyük. *IstMitt* 34: 66-91.

HUNTINGTON, E.
1902 Through the Great Canon of the Euphrates River. *The Geographical Journal* 20: 175-200.

KELLY-BUCCELLATI, M.
1978 The Early Bronze Age pottery. Descriptive and comparative analysis. In van Loon, M.N. (ed.), *Korucutepe. Final Report on the Excavations of the Universities of Chicago, California (Los Angeles) and Amsterdam in the Keban Reservoir, Eastern Anatolia 1968-1970, Vol. 2*: 67-88. Amsterdam.

KIKVIDZE, Ia. A.
1972 *Rannebronzovoe Poselenie Khizanaantgora.* Tbilisi (Georgian with Russian summary).

KoŞAY, H.Z.
1976a Yeniköy Höyüğü Kazısı 1972. Yeniköy
       Mound Excavations, 1972. *Keban 5:*
       175-183 (Turkish), 185-193 (English).
1976b *Keban Projesi, Pulur Kazısı 1968-70.*
       Keban Project, Pulur Excavations
       1968-70: 1-109 (Turkish), 113-230
       (English). Ankara (METU Keban
       Project Publications, Series 3, No. 1).

KUSHNAREVA, K. Kh.
1970   *Drevnie Kul'tury Iuzhnogo-Kavkaza (V-*
       III Tysiacheletii do n.e.). Leningrad
       (Russian with English summary).

McNICOLL, A.W.
1983   *Taşkun Kale; Keban Rescue*
       Excavations, Eastern Anatolia. Oxford
       (BIAA Monograph 6, BAR International
       Series 168).

McNICOLL, A.W. and HELMS, S.
1974   Taşkun Kale and Taşkun Mevkii.
       AnatSt 24: 6-9.

MALLOWAN, M.E.L.
1936   The Excavations at Tell Chagar Bazar
       and an Archaeological Survey of the
       Habur. *Iraq* 3: 1-59.
1937   The Excavations at Tell Chagar Bazar
       and an Archaeological Survey of the
       Khabur Region. *Iraq* 4: 91-154.
1964   Ninevite 5. In Bittel, K. et al. (eds),
       Vorderasiatische Archaölogie Studien
       und Aufsätze Anton Moortgat zum 65.
       Geburtstag gewidmet: 142-54. Berlin.

MARFOE, L.
1987   Cedar Forest to Silver Mountain: Social
       Change and the Development of Long
       Distance Trade in Early Near Eastern
       Societies. In Rowlands, M., Larsen, M.
       and Kristiansen, K. (eds), *Centre and*
       Periphery in the Ancient World: 25-35.
       Cambridge.

MARFOE, L. et al.
1986   The Chicago Euphrates Archaeological
       Project 1980-1984: An Interim Report.
       Anatolica 13: 37-148.

MATTHIAE, P.
1977   *Ebla. An Empire Rediscovered.* London.

MAXWELL-HYSLOP, K.R.
1971   *Western Asiatic Jewellery c.3000-612*
       B.C. London.

MELLINK, M.
1962   The Prehistory of Syro-Cilicia.
       Bibliotheca Orientalis 19: 219-26.

MITCHELL, S.
1980   *Aşvan Kale; Keban Rescue*
       Excavations, Eastern Anatolia. I. The
       Hellenistic, Roman and Islamic Sites.
       Oxford (BIAA Monograph 1, BAR
       International Series 80).

MUNCHAEV, R.M.
1975   *Kavkaz na Zare Bronzovogo Veka.*
       Moscow (Russian).

NAVAL INTELLIGENCE DIVISION
1942   *Geographical Handbooks, Turkey.*
       London.

ORDZHONIKIDZE, A.E.
1981   *Samtskhe-Dzhavakheti v Epokhu Rannei*
       Bronzy. Tbilisi (Avtoreferat).

ÖZDOĞAN, M.
1977   *Lower Euphrates Basin 1977 Survey.*
       Istanbul (METU Lower Euphrates
       Project Publications, Series, 1 No. 2).

PALMIERI, A.
1967   Insediamento del Bronzo Antico a
       Gelinciktepe (Malatya). *Origini* 1: 117-
       93.
1968   Scavi a Gelinciktepe. *OA* 7: 133-47.
1969   Recenti Dati sulla Stratigrafia di
       Arslantepe. *Origini* 3: 7-66.
1973   Scavi nell'Area Sud-Occidentale di
       Arslantepe: Ritrovamento di una
       Struttura Templare dell'Antica Età del
       Bronzo. *Origini* 7: 55-178, 225-228.
1981   Excavations at Arslantepe (Malatya).
       AnatSt 31: 101-119.
1985a Arslantepe, 1984. *AnatSt* 35: 181-82.
1985b Eastern Anatolia and Early
       Mesopotamian Urbanization: Remarks
       on Changing Relations. In Liverani, M.,
       Palmieri, A. and Peroni, R. (eds), *Studi*
       di Paletnologia in Onore di S.M.
       Puglisi: 191-214. Rome.

PORADA, E. and BUCHANAN, B.
1948   *Corpus of Ancient Near Eastern Seals*
       in North American Collections: The
       Collection of the Pierpont Morgan
       Library. Washington.

ROWTON, M.B.
1967   The Woodlands of Ancient Western
       Asia. *JNES* 26: 261-77.

SAGONA, A.G.
1984 *The Caucasian Region in the Early Bronze Age.* Oxford (BAR International Series 214).
1993 Settlement and Society in Late Prehistoric Trans-Caucasus. In Frangipane, M., Hauptmann, H., Liverani, M., Matthiae, P., and Mellink, M. (eds), *Between the Rivers and over the Mountains. Archaeologica Anatolica et Mesopotamica. Alba Pamieri Dedicata*: 453-73. Rome.

SAGONA, A.G., PEMBERTON, E. and McPHEE, I.
1992 Excavations at Büyüktepe Höyük, 1991: Second Preliminary Report. *AnatSt* 42: 29-46.

SERDAROĞLU, U.
1977 *Aşağı Fırat Havzasında Araştırmalar 1975. Surveys in the Lower Euphrates Basin*: 1-48 (Turkish), 49-97 (English). Ankara (METU Lower Euphrates Project Publications, Series 1 No. 1).

SPEISER, E.A.
1933 The Pottery of Tell Billa. *The Museum Journal* 23: 249-308.

SÜRENHAGEN, D.
1986 The Dry-Farming Belt: The Uruk Period and Subsequent Developments. In Weiss, H. (ed.), *The Origins of Cities in Dry-Farming Syria and Mesopotamia in the Third Millennium B.C.*: 7-43. Guilford.

THOMPSON, R.C. and HAMILTON, B.A.
1932 The British Museum Excavations on the Temple of Ishtar at Nineveh, 1930-31. *LAAA* 19: 55-116

THOMPSON, R.C. and MALLOWAN, M.E.L.
1933 The British Museum Excavations at Nineveh, 1931-32. *LAAA* 20: 71-186.

UZUNOĞLU, E.
1985 İmamoğlu Kazıları 1984 Yılı Çalışmaları. 7. *Kazı Sonuçları Toplantısı*: 181-199. Ankara.

VAN LOON, M.N.
1978 Architecture and Stratigraphy. In van Loon, M.N. (ed.), *Korucutepe. Final Report on the Excavations of the Universities of Chicago, California (Los Angeles) and Amsterdam in the Keban Reservoir, Eastern Anatolia, 1968-1970, Vol. 2*: 3-45. Amsterdam.

VON LUSCHAN, F.
1943 *Die Kleinifunde von Sendschirli V.* Berlin (Mitteilungen aus den Orientalischen Sammlungen, vol. 15).

WAGSTAFF, M.
1973 Physical Geography and Settlements. In French, D.H. et al., Aşvan 1968-1972: An Interim Report. *AnatSt* 23: 197-215.

WHALLON, R.
1979 *An Archaeological Survey of the Keban Reservoir Area of East-Central Turkey.* Ann Arbor (Memoirs of the Museum of Anthropology, University of Michigan, no. 11).

WHALLON, R. and KANTMAN, S.
1969 Early Bronze Age Development in the Keban Reservoir, East-Central Turkey. *Current Anthropology* 10: 128-133.

WHALLON, R. and WRIGHT, H.T.
1970 1968 Yılı Fatmalı-Kalecik Kazısı ön Raporu; 1968 Fatmalı-Kalecik Excavations Preliminary Report. *Keban* 1: 61-65 (Turkish), 67-71 (English).

WILLCOX, G.
1974 A History of Deforestation in East Anatolia. *AnatSt* 24: 117-33.

WOOLLEY, C.L.
1914 Hittite Burial Customs. *LAAA* 6: 87-98.

WOOLLEY, C.L. and BARNETT, R.D.
1952 *Carchemish. Report on the Excavations at Jerablus on Behalf of the British Museum. Part III. The Excavations in the Inner Town.* London.

YENER, A.
1984 *Third Millennium B.C. Interregional Exchange in Southwest Asia with Special Reference to the Keban Region of Turkey.* Ph.D. 1980, Columbia University (UMI). Ann Arbor.

CHAPTER 1

Introduction

The Aşvan region constitutes an enclosed basin of the Lower Murat valley formed as the river cut a deep course between the Munzur Mountains to the north and the hilly terrain to the south. Structurally, the area is the northern extension of the Anti-Taurus ranges, and comprises the western fringe of the eastern Anatolian highlands (Fig. 1). Human settlement within the Aşvan district, situated at an altitude of 720m, is concentrated on a crescent of land that follows the Kuru Çay, a tributary of the Murat which enters it by the south bank (Figs 2 and 3). Aşvan Kale, situated in a delta within a bend of the Murat, is the largest site in the area. Further upland in undulating terrain, about 4km to the south-east along the Kuru Çay, is Taşkun Kale, and 1km beyond, adjacent to a spring, lies Taşkun Mevkii. Eastwards of Aşvan, some 15km downstream, the Euphrates (or Fırat) and Murat rivers meet above the great gorge of Keban, now the site of the hydroelectric dam. The northern boundary of the Aşvan region is defined by the Murat river, the main tributary of the Euphrates.

Although spurs of the fringing hills prevented an unbroken view of the surrounding district from any one archaeological site, communication in the Aşvan neighbourhood was relatively easy, though the topography restricted direct access to certain surrounding regions. A route through the mountains which linked Elazığ, to the southeast, with Çemişgezek, on the northern side of the Murat, passed through Arslanbey Hanı. From there one track followed the Kuru Çay and led directly to Aşvan Kale, while another skirted the western hills and crossed the Murat near Ahurik. Travel in an east-west direction following the banks of the Murat has been described as difficult.[1] Likewise the fast current of the Murat itself rendered it navigable only downstream.[2] There is a strong likelihood, of course, that in antiquity the timber industry utilized major water courses such as the Murat for the transportation of logs.[3]

Before the Aşvan district was inundated, the landscape was likened more to the Central Anatolian plateau than to the highlands further east.[4] The climate, too, although extreme in winter, with temperatures often below freezing, is not as harsh as in some regions further east. According to Wagstaff, the modern physiography of the Aşvan district comprised five units: Valley of the Murat, Upper Flood Plain, Village Plain,

Fringing Hills and Undulating Upland Basin.[5] In terms of land usage, Aşvan Kale was situated in the most fertile section, at the interface between the Upper Flood Plain (the delta) and the Village Plain. In recent times, the village of Aşvan was almost entirely surrounded by irrigated gardens and field crops, while Taşkun Kale and Taşkun Mevkii, founded in the middle section of the Upland Basin, were in areas most suited for grazing (T.K.) and dry-land field crops (T.M.).[6] Past climatic and environmental conditions in the region are difficult to determine, owing to the poor preservation of pollen. But a study of charcoal samples collected at the Aşvan sites has indicated that the region was once surrounded by forest, in stark contrast to today's relatively austere and barren landscape.[7] While the results of Wagstaff's study pertain specifically to timbers utilised for fuel and building, certain tentative inferences can be put forward on the composition of the woodlands. It seems that in the Chalcolithic period and Early Bronze Age the forest was predominantly oak (*Quercus*). This agrees with the analyses of a series of wide-ranging pollen cores that have defined a broad Kurdo-Zagrosian zone, which encompasses the Upper Euphrates basin. The range of temperate species preserved in the Aşvan charcoal sample suggests a milder palaeo-climate for the district. If we are to believe the evidence of fluvial downcutting, however, the distribution of precipitation was apparently uneven, which, in turn, would have promoted changes in the ecosystem and land use.[8] River terraces and aggradation deposits indicate that the geomorphology was also different.[9] It is clear that both the Murat and Kuru Çay have substantially altered their courses over the millennia, at times undermining the sites closest to them. Moreover the considerable sedimentation in the Upper Flood Plain suggests large scale erosion in the higher areas caused by deforestation.

Although not as extensive as the fertile Altınova near Elazığ, preliminary analysis of environmental data from the Aşvan district suggests that it did hold attractions for the ancients: a plentiful supply of fresh water and acquatic resources — in addition to the Kuru Çay, the district is dotted with springs which issue from beneath the valley floor; agricultural prospects of a fertile depression; extensive pasturages in the surrounding hills then covered with a thicker layer of topsoil; and tracts of timber beyond. It would be otiose to proceed any further with details on the physical setting of the Aşvan region itself, as these have been already dealt with in specialised preliminary reports in *Anatolian Studies* vol. 23, 1973. So too for historical geography, which in any case falls well outside the limits of this report.[10] Given the wide-ranging connections that the Early Bronze Age cultures of Aşvan had with surrounding regions, however, it would be well to place Aşvan in the broader geographical context of eastern Anatolia.[11]

Topographically east Anatolia is very complex and rugged, with mountain ranges and plateaux rising some 2,000m above sea level. The trend line of the masses which constitute the highlands is pronouncedly east-west, as are the main communication routes which they control. Natural highways in this region follow the deep valleys and enclosed basins (or *ovalar*), themselves situated at high altitudes ranging from 700m in the East-Central part of the country to 1500m in the far eastern quarters near Trans-Caucasus.

The southern half of eastern Anatolia comprises a series of ranges east of the Euphrates which are essentially a continuation of the Anti-Taurus system. Basins around and between Malatya and Elazığ effectively breach the Anti-Taurus, separating the main chains to the west from the less structurally consistent mountains east of the river's bend. Both the Euphrates and the Murat flow into these basins, strategically positioned within the communications network of eastern Anatolia. From the plain of Malatya, several routes afford access to Sivas, Kayseri and Maraş, regions beyond its western flank. A southern passage from Maraş connects up with the great route that leads to the Amuq. Crossing the Euphrates east of Malatya leads to the Murat valley above Elazığ, which is in effect the lower end of one of two main routes that traverse the eastern highlands; the other runs along the southern foothills of the Pontic ranges to the north. The Murat rises eastwards through a steep-sided valley widening only at the plains of Palu and Genç till it reaches the broad Muş watershed. At this point, the Upper Murat begins to drain undulating lava plateaux, the characteristic land form around Bingöl and Kars, and over the modern frontier, in Armenia. Travelling across the expanses of lava terrain is not arduous. Following the meandering northward course of the Upper Murat leads one to Karaköse, and from there to the north-eastern regions and beyond, to Trans-Caucasus. Alternatively, skirting the prominent volcanic cones that punctuate the plateaux along the south-eastern side of the Muş

plain brings one to the southern shore of Lake Van, whence the way is open to the Urmia basin through the Kotur gap.

The east Anatolian highlands are sharply defined along the northern boundary by the formidable Pontic ranges rising in excess of 3500m above the south eastern Black Sea coast which it straddles. Access to the littoral region is afforded by two routes — the historic one through the Harsit valley to Trabzon, and the more difficult passage along the lower Çoruh. Between the Pontic ranges (comprising the Gümüşhane and Rize *dağları*) and those further south (the Kesis and Cimen-Kop *dağları*) is the sharply incised and narrow Kelkit-Çoruh trough, the northern counterpart of the Murat Valley. In terms of çommunication the trough effectively links Sivas to Doğubayazıt, following a fairly regular course through Suşehri, the elongated Bayburt plain, and then to Erzurum, on the edge of the lava plateaux. Near Erzurum is the watershed of the Kara Su, the northern extension of the Euphrates, which follows a tortuous course through mountain defiles to Erzincan.

South of the Anti-Taurus arc the terrain is substantially different. There the landscape is dominated by a broad lava plateau sometimes named after Karacalı Dağ, an extinct volcano situated in its centre. Communication to the Malatya region, north of the ranges, is limited to a few passes along the Euphrates valley which traverses the north-west sector of the plateau. Lands further south, however, in particular the Harran basin, the Balikh valley and the north Syrian plain are easily reached through a number of corridors such as the İncesu valley. It appears that in antiquity the human occupation of the Karacalı plateau was restricted primarily to the wide alluvial depressions, with minor valleys and river terraces absorbing the spill over from the main centres of settlement. The steppe regions above the valley floors were presumably utilized as pasture-lands, as they are today.

Ceramic Classification

A total of 8 different wares attributable to the Early Bronze Age period have been identified at the three Aşvan sites (Figs 13-26). Of these wares the overwhelming majority belongs to the hand-made variety referred to here as Red-Black Burnished, though variously termed Early Trans-Caucasian, Karaz and Kura-Araks. The retention of all sherds from the Aşvan excavations affords the opportunity to study with some quantitative precision the relative changes in fabric and shape across the three essentially overlapping sequences. Only diagnostic sherds — mostly rims and bases — have been used to tabulate the frequencies mentioned in this study (Tables 1-8). The greatest difficulty in the classification of the assemblage of hand-made pottery is posed by the seemingly innumerable array of shapes and sizes — variations that are no doubt the direct result of the method of manufacture and perhaps, in most cases, by a domestic potting tradition.

In developing the type series, primacy in classification has been given to basic shape.

Although variations demonstrated in the size of a form, or in minor changes of rim profile and ornamentation were not considered to be useful criteria on which to construct a type series, they have all been noted for purposes of internal stratigraphy and comparative chronology. Whenever size variations occurred, a 15cm rim diameter was found to be a useful arbitrary divider between what is here described as 'small' (15cm or less) and 'large' (greater than 15cm) vessels.

NOTES

1. Mitchell, 1980: 23
2. Both Wagstaff 1973: 208 and Mitchell 1980: 23 draw attention to *kelekler*, skin-covered riverine crafts of the Upper Euphrates region which were observed and photographed in the Murat by early geographers. See Huntington 1902, and Naval Intelligence Division 1942: 184.
3. Willcox 1974: 130 suggests that during the Medieval period pine was probably imported from the region of Erzincan. While according to Rowton 1967, the wooded mountains of the Anti-Taurus quite likely supplied timber to the Sumerian city states.
4. Wagstaff 1973: 197.
5. ibid., pp. 207-211.
6. Hillman 1973: Fig. 1.
7. Willcox 1974.
8. Wagstaff 1973: 203.
9. ibid., pp. 211-212.
10. Mitchell 1980: 7-12.
11. For detailed accounts of the geography of Eastern Anatolia see Brice 1966: 127-41, 155-65, and Dewdney 1971: 198-201.

CHAPTER 2
Stratigraphy and Chronology

TAŞKUN MEVKİİ

The mound of Taşkun Mevkii is low and broad, and roughly circular in plan. Measuring about 110m in diameter, it falls within the category of medium-sized settlements in the Keban region (Fig. 4).[1] Its highest point is to the north where it rises 5.6m above the plain, with the lower southern flank averaging 3.2m in height. Excavations at the site were limited to a small area along the northern edge of the mound, and comprised about two months of work stretched over three relatively short seasons in 1970, 1971 and 1973. In the first campaign, subsequent to the establishment of the overall site grid comprising 10 x 10m squares, a series of exploratory trenches were made in squares K10, K11 and L10 (Figs 5-7). Work was extended in the following seasons to include J11 (Fig. 7). Despite claims by R. Whallon of major concentrations of Early Chalcolithic and Hittite material collected at Taşkun Mevkii during his survey of Keban sites, all the material excavated by S. Helms can be accommodated within the early phase of the Early Bronze Age.[2] Perhaps this anomaly can be explained by the fact that the restricted excavations fall outside the controlled collection areas established by Whallon.[3]

Helms has distinguished four major stratigraphic phases at Taşkun Mevkii. He divided the latest occupation, Phase 1, in two on the basis of painted pottery sherds (Fig. 54 nos 17-19) which were found in the uppermost deposits, in Phase 1A, but not in the preceding level, Phase 1B.[4] Phase 1A is represented by topsoil and pits (no floor levels or structures were found), while the deposits below it yielded traces of substantial dwellings established on stone foundations (Fig. 8). Most of the walls were between 0.75m and 1.00m thick, although the stone corner of a house in K11 is about 2m thick at its widest point. A burial was found very close to the surface in the baulk between K10 and K11 (deposit 610.3). The corpse was laid in a contracted position in a simple pit, and accompanied by some grave furnishings. Soil in this phase comprised a matrix of mottled greys and browns, varying in texture from ashy through lumpy to coarse. Given the relative importance accorded to the Painted Ware in determining the stratigraphic sequence, it is perhaps proper to point out that, of the considerable quantity of

fragments recovered from Phase 1 overall (about 3857 diagnostic pieces were catalogued), only three (body) sherds are painted. As we shall see, whilst these sherds carry important chronological ramifications by bearing designs stylistically similar to those found on vessels at the neighbouring sites of Aşvan Kale and Taşkun Kale, they appear to have little significance for purposes of internal stratigraphy. Nor is the division of Phase 1 supported by the relatively homogeneous distribution of other wares throughout its deposits.

Occupation surfaces belonging to Phase 2 were encountered in all the squares excavated, although only minor traces of structures were found, in J11 and K11. This phase, too, is divided by Helms into an upper (Phase 2A) and lower (Phase 2B) level. Phase 2A essentially comprises pits and tiplines that accumulated as the 2B settlement petered out (Figs 5-7). We have no idea of the nature of domestic structures during this period, which are presumably located further down the southern flank of the mound. The area excavated was open, possibly a courtyard, and encompassed what appear to be two small (2m x 2m) storage bins built on top of the burnt debris of Phase 3 (Fig. 9). Both bins had small openings facing the north-west, and mud brick walls measuring 40cm in thickness. Fragments of two storage jars — one handmade and black burnished, the other wheelmade and pinkish cream — were found within the southern bin. Above the burnt debris, the soil varied in colour from yellowish brown to a deep red.

Phase 3 at Taşkun Mevkii has yielded the most interesting architecture, a mixture of wattle-and-daub and mud brick dwellings. Fire had burnt the settlement, preserving the remains of four freestanding structures (Fig. 10). Although the small area excavated allowed only one building, Structure 3, to be fully excavated, enough architectural details were exposed to clarify the plans of the various buildings. Structure 1 comprised one main room, rectangular in shape with rounded corners. It had walls built of wattle-and-daub supported by wooden posts clearly discernable as a single row of holes placed close together along the outside of the wall. Although only the southern (back) half of the building has been excavated, similar post houses found in the Altınova and Trans-Caucasus, mentioned below, suggest that the front of this house probably had an attached rectangular annex about half the size of the main room. Access to the annex would have been through a doorway situated in the middle of the outer wall. Another doorway directly opposite would have led to the main room. Most dwellings of this type would have had a stone or clay step in front of the threshold. The Taşkun Mevkii house preserves some of the installations commonly found in these wattle-and-daub structures. Built into the floor, in the middle of the main room, was a circular plastered hearth probably to accommodate a horned andiron (Fig. 71 nos 2, 4). While along the back wall, opposite the entrance, was a mud bench with a niche placed at either end forming the back corners of the room. Insignificant though it may seem, the post hole immediately to the west of the hearth supported a roof presumably constructed of beams and thatch. Whether the roof was ridged or flat is difficult to determine, but house-models from south-eastern Europe of similar structures suggest a sloping gabled roof. Among the floor deposits were a storage jar of the black burnished variety and a pitted saddle quern (Fig. 71 no. 1).

This house and others like it in neighbouring regions are arguably the clearest manifestation of Trans-Caucasian influence during the east Anatolian Early Bronze Age. Their construction and conception are so strikingly different to conventional Anatolian mud brick architecture that they suggest an exotic origin. In Anatolia they have been found at Arslantepe VIB1, and, slightly later, in contexts with painted pottery of local style at Norşuntepe XXII-XIV and Değirmentepe III and I.[5] Their origin is to be found in the northern part of Georgia known locally as Shida Kartli (or Inner Georgia), where entire settlements of post houses have been excavated. There, along the banks of the Kura river, one can trace a development from the roughly made circular affairs at Khizanaant Gora D to the round-cornered rectangular structures immediately above, in Levels C-B, and nearby at Kvatskhelebi C-B.[6] Wattle-and-daub structures have also been reported further south in the Samtskhe and Dzhavakheli regions, at Sioni in Kakheti, Baba Dervish 1 in Azerbaijan and at Haftavan in north-west Iran.[7] It has been suggested that the Early Trans-Caucasian culture, characterised by a diverse range of Red-Black Burnished ceramics and architectural forms, had a vacillating nomadic element in its subsistence economy.[8] This idea is supported not only by the construction of free-standing wattle-and-daub dwellings, but also by the settlement plans of sites such as Kvatskhelebi which bear a remarkable similarity to orientation of certain modern nomad camps. Other regions of Trans-Caucasus,

including the heavily settled plains around Tbilisi and Erevan, seem unaffected by this method of house construction, preferring instead the circular and rectangular mud brick houses.[9]

At Taşkun Mevkii the buildings to the south of the wattle-and-daub house were built of mud bricks. Structure 3 was rectangular in plan (9.50 x 7.25m), and centred with a plastered circular hearth similar to the one in the post-house. Two niches were built into one of its long walls on the interior, and on the outside a mud brick bench abutted its eastern half. This building also contained the best floor deposit (620.2) in the excavations, found when the south-eastern corner in K11 was cleared in 1973. Only a small portion of Structure 2 was uncovered. It, too, appears to have been rectangular in shape with remarkably thick walls, about 1m at the widest point. While both buildings conform to a plan common throughout the Keban region, the fourth structure is different. It was mud-brick built and stone-based, and comprised an inner raised platform (5.50 x 3.75m) separated from an outer encasing wall by a passage between 0.50m and 0.77m wide. The surrounding wall abutted a fifth structure with a burnt plaster floor. These features led Helms to suggest that the function of Structure 4 was to dry grains or possibly wool. The architectural layout of Phase 4 seems to be similar to that of Phase 3, though very little of these earliest deposits (located in K10 and J11) were excavated. The most significant feature was part of a mud brick wall which was exposed in a small trench sunk into the floor of Structure 3 (Phase 3).

The distribution of architecture in the areas excavated — namely the occurrence of buildings in Phases 3 and 4, and, conversely, their absence in the later deposits — has suggested to Helms that the focus of settlement at Taşkun Mevkii was originally along the northern edge, which was subsequently left as an open area.

Though the ceramic horizon at Taşkun Mevkii is defined by a number of distinctive wares, some quite rare, two groups of pottery predominate: hand-made Red-Black Burnished (Early Trans-Caucasian) Ware and light-coloured wheel-made Plain Simple Ware, which account for 87% and 17% respectively of the total quantity. Both are found in all four phases, with the greatest amount of either type located in the topsoil and associated pits of Phase 1.

Red-Black Burnished pottery at Taşkun Mevkii has a limited repertoire of shapes. By far the commonest form is the simple rounded bowl which comes in three variations best described by their profile: convex conical (Fig. 16 Type 1), standard hemispherical (Fig. 16 Type 2), and vertical-sided (Fig. 16 Type 3). Of these, the small bowl whose walls assume a convex curve proved to be most popular. Generally it is thin-walled and has a fine, well-levigated, hard fabric, which, to the naked eye, contains mostly grit and some chaff temper. Many pieces are entirely black and well polished on both surfaces. Others are fired red (2.5YR 5/8), brown (7.5YR 5/2), or to shades in between (2.5YR 6/4 to 2.5YR 5/4; 5YR 6/4 to 5YR 5/3) on the exterior below the rim, which remains black and highly burnished like the interior. Handles are exceedingly rare. Two bowls have small loop handles set below the rim (Figs 27 no. 2; 34 no. 2), while a few others were presumably suspended by a string passed through pierced lugs (Figs 30 no. 2; 33 no. 10), or holes at the rim (Figs 29 no. 4; 34 no. 1). These rounded bowls also bear most of the seldomly occurring ornamentation at Taşkun Mevkii. The decorative scheme consists of circular or elliptical knobs invariably attached to the rim, or immediately below it (Figs 27 nos 3, 9-11, 15; 29 no. 8; 30 nos 4, 8, 12, 17; 32 nos 10, 12, 13; 34 nos 4, 16). Such ornamentation recalls the protuberances on the Chalcolithic pottery at Çayboyu, Fatmali-Kalecik and Korucutepe.[10] Incised decoration is even rarer. The design of a chequer board and chevron pattern filled with a white paste illustrated in Fig. 3 no. 6 is redolent of the pattern on a Late Chalcolithic bowl at Tepecik.[11] A few sherds also preserve an arrangement of chevrons and punctures (Figs 34 no. 5; 54 nos 12-14). The standard and vertical-sided bowls are much fewer in number (Table 1), but they too have plastic ornaments, occasionally knobs that have been fused together (Figs 31 no. 6; 14; 32 nos 1, 11; 34 no. 14; 35 nos 5, 6). Hemispherical bowls are commonplace throughout the East-Central Anatolian region, in the north-eastern Bayburt province and in the Amuq. Arslantepe VI B2 has a good range of all three types, but its vertical-sided bowl with slightly incurving rim, a shape found also at Tepecik and Pulur, is a particularly close parallel.[12]

Among the larger vessels the ovoid-bodied, or bag-shaped, cooking pot supported on a flat base (Fig. 17 Type 10), and the low-bellied jar with a tall, sloping neck (Fig. 17 Type 11) are the most numerous. Both types tend to have a heavy, coarse, gritty fabric that fractures with a rough and irregular edge, displaying a black or grey core. Virtually all pieces conform to a visually effective contrasting colour scheme — a dark colour on the exterior (generally black on the low-bellied jar), and red (2.5YR 6/8), or one of the various shades of beige (7.5YR 7/2) and brown (7.5YR 5/2) on the interior. Mottled colours are not uncommon, particularly on the cooking pots. Lightly burnished exterior surfaces are usual, while the interior is either smoothed or left plain. Cooking pots come in a range of sizes and dimensions. Small kitchen cups with profiles similar to the pots belong to the same family. Triangular ledge handles are frequently attached to a simple rim, which is slightly out-turned at an angle that varies from one example to another. Fig. 16 Type 6 and Fig. 17 Type 8 illustrate two other kitchen pots, neither of which gained prominence. Both are round-bodied and hole-mouthed, and can be distinguished from each other on the basis of the rim, which is short but clearly differentiated in Type 8. In profile, the pendulous jar (Fig. 17 Type 11) is generally sinuous, although a development toward a well-defined juncture between the neck and shoulder is evident (Figs 48 no. 11; 49 nos 4, 6-8). Quite possibly a variant is the vessel whose fragments are characterised by a markedly everted rim and a slightly convex neck (Fig. 48 nos 2-4). To be noted is the conspicuous absence at Taşkun Mevkii of jars with a sharply squared 'rail' rim and marked recessed necks (Fig. 18 Type 14), so abundant at the two nearby Aşvan sites.

Decoration on the cooking pots and jars is neither common nor elaborate, and usually consists of a pair of small pellets (Figs 42 no. 11; 49 no. 8; 54 nos 3, 4, 6), or plastic lines (Figs 36 no. 11; 40 no. 1; 54 nos 5, 7-10) placed on the shoulder. Curious is a sherd of greenish Cream Ware with a fine relief pattern that is normally applied to black burnished rail rim jars (Fig. 65 no. 21).[13] Cooking pots are more widely distributed in the Upper Euphrates region than are the low-bellied jars. Ovoid-bodied and bag-shaped pots with a developed neck (Fig. 17 Type 10) have been found in the Malatya and Elazığ regions, in provinces further south, and in the Amuq plain.[14] The jars, on the other hand, are best compared to examples from Arslantepe VI B and Pulur XI.[15] No fragments from Taşkun Mevkii can be identified with any certainty as pot stands. Three small pieces bearing traces of an incised and punctured design, however, are reminiscent of the elaborately patterned stands found in considerable quantity at Pulur XI, which appear in the terminal phase of Arslantepe VI B.[16] At Taşkun Mevkii lids are discoid and flat, though occasionally convex (Fig. 19 Type 21 and 22), but never with a central depression (Fig. 19 Type 23). Finally, attention should be drawn to two fine and highly polished black spouts (Fig. 65 nos 2, 3), which have no parallels in East-Central Anatolia.

Plain Simple Ware at Taşkun Mevkii has a number of the typical qualities which characterise this pottery over much of the Turkish Upper Euphrates and north Syrian region. Its fabric is crisp, dense and well-fired to a buff or pink (10YR 7.5/3, 5YR 7.5/4) colour. Noticeably absent is the greenish buff variety. Temper is usually grit, and can be of a very fine quality in some of the smallest vessels. Wheel-marks are clearly evident on the walls, whose surfaces are smoothed and left either plain or finished with a slurry. The smooth-profiled cup on a flat base, with a short, sharply out-turned or rounded rim (Fig. 20 Type 8) is the hallmark of this group. Slightly rounder is Fig. 20 Type 9. Minor rim variations are found in both groups, but the most distinct is the groove along the inside rim (Figs 60 nos 3, 8, 16). Many comparisons of these bowls can be drawn with examples from Arslantepe VI B2, the Altınova, south-east Anatolia, and the Amuq.[17] Kurban Höyük V and IV, however, provide the most complete range of, and some of the closest parallels to, the deep bowls with the slightly convex walls (Fig. 20 Types 2 and 3). Conical bowls with a rounded rim (Figs 20 Type 2; 61 no. 12; 62 nos 9-13) do not occur at Arslantepe, and have been found only at Norşuntepe in the Keban area.[18] Those with a folded over rim are more widespread, but the Taşkun Mevkii profiles can be matched up best with pieces from Kurban Höyük.[19] One bowl with a ribbon of clay applied horizontally below the rim (Figs 20 Type 3; 61 no. 9) is particularly close to a Kurban Höyük vessel.[20] The technique of folding over the rim has been accentuated in the manufacture of the tall cup of Type 6 (Figs 20; 62 nos 2, 6), which stands alone in the Plain Simple Ware horizon of this region. The holemouth cup (Fig. 20 Type 5), too, a common form at Taşkun Mevkii, is difficult to equate with examples elsewhere. Although not quite 'rilled', a number of short, thick rims fluted either on the exterior or interior, or both, do occur (Figs 18 Type 10; 61 nos 4-7). A fine, close-textured fabric distinguishes the vertical-sided cup with slightly out-turned rim (Figs 20 Type 7; 58 nos 15, 16; 60 no. 11), which, though absent from the Arslantepe assemblage, is found in the Altınova and at Kurban Höyük V.[21] There is no complete specimen of the equally fine hemispherical cup of Type 4 (Fig. 20), but a number of flanged bases (Fig. 21 Types 14 and 16) suggests that they might be footed goblets.[22] In contrast to the bowls, the range of Plain Simple Ware jars is rather limited and includes two necked types: one has an everted neck and a rounded (Figs 21 Type 12; 63 nos 12-16; 64 nos 2-8, 10) or pinched rim (Fig. 64 nos 1, 9); the other is characterised by a flaring neck ending in a plain rim (Figs 20 Type 11; 63 nos 8-11).[23]

Except for a complete ovoid-bodied necked jar, Reserved Slip Ware is represented by fragmentary material of a late date found in deposits of Phases 1 and 2 (Figs 56; 57).[24] The paste of this ware is very similar to the Plain Simple variety, though its colour is slighty darker, tending towards a pale pinkish brown (5YR 6/4) rather than buff. In the strict sense of the term, this class of pottery, distinguished primarily by its light-coloured exterior slip and distinctive decoration, is not a ware type, but a variant of the Plain Simple Ware family. Only two shapes are represented: small-necked jars and rounded cups with an out-turned rim. (Figs 21 Types 1-2). Lacking are the large-mouthed necked jars and cups of different dimensions attested at other Euphratian sites. Further, the decorative scheme does not incorporate incised motifs, fairly common at those sites. Rather the reserved slip pattern at Taşkun Mevkii generally consists of a horizontal band round the neck and a series of oblique lines running radially down the body (Fig. 57 nos 8-12). One jar (Fig. 57 no. 11) has a virtually identical counterpart at Hassek Höyük.[25] Some of the cups have reserved vertical lines pendent to the rim (Fig. 57 nos 1, 2, 4), while certain pieces bear reserved zones of segmented bands (Fig. 56 nos 1, 6, 7, 10).

At this stage it is worth mentioning six painted sherds, possibly from a single vessel, found amongst the floor deposit of Phase 3 (Fig. 54 nos 20-24). Their fabric is beige-brown and cream-slipped on the exterior. They are decorated with bold designs in reddish brown with patterns akin, but not identical, to those painted on jars from Arslantepe VI B2.[26]

A tantalising glimpse of distant inter-connections is provided by distinctive Syro-Mesopotamian affinities in the form of four-lugged jars and high-stemmed fruit stands (Fig. 23), from a peripheral Ninevite 5 horizon, and the subject of a paper by Behm-Blancke.[27] The fabric of the jars is fine and varies from a plain greenish cream to a pale orange brown (2.5Y 7.5/4; 5YR 5.5/8). Vertically pierced lugs are set on the shoulder which can be sharply profiled (Fig. 65 nos 7, 9, 10-12, 15, 16), rounded (Fig. 65 no. 13), or high (Fig. 65 no. 8). Two fragments, decorated with paint, are comparable to pieces at Hassek Höyük[28]: one, in reddish brown, has a chevron and dot design, the other, in red, a net pattern. The fruitstands have a strikingly different fabric. Found in Phases 2 and 3 they are red-slipped (10R 4/6) and either burnished or smoothed. Their bowls have a sharp, carinated outline (Fig. 55 nos 1-7), and are attached to tall stems that end in a flanged foot (Fig. 55 nos 10-18). A series of horizontal ridges decorate the stem underneath the bowl and above the foot. A different stemmed fruitstand is illustrated in Fig. 55 nos 8 and 9. Its bowl is conical or slightly convex in shape, with surfaces that are either red-slipped or left plain reddish brown. And it was probably attached to a pedestal similar to the black burnished type illustrated in Fig. 55 no. 14. The straight spouted jar with an ovoid body on a flat base is represented by four sherds. It is manufactured from a creamy pink or orange brown paste (5YR 7/4, 5YR 6/6) that is granular to touch. Although none of the Taşkun Mevkii examples preserves the neck, it was probably cylindrical or outflaring.[29] A strainer spout made of the same clay as the straight spout is illustrated in Fig. 67 no. 9. These exotic vessels are best compared, in Anatolia, to examples from Arslantepe and Hassek Höyük, although minor differences of form are apparent in all three assemblages.[30] At Kurban Höyük only a few fruitstand stems have been found.[31] Stemmed fruitstands both plain and grooved occur at a number of north Syro-Mesopotamian sites including the cist graves on the acropolis at Carchemish (where Woolley termed them 'champagne glass pots'), Thalathat and Nineveh.[32] The end of the Taşkun Mevkii sequence can perhaps be defined by a single fragment of a *cyma recta* bowl found in a topsoil deposit (Fig. 63 no. 6). A feature of Amuq H, the *cyma recta* bowl is found at Kurban Höyük V and late in the Hassek Höyük sequence; at Arslantepe one piece appeared in a pit stratigraphically later than Level 0.[33] Thus despite the diversity of wares, the overall ceramic horizon at Taşkun Mevkii displays no abrupt changes and suggests a continuity of occupation.

Glyptic art is represented by two clay cylinder seals and an incised stone stamp seal (Fig. 69 nos 6-8). One cylinder seal has a geometric design that places it within the same family as those patterned seals from Norşuntepe and Arslantepe, while an unstratified example of related 'Piedment' style with floral elements comes from Pulur.[34] These seals, whether imports or local imitations of foreign types, are clearly derived from the geometric patterned style of the Jemdet Nasr period attributed in Mesopotamia and Iran to the late fourth-early third millennium BC.[35] Generally, their appearance in Anatolia and Syria is later, but they persist over most of the third millennium BC.[36] As noted by Helms, the other cylinder seal with three animals in paratactic style has Jemdet Nasr affinities.[37] Other terracotta objects include part of an animal figurine (Fig. 68 no. 3), spindle whorls (Fig. 70 nos 1-3) and loom-weights (Fig. 70 nos 4-10). Metal objects are few and comprise a double-spiral ornament (possibly

an earring) (Fig. 68 no. 4), a ribbon of copper shaped into a form of a snake (Fig. 68 no. 1), and two pins. The first type of pin has a loop-head and a coiled upper shank (Fig. 68 no. 8), whilst the second has a conical head which, like the upper shank, is incised (Fig. 68 no. 9). Frangipane has already noted the distribution of these pins — at Arslantepe VI B, Norşuntepe and a Ninevite 5 grave at Arbit in the Khabur region.[38] Bone points (Figs 68 nos 2, 5-7, 10; 69 nos 4, 5), three parallel-sided stone blades (Fig. 69 nos 1-3) and an edge-ground axe (Fig. 70 no. 3), all of which belong to long traditions, complete the assemblage at Taşkun Mevkii.[39]

The Taşkun Mevkii sequence is best defined in Anatolia by connections with a number of cultures including Arslantepe VI B, Hassek Höyük Levels 4-1 and Kurban Höyük V. It also displays affinities, however marginal, with the late Reserved Slip, Jemdet Nasr and Ninevite 5 horizons of Syro-Mesopotamia. In the absence of radiocarbon dates for Taşkun Mevkii, one must turn to Arslantepe VI B to secure the sequence within an absolute chronology. After MASCA calibration, the readings from Arslantepe VI B fall comfortably within the period 3000-2800 BC, suggesting an early 3rd millennium date for Taşkun Mevkii too.[40]

AŞVAN KALE

The site of Aşvan Kale overlooks the floodplain on the southern side of the Murat River from a high point on the edge of a terrace. The mound is flat-topped and steep-sided, measuring about 130m (northeast-southwest) by 110m (northwest-southeast) at its base.[41] Although Early Bronze Age occupation at the mound is extensive, occupying some two thirds of its deposit, work focused on the Roman levels. The Early Bronze material was obtained from a long slice running down the northern slope comprising a series of step trenches — G1b, G1d, G2b, G2d, G3b, G3d (Fig. 12).[42] While the stratigraphic sequence within most trenches is relatively clear, it is not always possible to link adjacent sequences on this northern scarp. No features that could be attributed to substantial structures were found in any of the trenches. The clearest sequence, in G2b, consisted of a series of tiplines, surfaces and pits (Fig. 13). Some of the other trenches, G2d and G3b in particular, provided little more than mud brick debris and pits.

At a glance the pottery repertoire of Aşvan Kale is markedly different from that of Taşkun Mevkii in three ways. In the first place, it comprises large black burnished jars with squared rail rim which are conspicuously absent from Taşkun Mevkii; second, by the occurrence of a substantial quantity of hand-made Cream Wares which in the variations of shape and decoration have characterised a local painted style; third, by the minimal amount of Syro-Mesopotamian wheel-made wares. A close examination reveals further differences between the two horizons.

The Red-Black Burnished group is more varied than at Taşkun Mevkii, with all the main types illustrated in Figs 16-19 present, bar three (Table 1). Its fabric, generally tempered with grit and chaff inclusions, is open textured in the large jars and denser in the smaller vessels. Many pieces display a scheme of contrasting colours. The exterior is usually black burnished, but brown (7.5YR 5/2) and red (2.5YR 5/8; 2.5YR 6/4) surfaces are not uncommon, while the interior is reddish brown (5YR 6/4) or beige (7.5YR 7/2).

Large recess-necked vessels comprise the most numerous group (Fig. 18 Type 14), but with so few reconstructed items it is difficult to discern precisely whether the tall jar or wide pot forms the principal type. However, judging from the number of tall-necked fragments, it appears that jars predominate. The defined juncture between neck and shoulder that certain precursors of this form at Taşkun Mevkii (Fig. 17 Type 11) display, now develops into a marked ridge. Apart from a few grooved sherds (Fig. 113 nos 3-6), there is no indication that these jars were elaborately decorated as was the fashion elsewhere in the Keban region. Recess-necked jars are found over a wide area in eastern Anatolia (except amongst the south-eastern horizons) and beyond, in Trans-Caucasus and north-western Iran.[43] Understandably, the tightest comparisons can be made with the relatively close sites of Korucutepe, Norşuntepe and Değirmentepe.[44] At Norşuntepe they appear in the late Early Bronze Age I deposits, but elsewhere in the Keban region they characterise the Early Bronze Age II and III periods.

While the Aşvan rail rim jars belong to a form too common to be of typological significance, a number of other elements indicate that the Aşvan Kale sequence straddles both the Early Bronze Age II and III periods. A few diagnostic sherds with a horizontally fluted upper neck (Fig. 17 Type 9) are related to pots found at Korucutepe, Norşuntepe and Tepecik, although none of the Aşvan fragments shows any trace of the broad bands of fluting across the belly that some pots of this type bear.[45] Potstands too are fluted (Figs 19 Type 20; 108 nos 5-10), in a manner that recalls those from Korucutepe.[46] Suggestive of a late

date in the Early Bronze Age is the bowl type with a pronouncedly incurving rim (Fig. 16 Type 4) found only in G3b, and a jar with a distinct swollen rim (Fig. 17 Type 12). The two are typical of the later part of the Early Bronze Age III (Period VI D, also known as Fase Recente) at Arslantepe.[47] Again no full profiles of either the jar or bowl could be recovered from the fragmentary material. But to judge from the published material, the jars tend to have a smooth, biconical profile, with the diameters of the rim and base approximately equivalent. Some of the bowls and jars at Arslantepe are decorated with rows of simple incised designs, though no such patterns have been found at Aşvan Kale. The bowls with incurving rim are also common at Korucutepe, where their popularity peaked during the Early Bronze Age IIIB (Phase F).[48] Looking at other Aşvan types, hemispherical bowls with a simple rim (Fig. 16 Types 1-3) were found throughout the sequence and are accompanied by bowls with rail rim (Fig. 16 Type 5). Round and ovoid-bodied cooking pots (Fig. 17 Types 8 and 10) were still manufactured, but the hole-mouthed variety (Fig. 16 Type 6) was clearly the favoured kitchen vessel. Pot lids usually have a depression around a central handle and a grooved decoration along the edge (Fig. 19 Type 23), although fragments of the flat variety do occur.

Both the painted and plain variety of Cream Ware are generally well-fired to a uniform colour (10YR 8/3), though some vessels have a pinkish-buff interior. Cream Ware is manufactured from a coarse paste, tempered with grit and some chaff. The range of cream forms is limited. Wide-mouthed pots (painted Fig. 25 Types 7-9; plain Fig. 26 Types 6-8) are the most common shapes, followed by open hemispherical bowls (painted Fig. 24 Type 1; plain Fig. 26 Types 1 and 2). Painted bowls with the incurving rim occur (Fig. 24 Type 3), but not the pronouncedly inturned variety, which is represented among the Plain Ware by one sherd (Fig. 26 Type 3).

Painted decoration, most often in matt reddish brown, is haphazardly executed and consists of simple patterns. A row of running triangles filled with oblique lines, sometimes superimposed by a wavy line, is the most popular design on the exterior. (Figs 117 nos 4, 6, 8, 14; 118 nos 2-4, 8-9; 120 nos 1, 7, 9; 121 nos 6, 10, 12). A number of variations of this basic design occur, but it will suffice only to point out a few: a series of horizontal and oblique lines in place of triangles (Figs 117 nos 3, 11; 123 no. 4); a row of short oblique lines round the shoulder (Fig. 118 no. 5); oblique lines from rim to shoulder (Fig. 118 no. 6); a row of running solid triangles (Figs 118 no. 7; 120 no. 10; 124 no. 10); inverted triangles above a wavy line (Fig. 120 no. 3). On the interior, many vessels have a row of oblique strokes or an inverted flame pattern pendent to the rim (Figs 116 nos 3, 10-12; 117 nos 1, 13; 118 nos 3, 9, 13-16; 119 nos 1, 3, 5, 7-15; 120 nos 1, 2, 4-6; 121 nos 1, 4, 6, 8, 9, 13; 122 nos 6, 7; 123 no. 8; 124 nos 2, 5, 8, 9; 125 nos 1-3, 6, 7). Isolated motifs include the radiating sun disc (Fig. 126 no. 17), butterfly (Fig. 127 no. 7) and swastika (Fig. 127 no. 22).

The centre of production of this particular style of painted pottery was the Murat basin, with only a few pieces manufactured in, or imported into, the Altınova plain.[49] The Aşvan material finds its closest affinities in the pottery from Pulur (Sakyol), Han İbrahim Şah and Kalaycık. Conversely, one sherd from Aşvan (Fig. 125 no. 6) displaying a more precisely executed decorative scheme, belongs to a related style widely represented in the Malatya and Elazığ regions, with the exception of the Murat basin. This design is characterised by a frieze of broad horizontal bands separated by narrow lines left in reserve.[50] Thus Malatya-Elazığ Painted is an apt term for both styles of this ware.[51]

Wheel-made wares are rare at Aşvan Kale. A handful of Plain Simple and Reserved Slip Ware sherds (Fig. 134) represent the end of that tradition. The few sherds of a fine, close textured pale orange brown ware are of chronological significance (Figs 22 Types 3-5; 133 nos 15-18). Two of the bowls decorated with a brown horizontal on the rim are similar to vessels from Kurban Höyük IV and, more importantly, Tell Mardikh II B2, where they form part of the Painted Simple Ware horizon.[52] According to Matthiae, Mardikh IIB2, built immediately after the destruction period IIB1 and the Royal Palace G, can be dated to the last quarter of the 3rd millennium BC, about 2250-2000 BC.

Among the small finds are two clay stamp seals with a design of a radiating sun disc centred by a circular impression deeply grooved on a convex face (Fig. 135 nos 1, 2). One has a thick stalk, the other is spindle-shaped with a design at each end of the stalk. Given their size, about 6 cm across the face, this seal type was possibly used to print textiles. Like the Aşvan variety of painted pottery these seals are concentrated in the Murat basin. They have been found at Han İbrahim Şah, Yeniköy and, in particular, Pulur where over fifteen were assigned mostly to the middle and upper levels.[53] In the Altınova, four have been reported, all from Early Bronze Age II-III levels at Tepecik.[54] Another two curious outliers come from Sendschirli, though their relationship to the Keban examples is not clear.[55] Aşvan Kale also yielded three small animal figurines (Fig. 135 nos

3-5) and a larger, pierced example that appears to have been an attachment of a hearth (Fig. 135 no. 6). Metal work is rare. The most significant piece is a bronze earring with overlapping ends (Fig. 135 no. 8) similar to those attributed to the Early Bronze Age III at Norşuntepe and Tepecik, which are sometimes stylistically related to the lunate earrings from the Akkadian graves at Ur.[56] The lithic industry is represented by one well-manufactured piece — a finely flaked triangular projectile point (Fig. 136 no. 2) not unlike a piece found at Arslantepe.[57] The rest of the flaked stones comprise crudely fashioned small pieces of obsidian (Fig. 136 nos 3-8) and debitage. An edge-ground axe completes the lithic assemblage (Fig. 136 no. 10).

On the basis of all these comparisons, and given the difficulty of linking up the various Early Bronze deposits at Aşvan Kale, the trenches are best understood as spot samples of the Early Bronze II-III periods. The handful of late Reserved Slip Ware and Plain Simple Ware sherds in the basal levels at Aşvan Kale suggest an overlap with the end of occupation at Taşkun Mevkii. This overlapping is corroborated by the very few pieces of Malatya-Elazığ Painted Ware in the top deposits at Taşkun Mevkii. Stylistically, the Aşvan material is comparable to Değirmentepe IV-I and Pulur VIII-I in the Murat Valley, Korucutepe C-F, Norşuntepe XXIII-VII and Tepecik (14-3-K) in the Altınova, and Arslantepe VI C-VI D and Gelinciktepe near Malatya. With radiocarbon determinations from the Early Bronze IIIB at Arslantepe (the latest half of VI D) averaging between 2300 and 2000 BC, Aşvan can be placed within the range 2800 and 2000 BC.[58] The extent of cultural continuity over this period at Aşvan Kale, however, is impossible to determine given the restricted area excavated.

TAŞKUN KALE

Taşkun Kale is a relatively high (20m), flat-topped mound with steep northern and eastern sides which fall abruptly to meet the western bank of the Kuru Çay. Its western and southern flanks are much less severe, fanning out to merge gently with the basin in which the site is situated. Early Bronze Age material occurred in a number of trenches, sometimes mixed with late Medieval deposits. The clearest stratigraphic sequence is discernable in trenches S9 and S11 (Fig. 14). Substantial architectural features were found only in S9 which yielded a rectangular mud brick building (c. 6.5 x 4.5m) oriented northwest-southeast (Fig. 15). It comprised a roughly square main room and a rectangular annex entered through an offset doorway. The main room had plastered walls, a pisé bench in the east corner, and, towards the end of the room, a horseshoe-shaped oven.

The very small area excavated at Taşkun Kale necessarily yielded only a small quantity of pottery, some 280 diagnostic pieces in all. Yet the repertoire is quite clearly comparable to Aşvan Kale. Red-Black Burnished pottery is far and away the principal group, with large squared, rail rim jars again the dominant form (Fig. 18 Type 14). Open hemispherical bowls with plain, squared and inturned rim are all present (Fig. 16 Types 1-5). However, the practice of running the finger under the rim on the exterior of a vessel during its manufacture thereby creating a shallow groove (Fig. 139 nos 5, 7, 10) is peculiar to Taşkun Kale. The only cup with a handle is illustrated in Fig. 140 no. 6. Cooking pots are common, as are triangular ledge handles. Here too are represented pots with a horizontally fluted upper neck (Fig. 15 nos 1 and 2), and both the flat and centrally depressed pot lids (Figs 155 nos 3-5; 156).

Only four types of vessels are painted in the local style: the bowl with inturned (Fig. 24 Type 4) and everted (Fig. 24 Type 5) rim, and the globular pot (Fig. 25 Type 7) and jar (Fig. 25 Type 9) with developed necks. Both styles of decoration found at Aşvan Kale are represented here. One bowl has had its vertical lug handle incorporated into the design (Fig. 157 no. 8). Worth noting is the association of the reserved paint decoration with the incurving bowls (Fig. 157 no. 4), suggesting a date in the second half of the third millennium BC. Two globular pots also bear finely executed decoration (Figs 157 no. 12; 158 no. 1). The bronze chisel found in S9 is in excellent condition (Fig. 160 no. 1). It has a square haft, an octagonal shaft, and a flattened and flaring chisel edge. The only stone object is a winged projectile point finely fashioned from flint (Fig. 160 no. 2). Similar points reported from Norşuntepe and Körtepe have been attributed to the Late Chalcolithic period suggesting a long history for this type.[59] The Taşkun Kale material matches closely that from Aşvan. Like the Aşvan material, its precise location within the Early Bronze II-III period is difficult to determine.

NOTES

1. In his survey of the Keban reservoir area, R. Whallon described the site as 'oval' measuring 190m from north to south and 120m along the east-west axis; Whallon 1979: 161 (site N52/1). For preliminary notices of excavations see Helms 1971; idem 1972; idem 1973; McNicoll and Helms 1974; Helms in French et al. 1972: 60-62; Helms in French et al. 1979: 11.

2. loc. cit.

3. ibid., p. 297; Figs 56-60, pp. 162-164.

4. Helms 1973: 109.

5. Frangipane and Palmieri 1983b: 523-24; Palmieri 1985a: 181. Hauptmann 1979: 70-71, Pl. 26; idem 1982: 48-49, Pls 29, 30; Duru 1979: 70, 72, Pls 69, 71.

6. Kikvidze 1972: Pls 2-5; Dzhavakhishvili and Glonti 1962: Pls 6-23; Dzhavakhishvili 1973: pp. 113ff, Pls 13-15.

7. Ordzhonikidze 1981: 10.

8. Cribb 1991: 220-223; Burney and Lang 1971: 57; Whallon and Kantman 1969: 103; Sagona 1993: 453-73.

9. Dzhavakhishvili 1973: 1-90 for Late Neolithic - Chalcolithic architecture; 163ff for the Early Bronze Age traditions.

10. Aksöy and Diamant 1973: Fig. 4 nos 3, 4, 8, 9; Whallon and Wright 1970: Pl. 4b; Brandt 1978: Pls 104 no. 7; 105 nos 3, 5, 13.

11. Esin 1976a: Pl. 72 no. 2.

12. Type 1: Arslantepe VI B2 (Frangipane and Palmieri 1983b: Fig. 22 nos 2, 3); Değirmentepe III (Duru 1979: Pl. 27 no. 9). Type 2: Arslantepe VIB2 (Frangipane and Palmieri 1983b: Fig. 22: 1-6, 8-10), Değirmentepe IV (Duru 1979: Pl. 25 nos 8, 9), III (Pl. 27 nos 10-15), II (Pl. 29 nos 10-14), I (Pl. 31 nos 22-25); Norşuntepe EB I (Hauptmann 1979: Pl. 43 no. 4 — these pieces have horizontal handles not found at Taşkun Mevkii; idem 1972: Pl. 72 no. 4), EB III (idem 1972: Pl. 75 no. 1). Type 3: Arslantepe VI B2 (Frangipane and Palmieri 1983b: Fig. 22 no. 5); Pulur (Koşay 1976b: Pl. 51 no. 197); Tepecik (Esin et al. 1979: Pl. 61 no. 2); Büyüktepe Höyük-Bayburt

(Sagona, Pemberton and McPhee 1992: Fig. 4 nos 1, 2).

. 13.   Cf, for example, the 'face' designs from Pulur (Koşay 1976b: Pls 83 nos 58, 59; 86 no. 38); Sagona 1984: Fig. 122.

14.   Malatya: Arslantepe VIB2 (Frangipane and Palmieri 1983b: Fig. 23). Elazığ: Değirmentepe (Duru 1979: Pls 25 nos 18, 30; 27 no. 17; 29 nos 15, 25, 26; 31 no. 27); Norşuntepe EB I levels (Hauptmann 1972: Pl. 72 no. 2; idem 1982: Pls 42 nos 9,10; 44 no. 1), some of the Norşuntepe examples have four ledge handles set at the rim; Pulur (Koşay 1976b: Pls 40 nos 42, 53, 55; 41; 42); Tepecik (Esin et al. 1979: Pl. 62 no. 20; eadem 1982b: Pl. 75 nos 3-5). South-East Anatolia: Hassek Höyük (Hoh 1981: Fig. 15 no. 8; idem 1984: Fig. 13 no.9); Kurban Höyük IV (Algaze 1990: Pls 93; 94). Amuq, Phase G (Braidwood and Braidwood 1960: Fig. 283 nos 9, 12-16).

15.   Arslantepe (Frangipane and Palmieri 1983b: Fig. 21 no. 2); Pulur (Koşay 1976b: Pls 43 nos 74, 89, 97; 44 nos 91, 94; 46 no. 88).

16.   Pulur (Koşay 1976b: Pls 81; 82); Arslantepe (Frangipane and Palmieri 1983b: Fig. 24).

17.   Arslantepe (Frangipane and Palmieri 1983b: Fig. 20 nos 1-4); Norşuntepe EB1 (Hauptmann et al. 1972: Pl. 73 nos 8, 9, 12; idem 1982: Pls 40 nos 5-6; 42 nos 2-3); Tepecik EB (Esin 1970: Pl. 16); Hassek Höyük EB (Hoh 1981: Figs 9 nos 1-5; 16 no. 6; 1984: Fig. 10 no. 3); Kurban Höyük V (Algaze 1990: Pl. 44 A-K).

18.   Kurban Höyük V (Algaze 1990: Pl. 44 L-T); IV (Pls 55; 56 A-D, J); Norşuntepe EB I (Hauptmann et al. 1972: Pl. 73 no. 5; idem 1982: Pl. 42 no. 1).

19.   Kurban Höyük V (Algaze 1990: Pl. 46 M; more elaborate folded rims are found in Level IV, Pl. 57); Arslantepe VIB2 (Frangipane and Palmieri 1983b: Fig. 20 nos 6-8; 26 no. 2); Norşuntepe EB I (Hauptmann 1982: Pl. 40 no. 2); Hassek Höyük (Hoh 1981: Figs 11 no. 6; 12 no. 2).

20.   Kurban Höyük V (Algaze 1990: Pl. 57 C; and to a lesser extent Pl. 46 J, K from Level V).

21.   Kurban Höyük V (Algaze 1990: Pl. 43 J-P, especially N); Norşuntepe XXVI (Hauptmann 1982: Pl. 41 no.1; 42 nos 6-8); Değirmentepe II (Duru 1979: Pl. 30 nos 15, 17).

22.   Arslantepe VI B2 (Frangipane and Palmieri 1983b: Fig. 18 nos 1, 3; 26 no. 7); Norşuntepe EB I (Hauptmann 1982: Pl. 43 nos 8, 9); Kurban Höyük IV (Algaze 1990: Pl. 79 A, B); Hassek Höyük (Hoh 1984: Fig. 11 no. 7). For northern Mesopotamian affinities see Tell Billa (Speiser 1933: Pl. 53 no. 3); Nineveh (Thompson and Mallowan 1933: Pl. 52 no. 8); and Telul Eth-Thalathat (Fukai et al. 1974: Pl. 49 nos 1-5). For flat-based bowls, see Frangipane and Palmieri 1983b: Fig. 20 no. 5; Algaze 1990: Pls 45 C; 54 P.

23.   Type 12: Arslantepe VI B2 (Frangipane and Palmieri 1983b: Fig. 14 nos 4, 5); Norşuntepe XXVI, EB I (Hauptmann 1982: Pl. 41 no. 2); Kurban Höyük V (Algaze 1990: Pls 49 F, G, H-J; 50 D-J); Amuq G (Braidwood and Braidwood 1960: Fig. 290 no. 1). Type 11: Kurban Höyük V (Algaze 1990: Pl. 48 D).

24.   The division of Reserved Slip Ware into an early (Late Chalcolithic) and late (Early Bronze) phase has been suggested by Palmieri and Sürenhagen, who base their division on a change in the slip technique and nature of decoration respectively. Both use the Reserved Slip horizon at Hassek Hoyük as a benchmark (Palmieri 1985b: 192; Sürenhagen 1986: 26; Behm-Blancke et al. 1981).

25.   Behm-Blancke 1987: Pl. 86 no. 12. Other jar parallels include Arslantepe (Frangipane and Palmieri 1983b: Fig. 15 nos 2-4, 7, 8); Norşuntepe XXVI, EB I (Hauptmann 1982: Pls 40 no. 7; 41 nos 3, 4); Değirmentepe III (Duru 1979: Pl. 34 nos 18-21); Hassek Höyük (Hoh 1984: Fig. 15 nos 1, 3); Kurban Höyük V (Algaze 1990: Pls 49 K-M, O, P; 50 B, C); stylistically different examples also occur in Level IV, Pl. 75 H-N. For similar bowls see Arslantepe VI B2 (Frangipane and Palmieri 1983b: Fig. 20 no. 10); Norşuntepe XXVI, EB I (Hauptmann 1982: Pl. 43 no. 2); Hassek Höyük (Hoh 1984: Fig. 10 nos 13-15). See Sagona 1984: 114 on the distribution of Reserved Slip Ware in East-Central Anatolia.

26.   Frangipane and Palmieri 1983b: Fig. 17.

27.   Behm-Blancke 1988.

28.   ibid., Figs 4; 5 nos 1-4. See also Telul Eth-Thalathat (Fukai et al. 1974: Pl. 51 nos 17-18); Nineveh (Thompson and Hamilton 1932: Pl. 55 nos 1, 3, 6, 7; Thompson and Mallowan 1933: Pl. 53 nos 13, 14); Chagar Bazar (Mallowan 1936: Fig. 19 no. 3); Dhahab (Amuq A) (Braidwood and Braidwood 1960: Fig. 222).

29.   Arslantepe VI B2 has a wide range of spouted jars. The closest parallel is illustrated in Frangipane and Palmieri 1983b: Fig. 16 no. 6. See also the smaller version from Hassek Höyük (Hoh 1984: Fig. 13 no. 1).

30.   Arslantepe VI B2 (Frangipane and Palmieri 1983b: Figs 18 nos 2, 4, 5; 19; 26 no. 6); Hassek Höyük EB I (Hoh 1981: Figs 13 nos 2, 4, 6; 14 nos 2, 5; idem 1984: Pl. 16 nos 1-5; Behm-Blancke

et al. 1984: 57-58).

31. Algaze 1990: Pl. 79 L-F.
32. Carchemish (Woolley 1914: Pl. 19a; Woolley and Barnett 1952: Pls 57a, b; 58a; 59). The graves at Tell Kara Hasan and Yazir are dated by Woolley to the champagne glass pot group not on the occurrence of these vessels, but on the basis of other objects, especially metalwork. Telul Eth-Thalathat (Fukai et al. 1974: Pl. 48 nos 3, 4, 8, 10-15, 17, 18); Nineveh (Thompson and Hamilton 1932: Pl. 56 no. 5).
33. Amuq H (Braidwood and Braidwood 1960); Hassek Höyük (Hoh 1984: 67; Fig. 11 no. 8); Kurban Höyük V (Algaze 1990: Pl. 43 G, H); Arslantepe (Frangipane and Palmieri 1983b: 555).
34. Norşuntepe (Hauptmann 1974 et al.: Pl. 80 no. 1; Yener 1984: Fig. 21 nos 1-5); Arslantepe (Palmieri 1981: Fig. 10 no. 1); Pulur (Koşay 1976b: Pl. 110 no. 1063).
35. Buchanan 1966: 10-18; Yener 1984: 123-24.
36. Amiet 1963: 63-65; Mellink 1962: 223.
37. Helms in French et al. 1972: 62 n. 4 draws attention to Frankfort 1939: Pl. 8c; Porada and Buchanan 1948: Pls 4, 5.
38. Frangipane and Palmieri 1983b: 566; Fig. 27 nos 2, 3; Hauptmann 1972: Pl. 69 no. 6; idem 1982: Pl. 26 no. 4; Mallowan 1937: Fig. 12 no. 10; idem 1964: 147.
39. Blades: Arslantepe (Frangipane and Palmieri 1983b: Fig. 29 nos 4-6); Tepecik (Esin et al. 1979: Fig. 65); Pulur (Koşay 1976b: Pls 95 second row, and no. 498; 96 no. 463; 97 nos 476, 481). Edge ground axe: Tepecik (Esin 1982b: Pl. 78 no. 15); Tülintepe (Esin 1976b: Pl. 87 TL 72-422; Esin and Arsebük 1982: Pl. 98 nos 13-16); Pulur (Koşay 1976b: Pls 99 nos 761, 731, 746; 100 no. 765, 764, 763, 762).
40. Alessio et al. 1983: 579; see also p. 296.
41. French in French 1973; Mitchell 1980.
42. French 1971: 36-37; French and Helms 1973.
43. Sagona 1984: Figs 82 (Form 182); 83 (Form 183).
44. Korucutepe EB II-III (Kelly-Buccellati 1978: Pl. 112 A-C); Norşuntepe EB I (Hauptmann 1972: Pls 72 nos 8, 11; 74 no. 4); Değirmentepe (Duru 1979: Pls 25 no. 19; 27 no. 19; 29 nos 4, 19, 20).
45. Korucutepe (Kelly-Buccellati 1978: Pls 112 D; 115 G); Norşuntepe (Hauptmann 1972: Pl. 74 no. 7); Tepecik (Esin et al. 1979: Pls 61 no. 9; 62 no. 21).
46. Kelly-Buccellati 1978: Pl. 118 C, E and especially F; Sagona 1984: Form 215.
47. Palmieri 1969: Figs 14 no. 9; 15 nos 13, 15; 16 nos 15, 18, 19, 21, 28; eadem 1973: Figs 30 nos 3-5, 7; 31 nos 1, 3, 6; 39 nos 1, 3.
48. Kelly-Buccellati 1978: 70; Pl. 113 M.
49. Sagona 1984: 68.
50. ibid., p. 69.
51. Burney 1958: 169, 205.
52. Algaze 1990: Pls 81 A-E, G, I; Matthiae 1977: 109; Fig. 21. The Aşvan pieces are not a close match to the fabric of the Mardikh vessels, which are overwhelming pale yellow in colour and only rarely tending towards pink.
53. Han İbrahim Şah (Ertem 1974: Pls 59 nos 23; 60 nos 1, 2); Yeniköy (Koşay 1976a: Pl. 115 nos 3, 4); Pulur (Koşay 1976b: 89-90; Pl. 69 no. 360; 88 nos 365, 367, 368, 370.
54. Esin 1970: Pl. 70 no. 3; eadem 1972: Pl. 110 no. 3; eadem 1973: Fig. 28.
55. von Luschan 1943: Pl. 32 N, O.
56. Norşuntepe (Hauptmann et al. 1976b: Pl. 47 no. 1); Tepecik (Esin 1982b: Pl. 78 nos 11, 12); Maxwell-Hyslop 1971: 23-24.
57. Frangipane and Palmieri 1983b: Fig. 29 no. 2.
58. Alessio et al. 1983: 579; see also p. 296.
59. Hauptmann 1972: Pl. 68 no. 6; Hauptmann et al. 1976a: Pl. 48 no. 12.

CHAPTER 3
East-Central Anatolia in the Early Bronze Age

Strung together, the three overlapping Aşvan Early Bronze Age sites span the greater portion (if not all) of the third millennium BC, and provide a useful check on the deeper sequences in the region. Briefly, the main ceramic features of the Aşvan sites are: Taşkun Mevkii (3,000-2,800 BC) — a Plain Simple Ware and Late Reserved Slip horizon with provincial Ninevite 5 influence, in a strong east Anatolian-Trans-Caucasian Early Bronze I context typified by Red-Black Burnished pottery; Aşvan Kale (2,800-2,000 BC?) — a local Early Bronze II-III tradition defined by a varied range of Red-Black Burnished pottery and Malatya-Elazığ Painted Ware, with only a few wheel-made Syro-Mesopotamian derived pieces; Taşkun Kale (2,800-2,000? BC) — a horizon comparable to Aşvan Kale.

From the spate of excavations in the Anatolian Euphrates basin over the last few decades, it has become increasingly apparent that cultural developments in the Chalcolithic and Early Bronze Age in this region owe much to both local and foreign influences. Accessible through a number of major routes, the fertile and resource rich Euphrates basin attracted Trans-Caucasians, Syro-Mesopotamians and, to a lesser extent, central Anatolians. The degree and nature of Syro-Mesopotamian contact allow the region to be divided into two cultural zones.[1] One encompasses the Malatya-Elazığ region, north of the Anti-Taurus ranges, and falls within the expansive culture province of East Anatolia and Trans-Caucasia.[2] The other incorporates the Euphrates region south of the Anti-Taurus.

To judge from the Halaf-like sherds at Tülintepe in the Altınova, the beginnings of foreign contacts were already, by the commencement of the Early Bronze Age, at least fifteen centuries old.[3] But the nature of these relations, to be sure, was not uniform. The Ubaid character of Değirmentepe 5-11 and the Late Uruk-related status of Arslantepe VIA, for instance, are clear enough as to leave little doubt about the pervasive influence of Syro-Mesopotamian relations there.[4] Likewise the prosperity of Norşuntepe in the Early Bronze IIIa period, manifested in its imposing architecture and high quality of goods, suggests that it was part of the extensive commercial network of the so-called Late Protosyrian period centred at Tell Mardikh IIB2.[5] Generally, however, foreign influences throughout the Chalcolithic and Early Bronze Age were well diluted by the time they reached sites north of the Anti-Taurus, especially those in the relatively isolated Murat Valley. Indeed in the middle stretch of the third millennium BC, southern interconnections all but disappeared at most sites in this region, having given way to the local east Anatolian tradition. These factors support the idea that contact, whether mercantile or otherwise, in the sixth to third millennia BC was directional and discontinuous rather than uniform.[6] They also suggest that whilst Syro-Mesopotamian cultural influence permeated this region, it was adapted and transformed by the local population. This push into the Syro-Anatolian region appears to have emanated from the riverine settlements along the Euphrates and Khabur complexes where, in the Uruk period, for instance, Mesopotamian colonies were established at Habuba Kabira, Quannas and Jebel Aruda. From this nexus a series of links were established with centres in the highland region via the main waterways in a deliberate attempt to exploit the natural resources this area had to offer.[7] Further, the evidence suggests that the Malatya-Elazığ region was a frontier zone on the periphery of the Syro-Mesopotamian orbit, with the Murat acting as the northernmost boundary.

By contrast, the lower reaches of the Euphrates south of the Taurus, in the districts of Adıyaman and Urfa, quite clearly formed a contact zone between Anatolia and its southern neighbours. Throughout the Chalcolithic and Early Bronze Age material of local character is found in association with remains displaying strong Syro-Mesopotamian affinities. Three of the sites in this region may be signalled as particularly significant in the late prehistoric period: Kurban Höyük for its overall albeit discontinuous sequence ranging from Halaf to the end of the Early Bronze Age (Periods VIII to IV);[8] Lidar Höyük for extensive third millennium deposits (Early Dynastic and Akkadian, to use the excavator's Mesopotamian terminology);[9] and Hassek Höyük for evidence relating to Late Uruk colonisation (Level 5) and the Early Bronze I and II periods (Levels 4-1).[10]

A few words must now be said on how the three Aşvan sequences can best be accommodated into the cultural developments of the Malatya-Elazığ region. In a recent study the author attempted to establish, however tentatively, a basic outline of the development of the wide-ranging Early Trans-Caucasian (or Kura-Araks) culture, whose hallmark is Red-Black Burnished pottery.[11] Several cultural traditions were defined on the basis of ceramic and architectural styles, and incorporated into a chronological scheme ranging from the mid-fourth millennium BC to the end of the third millennium BC. While the basic synchronisms between the Trans-Caucasian, East Anatolian and Iranian sequences remain essentially unchanged, the unabated flow of annual reports and the partial publication of excavations at sites in the Turkish Euphrates basin, and indeed the author's own examination of the Aşvan material itself, have necessitated a major re-evaluation of cultural relations in East-Central Anatolia (Table 9).

Recently, Palmieri outlined the nature of developments along the Turkish Euphrates during the transition between the Late Chalcolithic and Early Bronze I, emphasising Mesopotamian relations and its proto-Urban context.[12] Palmieri defined this transition on the basis of the change from Early (Late Chalcolithic) to Late (Early Bronze I) Reserved Slip Ware which, in effect, documents a move towards a more sophisticated style of reserve decoration. Equally valid is the distinction made by the Kurban excavators between the chaff-tempered coarse ware of the Late Chalcolithic and the finer, grit-tempered Plain Simple Ware of the Early Bronze Age.[13] These ceramic distinctions reflect more significant cultural changes: first, a general move away from the public buildings of the late fourth millennium BC to dwellings of a more domestic nature in the early centuries of the following millennium; second, an increase in metallurgical activity in the Early Bronze Age; third, the gradual disappearance of clay seals and sealings during the Early Bronze Age, which, like the Uruk-related coarse bowls, are often associated with a centralised exchange system.

Only at Hassek Höyük do we find an apparently smooth transition from an Early Reserved Slip and Late Uruk horizon (Level 5 A-C) to a Late Reserved Slip phase (Levels 1-4).[14] Nearby at Kurban Höyük, a local Late Chalcolithic horizon (Period VI), distinguished by the appearance of Uruk-like vessels towards its end, is followed by Late Reserved Slip pottery.[15] Arslantepe, too, still the benchmark for cultural developments in the Malatya-Elazığ region, documents an abrupt change from Late Uruk (Period VIA) to Late Reserved Slip (VIB2).[16] Here the sequence is interrupted by a phase with strong Trans-Caucasian connections (VIB1). Similarly, at Norşuntepe Late Reserved Slip pottery is separated from local Late Chalcolithic wares by a hiatus.[17] In the early levels of the lengthy 'Early Bronze I' period (Levels XXVI-XXV), Plain Simple Ware is clearly dominant, but declines in quantity during the round house phase (Level XXIV), finally giving way to Red-Black Burnished Ware, and Malatya-Elazığ painted from Level XXIII onward, whose appearance initiated the Early Bronze II period.[18] The development pattern is different again at Tepecik where local Late Chalcolithic Ware (below Level 14) is followed by an interesting conjunction, in Building 1-2, of Uruk-derived pieces with material which recalls Central Anatolian tradition — 'fruitstands' and sherds with an incised, white-filled pattern.[19] Plain Simple Ware is also dominant at Tepecik during the Early Bronze I levels, comprising about two thirds of the assemblage, but dwindles to less than 10% by Early Bronze IIIA.[20] To this list of Early Bronze I sites can now be added Taşkun Mevkii 1-4, a Late Reserved Slip horizon, to use Palmieri's terminology.[21] Unlike the scene at Norşuntepe and Tepecik, however, Plain Simple Ware never predominates at Taşkun Mevkii. Not surprisingly the Taşkun Mevkii horizon matches more closely the picture at Pulur (XI-IX) and Han İbrahim Şah (XIV-XI), both located in the Murat valley, where Early Bronze I ceramics are represented almost entirely by the Red-Black Burnished variety.[22] Thus to judge from the concentration of Plain Simple Ware in the Altınova, the Murat valley around Aşvan was only of marginal interest to Syrian merchants at the turn of the third millennium BC.

During the Early Bronze II, a period best defined by the appearance of Malatya-Elazığ Painted Ware and a predominance of polished pottery, East-Central Anatolia distanced itself from activities further south and became well ensconced within the broader developments of the eastern highlands. Taşkun Mevkii was abandoned at the beginning of this period about 2800 BC, overlapping with Aşvan Kale and Taşkun Kale which continued on. None of the buildings found in the Malatya-Elazığ region can be designated as large or public. Indeed there is a noticeable decline in the number and size of structures. Architecture now generally comprised either fairly simple wattle-and-daub affairs, or rectangular structures made entirely of mud bricks; stones were rarely used as foundations. Although the dwellings at Pulur from Level VIII upwards are stylistically similar to those from the earlier periods, they are considerably fewer.[23] The same holds true for Han İbrahim Şah X-VIII, noted for its horseshoe-shaped and round hearths.[24] This period at Korucutepe (Period D) saw the establishment of several mud brick houses built round a courtyard with cooking installations.[25] At Tepecik buildings were rectangular and mud brick in Levels 4-11, Early Bronze II according to Esin, with only the larger walls having stones occasionally embedded in their foundations.[26] Of totally different character are the post structures erected at Norşuntepe and Değirmentepe which attest to the continuing influence of the north Georgian region.[27] No architecture has been as yet uncovered at Arslantepe VIC, which, to judge from a series of pits found in the level, was probably a semi-permanent settlement.[28] This transient settlement pattern at Arslantepe is perhaps highlighted by the re-occupation of the nearby rock shelter at Gelinciktepe last inhabited in the Chalcolithic.[29]

A resurgence of Syrian connections characterises the Early Bronze III period north of the Anti-Taurus, at a time when the commercial empire of Ebla (Tell Mardikh IIB1) was at its most expansive and influential.[30] Red-Black Burnished pottery now often displays a lustrous surface which, if decorated, is usually incised. Amongst the common forms of Red-Black Burnished pottery are bowls with inturned rim, and tall, ovoid jars with swollen rim. Painted pottery in the Malatya region bears a finer execution of draughtsmanship, though the rather crude style is still pervasive in the conservative Murat valley.

The prosperity of the period is clearly reflected in architecture and is best illustrated at Norşuntepe, the most significant site towards the end of the third millennium BC. In Levels XII and XIII, the site was characterised by a well-defined street flanked by mud-brick houses. Later, in Levels VII/VIII, the citadel area was dominated by a complex comprising a large storeroom filled with pithoi and a room with a platform and domed ovens.[31] Other areas (N-O/18-20) contained large blocks of rooms with large horseshoe-shaped hearths. Nearby, at Tepecik, the Early Bronze Age III levels were distinguished by a main street lined with blocks of rectangular houses, in certain cases rebuilt several times.[32] At Korucutepe the highlight of Period E was an imposing thick-walled building (6 x 9m) designated 'the hall'. Plastered on the inside, this structure contained a bench, hearth and three horseshoe-shaped andirons. It was rebuilt in Stratum LXXXIX, but not along the lines of its former structure.[33] Towards the end of the Early Bronze Age, Period F, the settlement at Korucutepe shifted to the base of the mound and was represented by rather undistinguished structures. In the Murat valley, the house at Taşkun Kale and the sturdy stone-based buildings

at Han İbrahim Şah VII-V clearly belong to this architectural tradition. Houses in the Malatya region, at Şemşiyetepe, İmamoğlu and Köskerbaba in particular, reflect the same prosperity with well constructed and plastered walls, large hearths and fine local painted pottery.[34] But Arslantepe had not yet fully recovered from the isolation of the Early Bronze II. Only the Early Bronze IIIB has thus far been attested at the site, but its architectural features, including a stone paved courtyard, are typical of the latter half of the third millennium BC.[35]

What attracted Syrian and Mesopotamian merchants and colonists to the highlands of East-Central Anatolia? With the rapid expansion of cities in Mesopotamia evidenced, in particular, by ambitious construction projects and an increase in luxury commodities, there appear to have been two likely reasons: first and foremost the procurement of metals, especially copper, and second the demand for timber. Sites with an Uruk cultural context in the Malatya-Elazığ region, contiguous to the rich mineral deposits in the Anti-Taurus, attest fairly advanced metallurgical activity during the second half of the fourth millennium BC.[36] Pre-eminent amongst the metalwork finds are the arsenical bronzes of nine swords, some decorated with silver inlay, twelve spearheads, and a series of small finds from Arslantepe VIA.[37] The swords, whose flat hilts suggest a ceremonial rather than functional use, stand alone in the Near Eastern metalwork repertoire, while the spearheads belong to a general class concentrated in southern Anatolia and northern Syria. Constituting some of the finest late fourth millennium pieces to be found anywhere in the Near East, these Arslantepe objects reflect skilled craftsmanship and an expertise in sophisticated smelting and alloying techniques. Silver metallurgy during this period is best represented by the jewellery found in two rectangular tombs belonging to the Chalcolithic cemetery of Korucutepe Phase B. Both the construction of the tomb and the style of other grave goods can be matched at Gawra in Strata XI-IX.[38] These finds from the Upper Euphrates basin do indeed support the argument made by some that advances in metal technology and craftsmanship were likely in those areas closest to the mining centres.[39]

Metallurgical activity continued unabated in the Early Bronze Age when interconnections extended beyond north Syria and Mesopotamia to include eastern Anatolia and Trans-Caucasus, themselves areas noted for their tradition of metal production.[40] This new impetus from the east is manifested by the utilisation of arsenical bronze which can be attributed to the influence or arrival of Early Trans-Caucasian folk in the Malatya-Elazığ region, who moved into the vacuum created by the collapse of Late Chalcolithic centres. Whilst the dagger found at Hassek indicates that weapons continued to be produced, pins are now the commonest metal type found at sites along the Upper Euphrates, with chisels equally well distributed geographically.[41] That this period had an active metalworking tradition is also reflected in the large quantities of metal slag at Arslantepe, and the crucibles from Norşuntepe and Pulur.[42]

Timber is also likely to have been exported. Working from admittedly scanty cuneiform sources of the third and second millennium BC, Rowton maintained that the eastern Taurus including the hills surrounding the region south of Malatya probably constituted the vast wooded expanse known to Mesopotamians as Mt. Hasur or the 'Wild Cypress Mountain', named after the *hasurru*-tree, the *Cupressus semperavens horizontalis*.[43] On the basis of the occurrence of the term in epics, myths and religious texts, Rowton has argued in favour of the 'antiquity' of the term which was probably used at the onset of the Bronze Age, if not earlier. The wild cypress, naturally confined to the foothill regions, was keenly sought by the Sumerians for the construction of their temples and palaces because of its wood's fragrance. Given Mesopotamian

interaction with settlements in the Elazığ region, it is not unlikely that trees were felled throughout the area south of the Murat and then floated down the major water courses to their destinations.[44] Later texts also refer to this area as an exporter of wine, oil and essences, though it is difficult to ascertain how far back the trade in these perishable items extends.[45] In regard to imports from Mesopotamia, again later texts suggest manufactured goods like textiles, and possibly bitumen and animal husbandry too. All this evidence points to a highly centralized exchange system up till the Early Dynastic III period, when the political situation in both the highlands of Anatolia and the lowlands further south was disrupted. In the Elazığ region, this transformation is characterised by the increase of Syrian wares and the establishment of substantial local centres.

To sum up, the Aşvan Early Bronze Age sites provide a useful series of overlapping sequences that flesh out the cultural developments in East-Central Anatolia in the 3rd millennium BC. Evidence suggests that the Murat region was relatively conservative compared to the Altınova plain and the Euphrates basin south of the Anti-Taurus. The district harboured a strong east Anatolian-Trans-Caucasian cultural tradition that was marginally influenced by Syro-Mesopotamian activities.

NOTES

1. Both Palmieri (1985b) and Sürenhagen (1986: 10-13, 30).
2. Among the seminal studies are: Arsebük 1979; Burney and Lang 1971; Burney 1980; Kushnareva 1970; Munchaev 1975; Sagona 1984.
3. Esin et al. 1979: 122-29; Esin and Arsebük 1982: 127-28.
4. Esin 1982a; eadem 1987; Frangipane and Palmieri 1983a: 287-448; Frangipane and Palmieri 1987; Palmieri 1985b: 194ff. Of the Anatolian sites attesting Uruk influence, Sürenhagen, concerned with the question of what constitutes an Uruk settlement, designates only Hassek Höyük as 'genuine' (1986: 13). The others, according to him, are 'Uruk-related'. See also Algaze 1989a.
5. Hauptmann et al. 1976b: 72-79; Hauptmann 1979: 69-73; idem 1982: 43-48.
6. Algaze 1986: 275; Marfoe 1987: 28
7. Burney 1980; Marfoe 1987: 29
8. Marfoe et al. 1986.
9. Hauptmann 1983; idem 1984; idem 1985.
10. Behm-Blancke et al. 1981; Behm-Blancke et al. 1984.
11. Sagona 1984.
12. Palmieri 1985b.
13. Algaze 1986: 278. See discussion on p. 312.
14. Behm-Blancke 1981.
15. Marfoe et al. 1986: 56-58.
16. Frangipane and Palmieri 1983b: 572. See postscript below.
17. Hauptmann 1972: 113-15; idem 1982: 59-61.

18. Hauptmann 1982: 53-57.
19. Esin 1976a: 114-16; eadem 1982b: 117.
20. Esin 1982b: 104-105.
21. van Loon 1978: 9-13. Although Korucutepe did not yield any Early Bronze I material (an unexcavated deposit of five metres comprising Strata XLV-LIV, Period C, has been tentatively assigned to this period), the site was occupied during the Late Chalcolithic, Period B, which attested Uruk ceramic forms.
22. Koşay 1976b: Pl. 56 no. 214 is the only recognisable Syro-Mesopotamian like piece. Note too the absence of wheel-made wares in the percentages on p. 150.
23. Koşay 1976b: 127-31.
24. Ertem 1974: Pl. 66.
25. van Loon 1978: 13-18.
26. Esin 1982b: 104.
27. Hauptmann 1979: 70-71; idem 1982: 48-49; Duru 1979: 70, 72.
28. Palmieri 1973: 110-12. See postscript below.
29. Palmieri 1967; eadem 1968.
30. This contact is apparent in the ceramic horizon by the occurrence of Simple Ware and Akkadian (or Metallic) Ware. Sagona 1984: 115-17.
31. Hauptmann 1979: 64-68; idem 1982: 45-48.
32. Esin 1982b: 100-104.
33. van Loon 1978: 18-23.
34. Darga 1982; eadem 1983; eadem 1985; Uzunoğlu 1985; Bilgi 1985.
35. Palmieri 1973: 83-93. See postscript below.
36. Frangipane 1985: 215ff.
37. Frangipane and Palmieri 1983a: 394-407.
38. Brandt 1978: 61-62; Frangipane 1985: 218.
39. Frangipane in Frangipane and Palmieri (eds) 1983a: 406.
40. Abesadze 1969.
41. Palmieri 1985b: 296.
42. loc. cit.; at Pulur crucibles are identified as 'cosmetic cups', Koşay 1976b: Pl. 59.
43. Rowton 1967: 268.
44. Whallon and Kantman 1969: 131-32.
45. Marfoe 1987: 29.

Postscript

At the same time as this volume was in press, two articles relevant to this chapter were published. One appeared in the Alba Palmieri memorial volume — CONTI, A. M. and PERSIANI, C., 1993, When Worlds Collide: Cultural Developments in Eastern Anatolia in the Early Bronze Age. In Frangipane, M., Hauptmann, H., Liverani, M., Matthiae, P., and Mellink, M. (eds), *Between the Rivers and Over the Mountains. Archaeologica Anatolica et Mesopotamica. Alba Palmieri Dedicata*, Rome: 361-413. The other is by MARRO, C., 1992, Introduction à la Céramique du Haut-Euphrate au Bronze Ancien. *In Anatolia Antiqua: Eski Anadolu II* (Bibliothèque de l'Institut Français d'études Anatoliennes d'Istanbul 38), Paris: 43-69. Although time has not allowed either paper to be discussed in the manner they deserve, the attention of readers is drawn to their conclusions and in particular to the outline of the Arslantepe sequence in the Conti and Persiani paper.

FIGURES AND CATALOGUES

The following abbreviations are used in the catalogues:

D = diameter

RD = rim diameter

BD = base diameter

H = height

L = length

W = width

Th = thickness

HM = hand-made

WM = wheel-made

max. = maximum

pres. = preserved

All measurements are in cm.

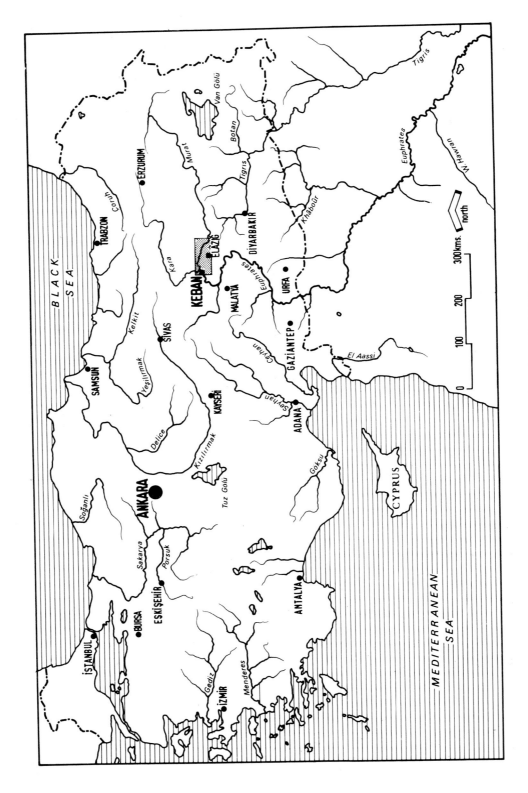

Anatolia and Keban area (after French 1973: Fig. 1)

Fig. 1

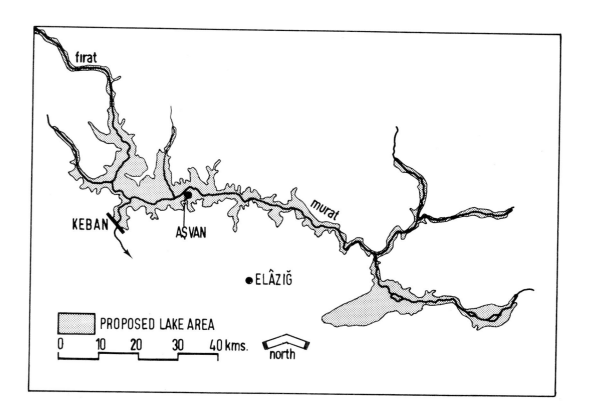

Keban area and Aşvan (after French 1973: Fig. 2)

Fig. 2

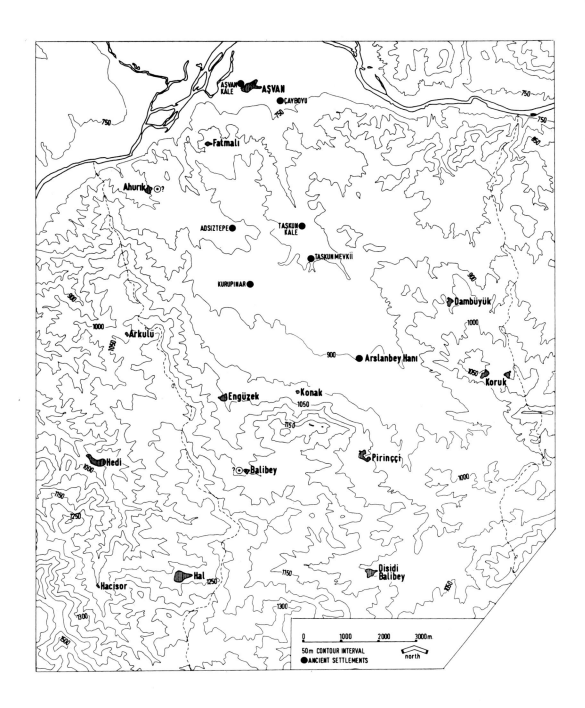

Sites in the Aşvan region (after French 1973: Fig. 3)

Fig. 3

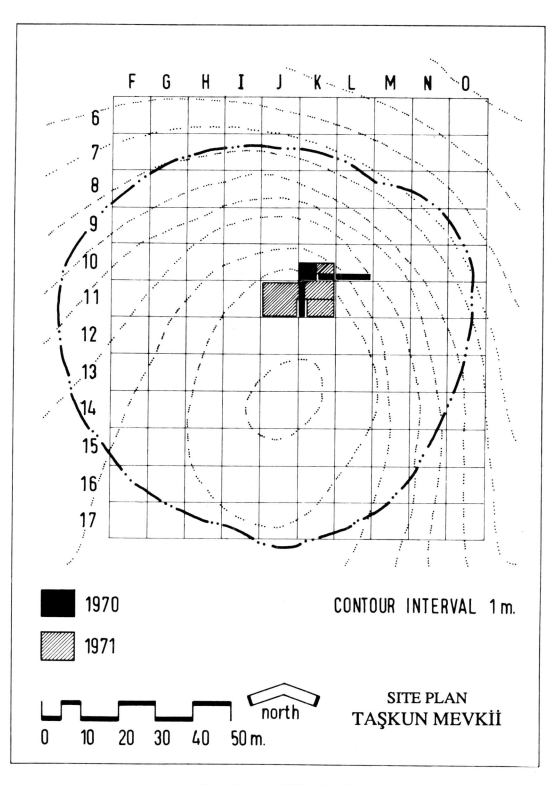

(after Helms 1973: Fig. 1)

Fig. 4

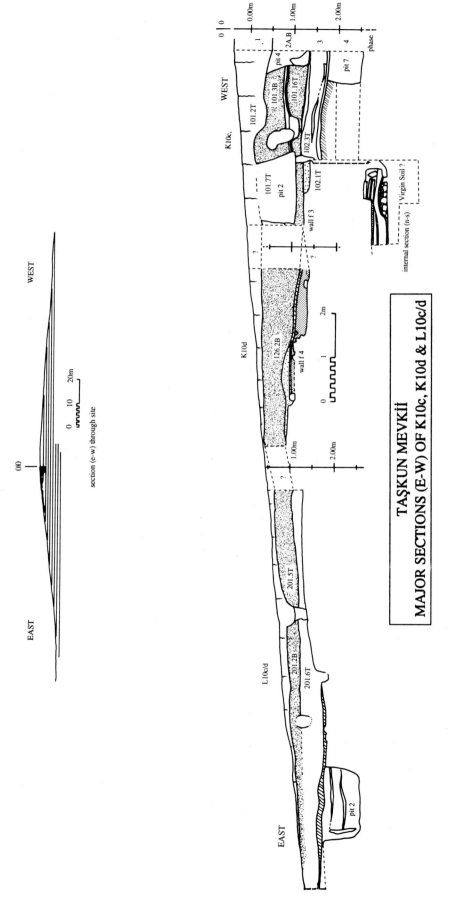

Fig. 5

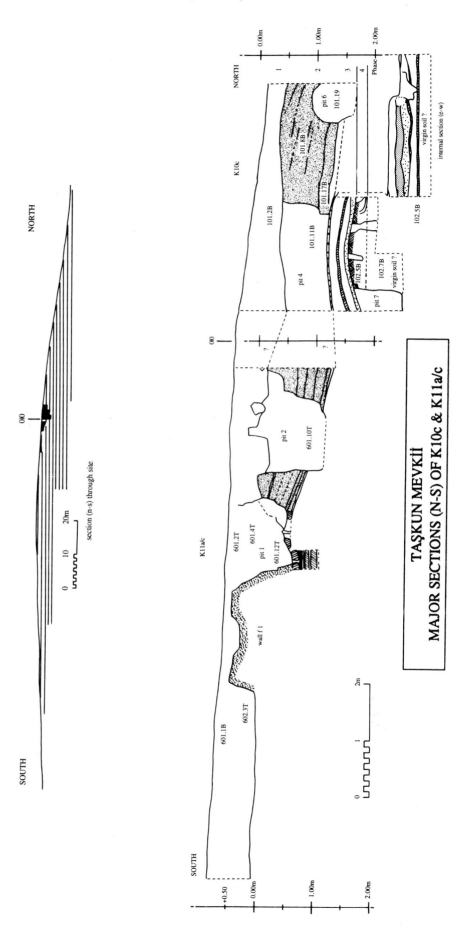

TAŞKUN MEVKİİ
MAJOR SECTIONS (N-S) OF K10c & K11a/c

Fig. 6

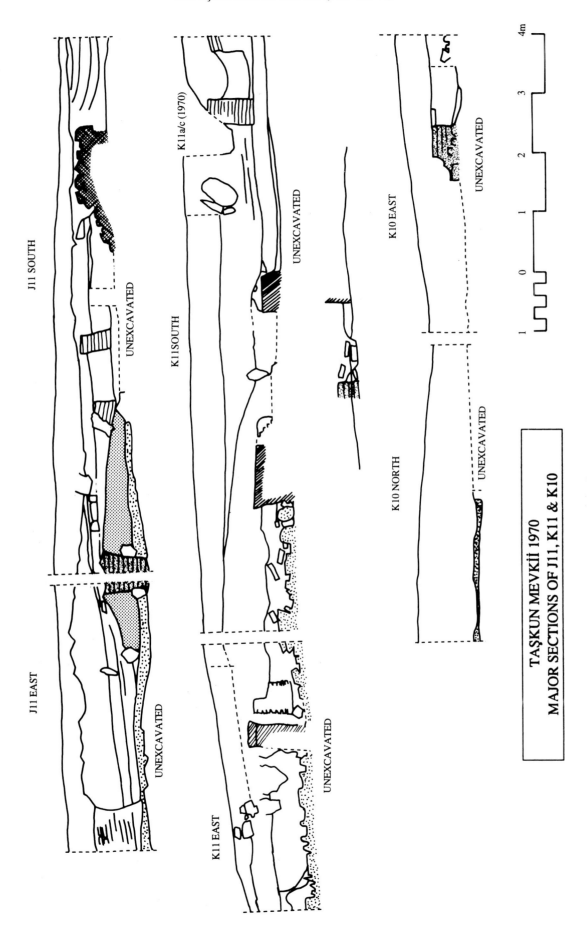

Fig. 7

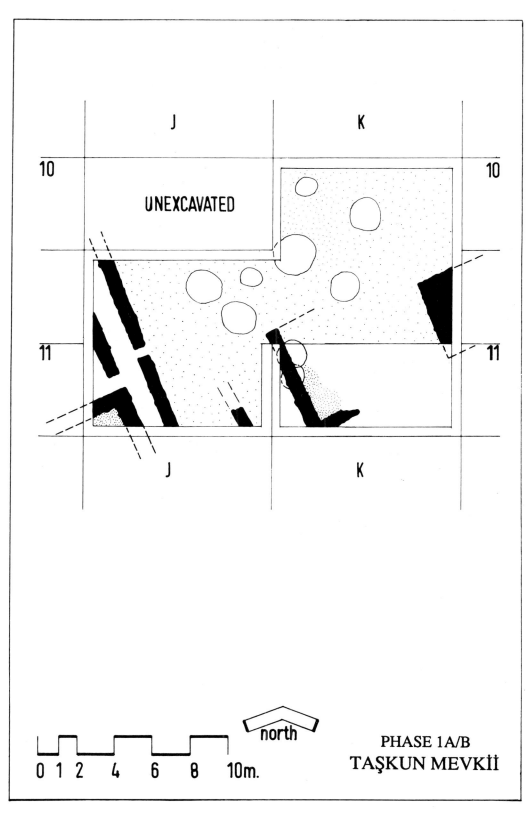

(after Helms 1973: Fig. 2)

Fig. 8

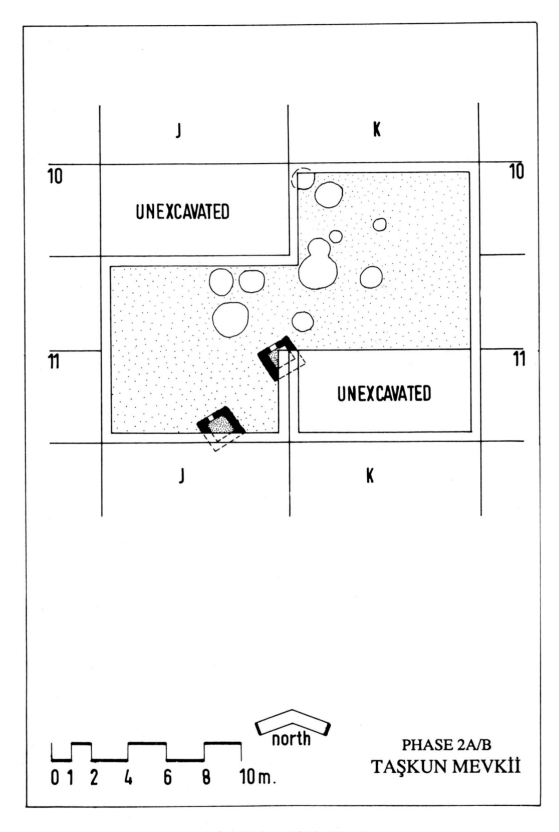

(after Helms 1973: Fig. 3)

Fig. 9

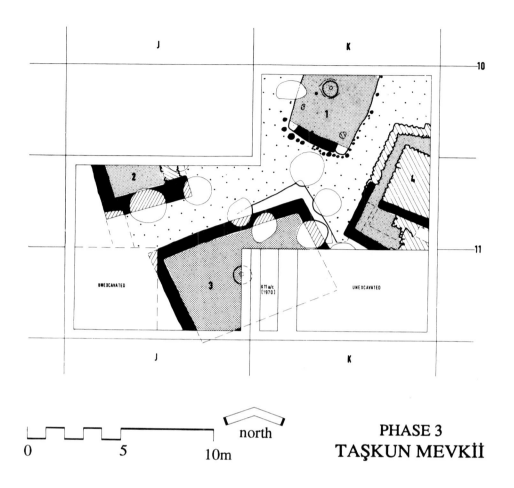

PHASE 3
TAŞKUN MEVKİİ

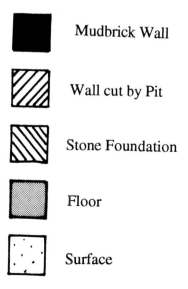

Mudbrick Wall

Wall cut by Pit

Stone Foundation

Floor

Surface

(after Helms 1973: Fig. 4)

Fig. 10

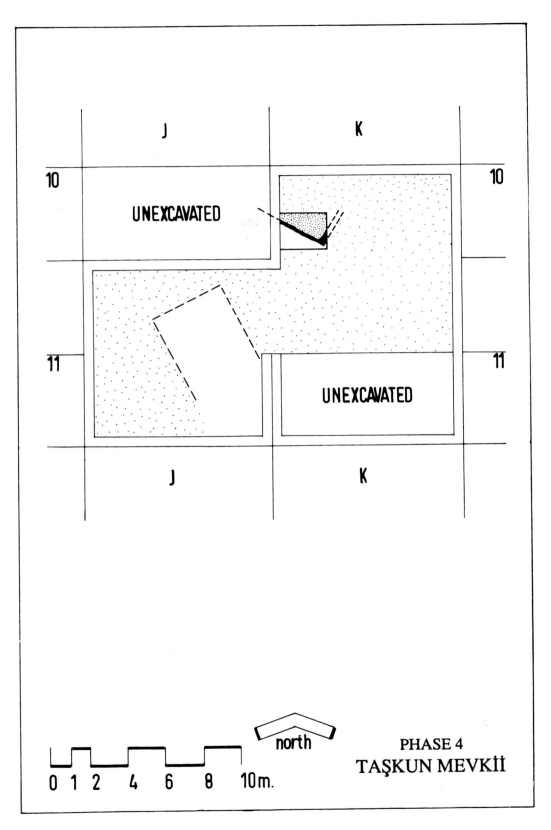

(after Helms 1973: Fig. 7)

Fig. 11

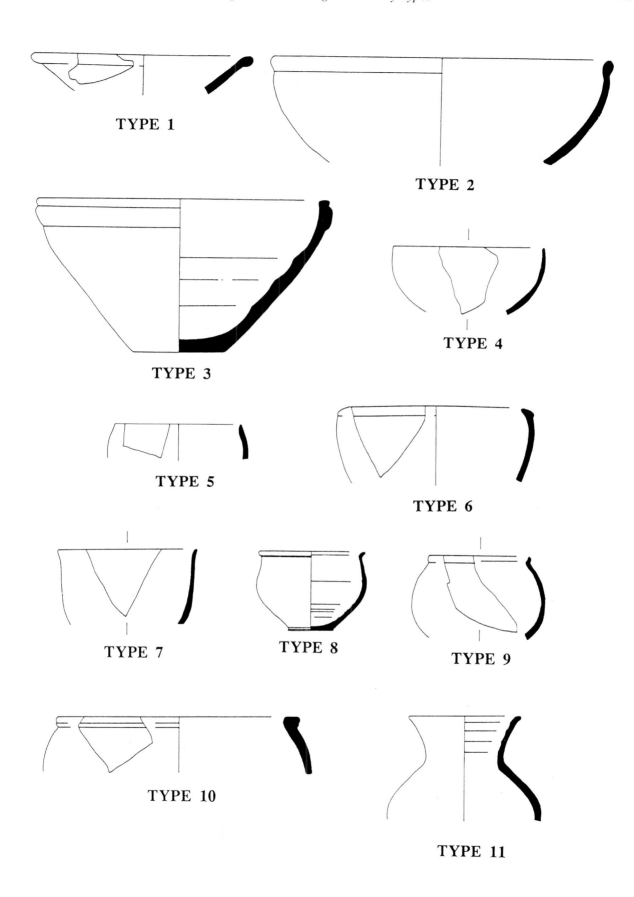

PLAIN SIMPLE WARE

Fig. 20

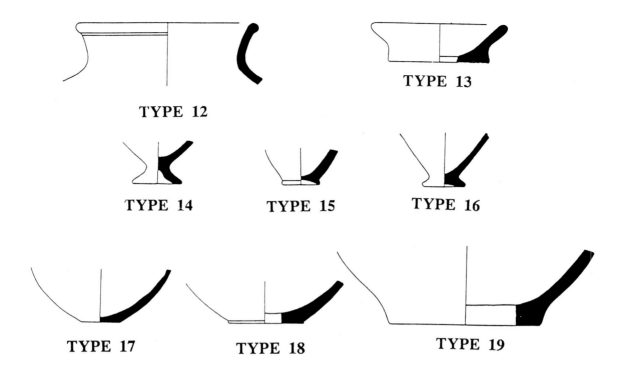

TYPE 12

TYPE 13

TYPE 14

TYPE 15

TYPE 16

TYPE 17

TYPE 18

TYPE 19

PLAIN SIMPLE WARE

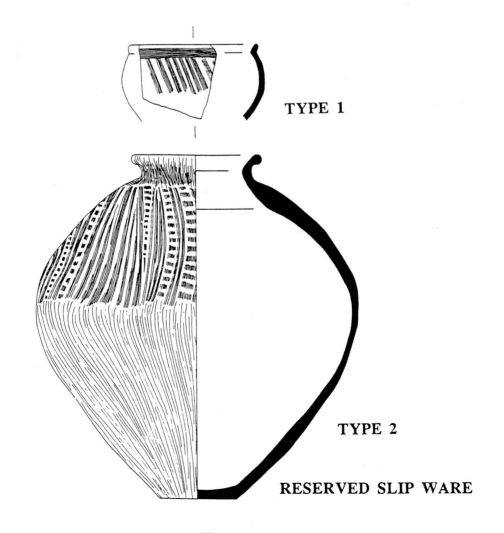

TYPE 1

TYPE 2

RESERVED SLIP WARE

Fig. 21

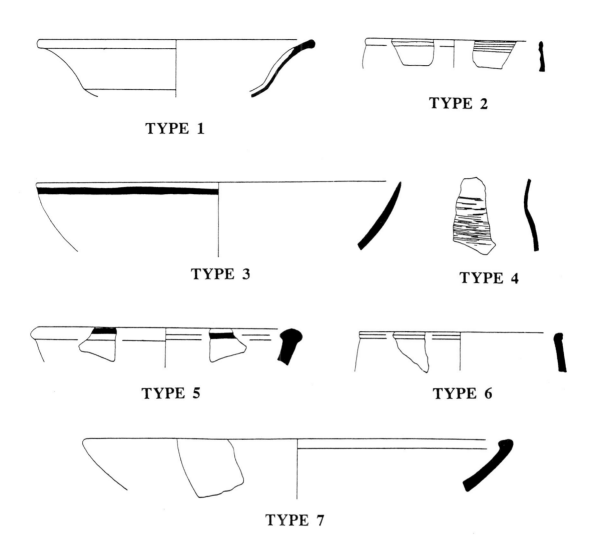

SIMPLE AND PAINTED SIMPLE WARE

PAINTED BEIGE-BROWN WARE

Fig. 22

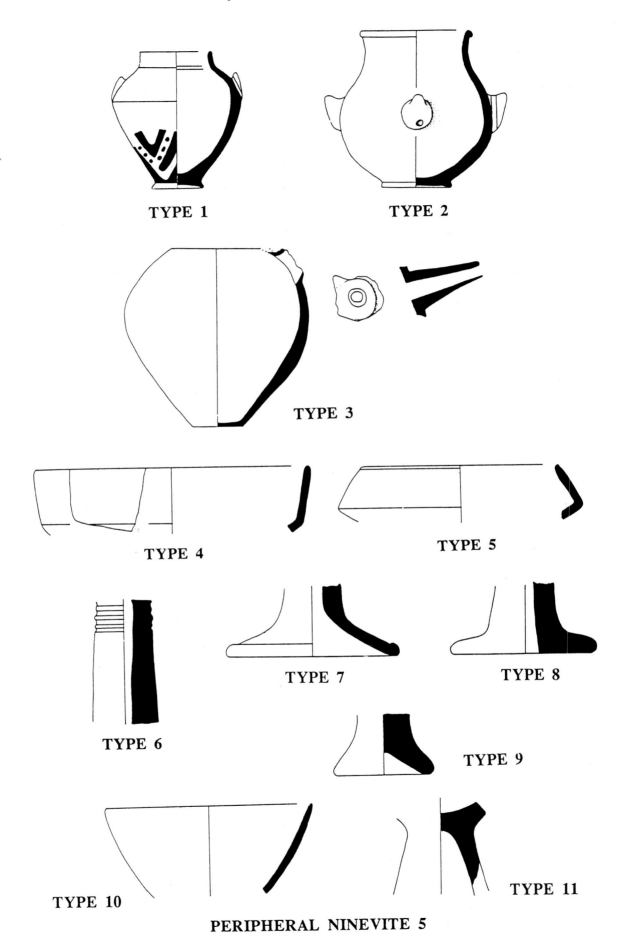

TYPE 1

TYPE 2

TYPE 3

TYPE 4

TYPE 5

TYPE 6

TYPE 7

TYPE 8

TYPE 9

TYPE 10

TYPE 11

PERIPHERAL NINEVITE 5

Fig. 23

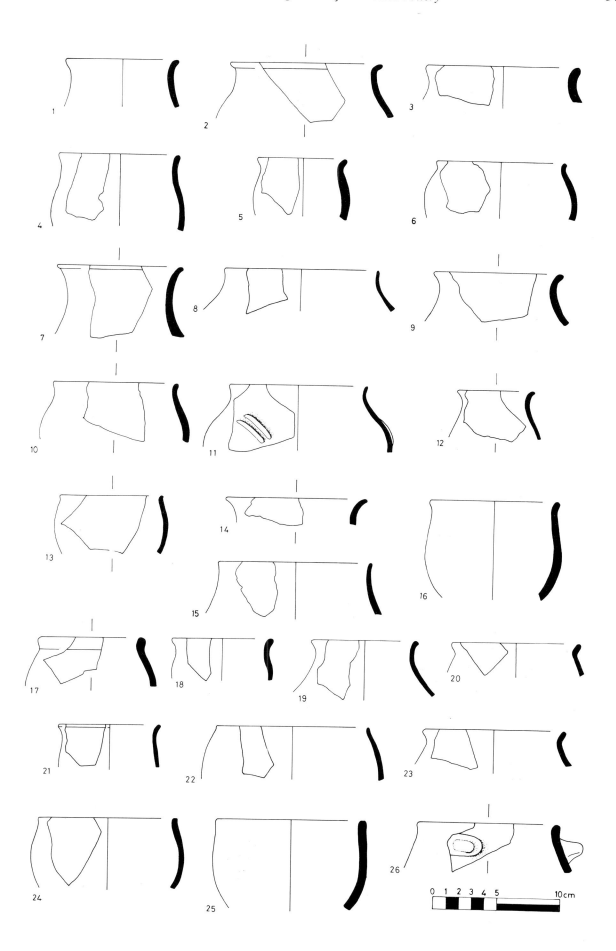

Fig. 36

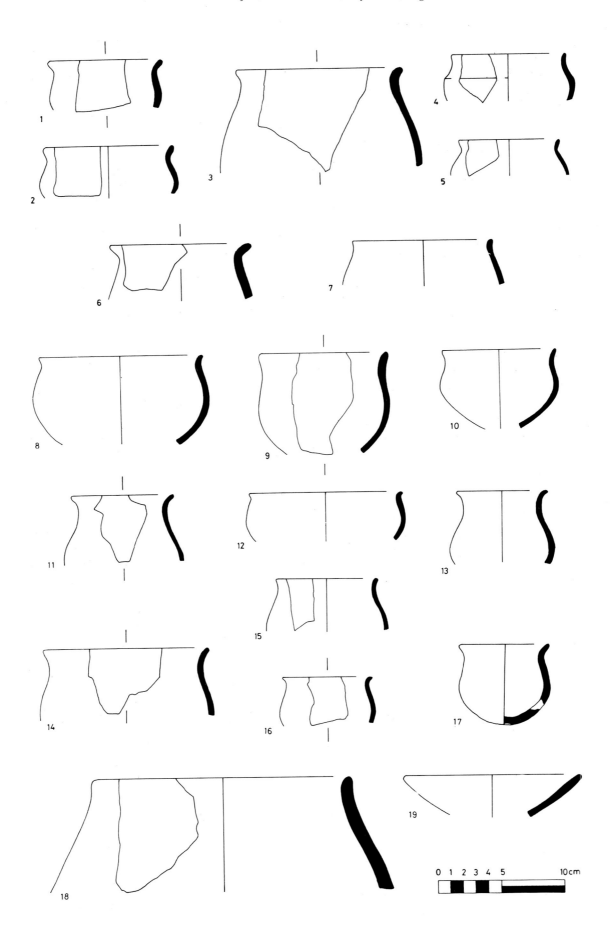

Fig. 37

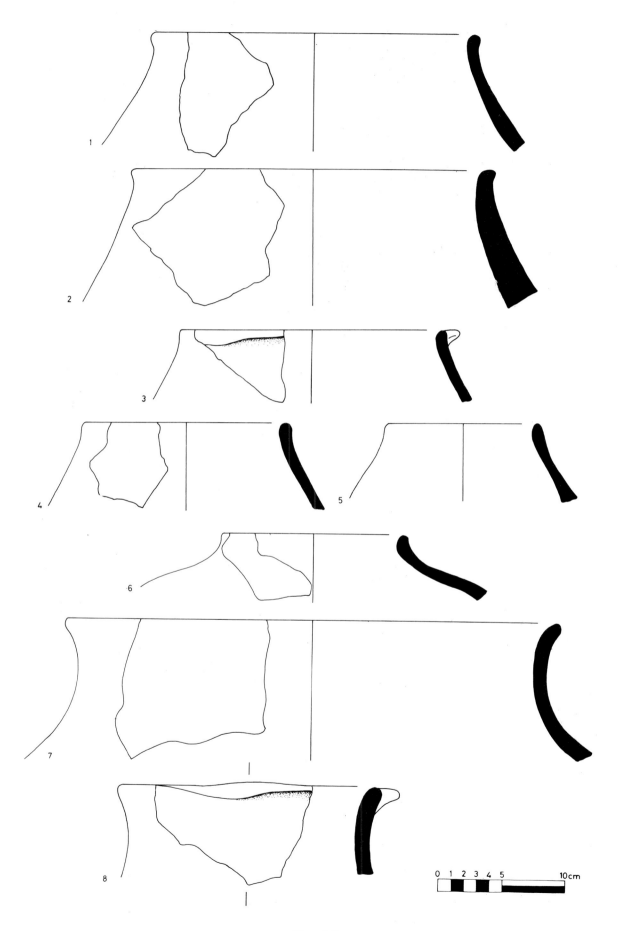

Fig. 38

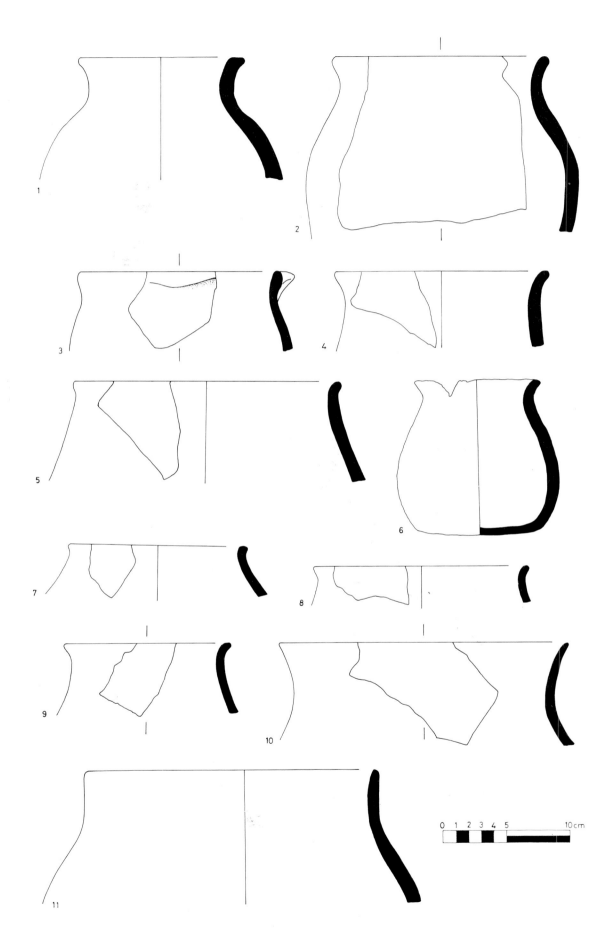

Fig. 39

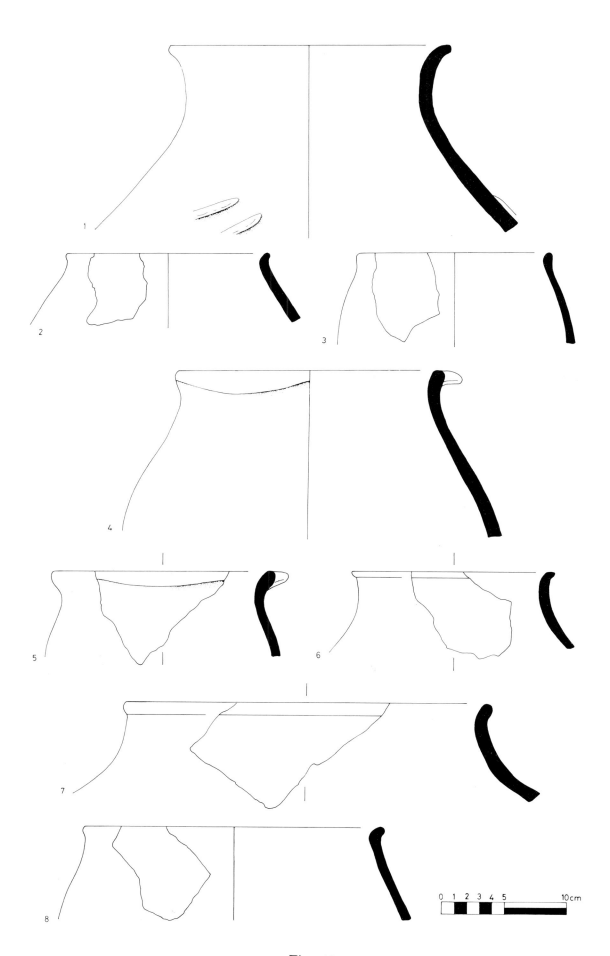

Fig. 40

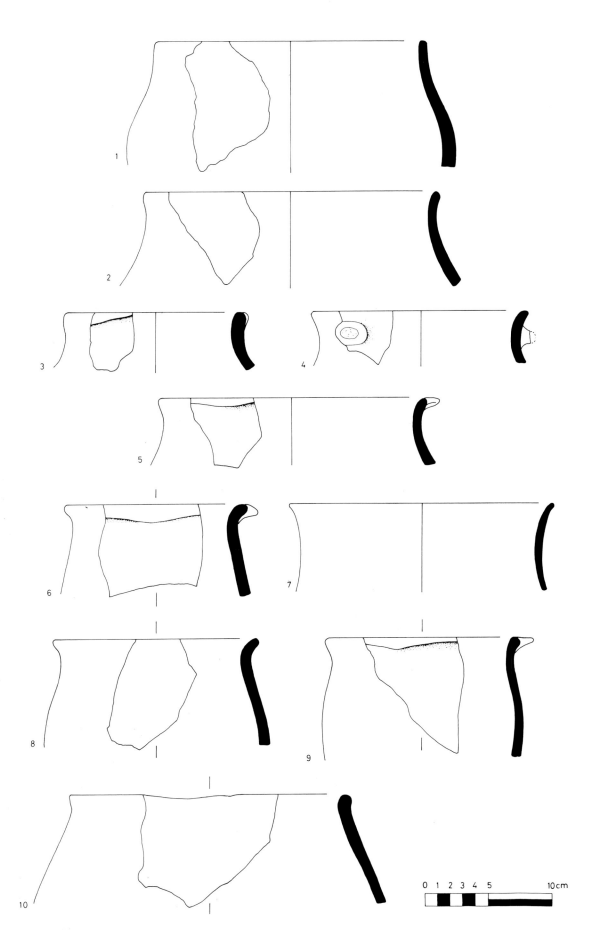

Fig. 41

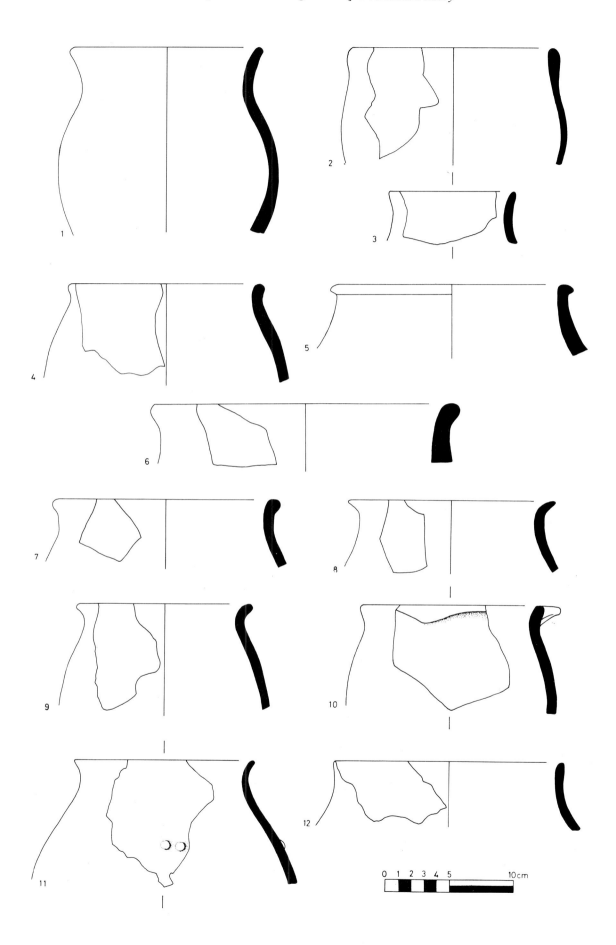

Fig. 42

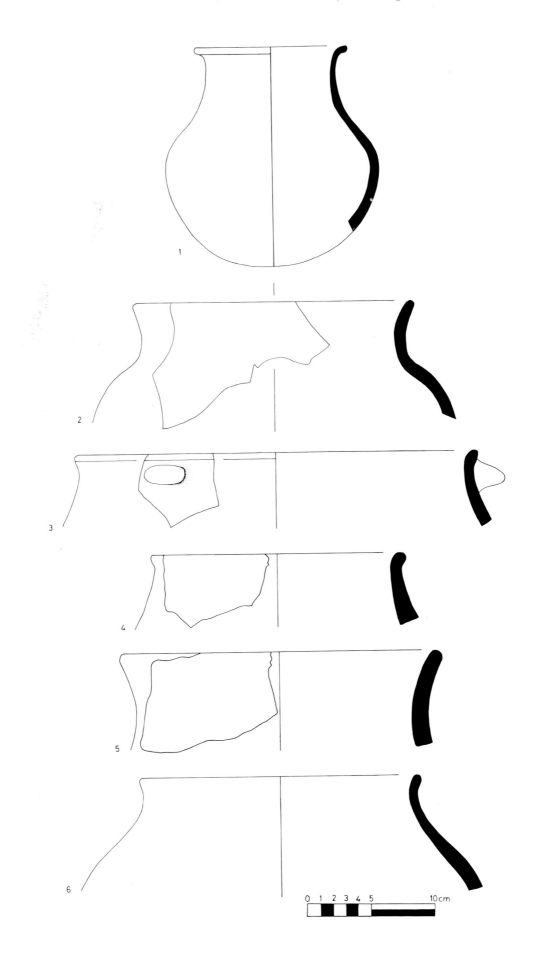

Fig. 43

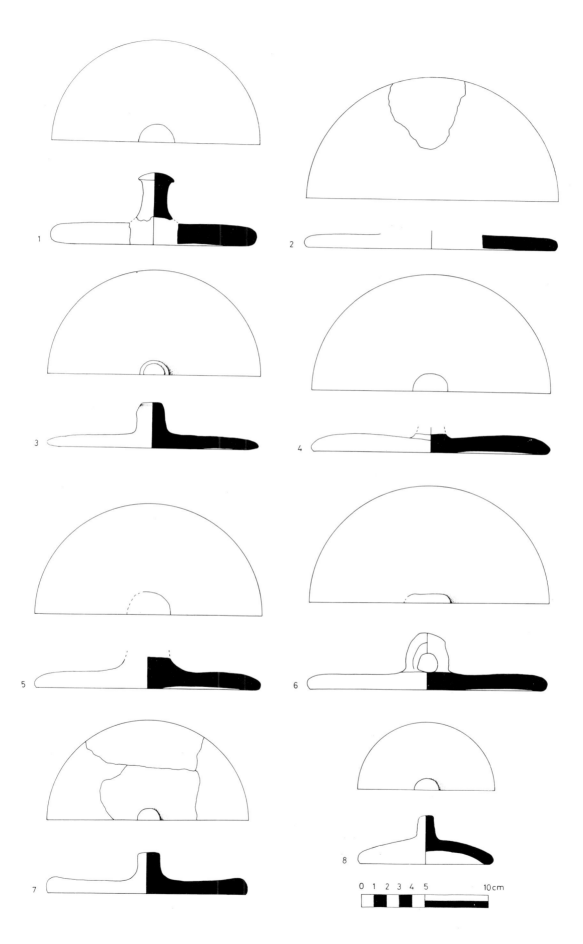

Fig. 52

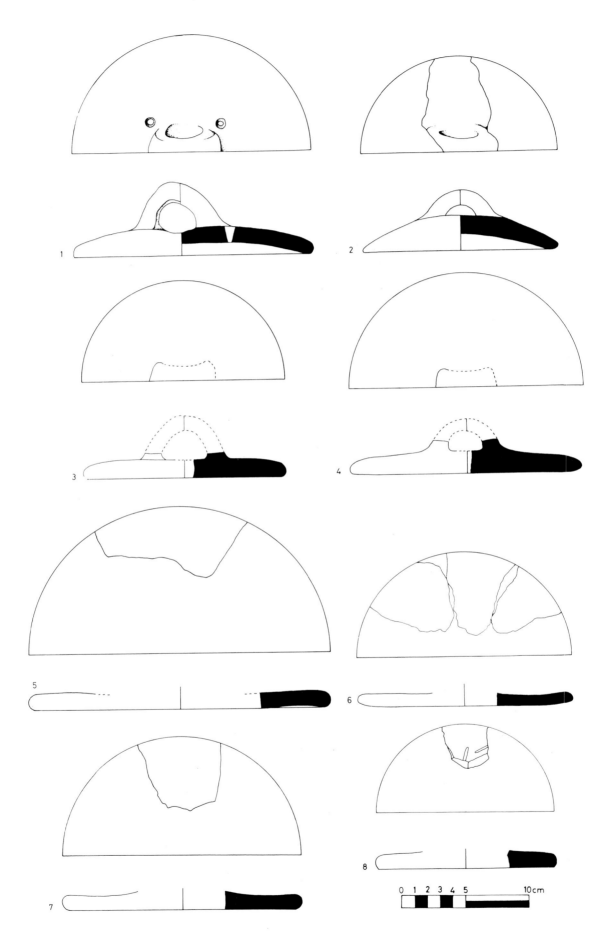

Fig. 53

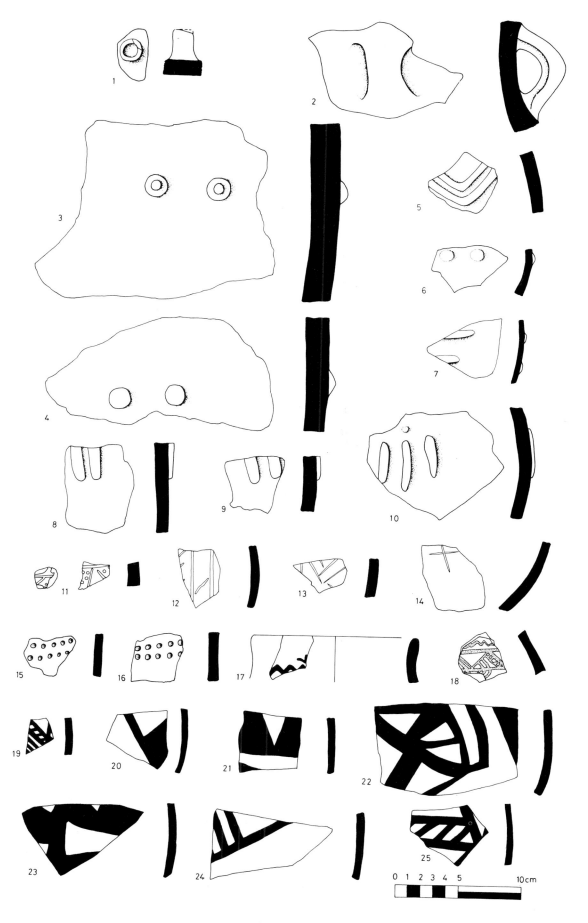

Fig. 54

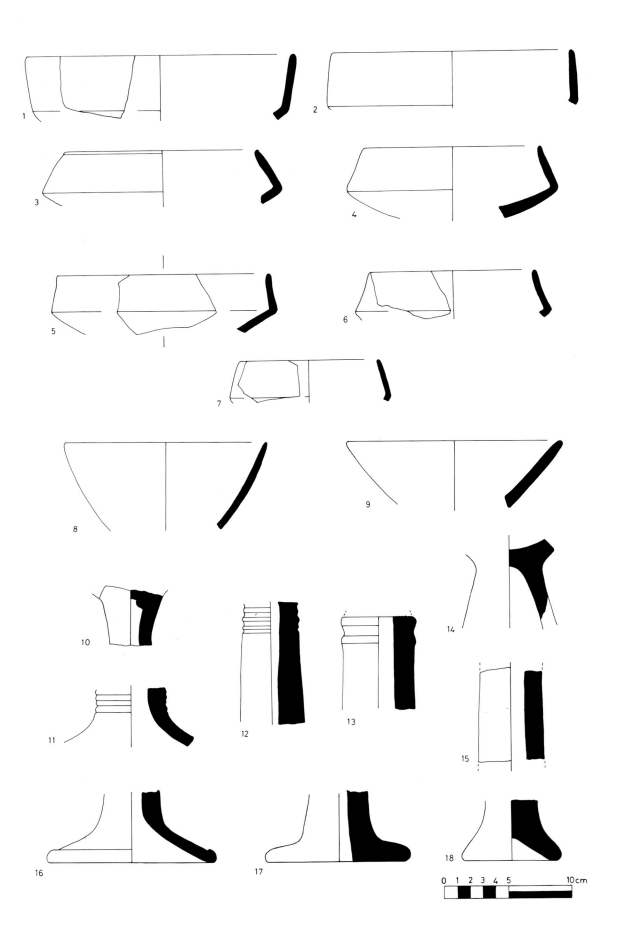

Fig. 55

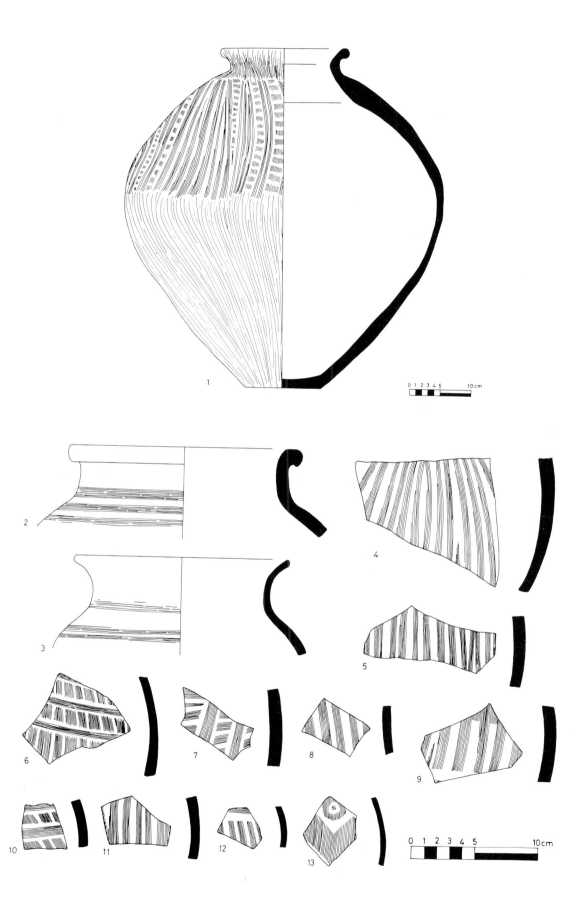

Fig. 56

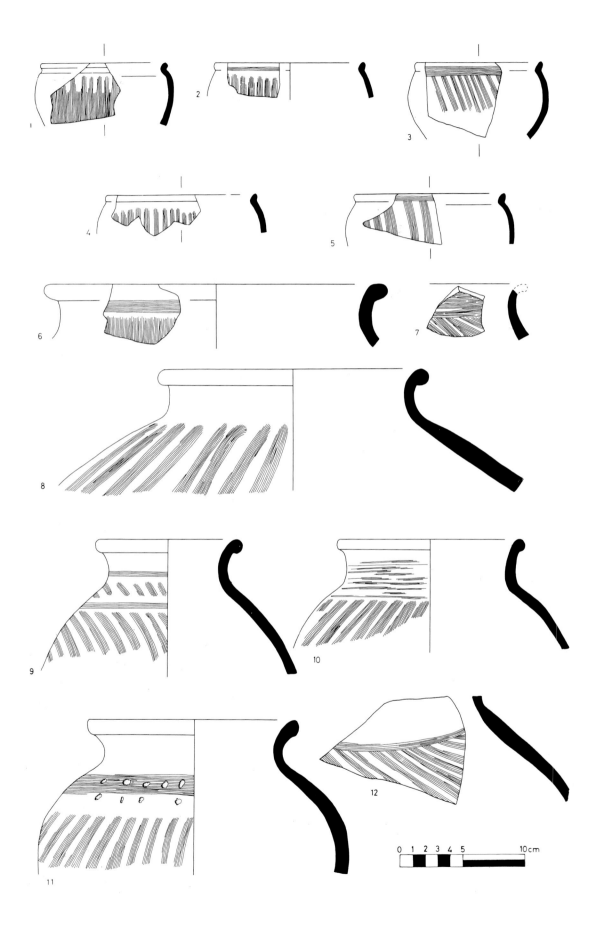

Fig. 57

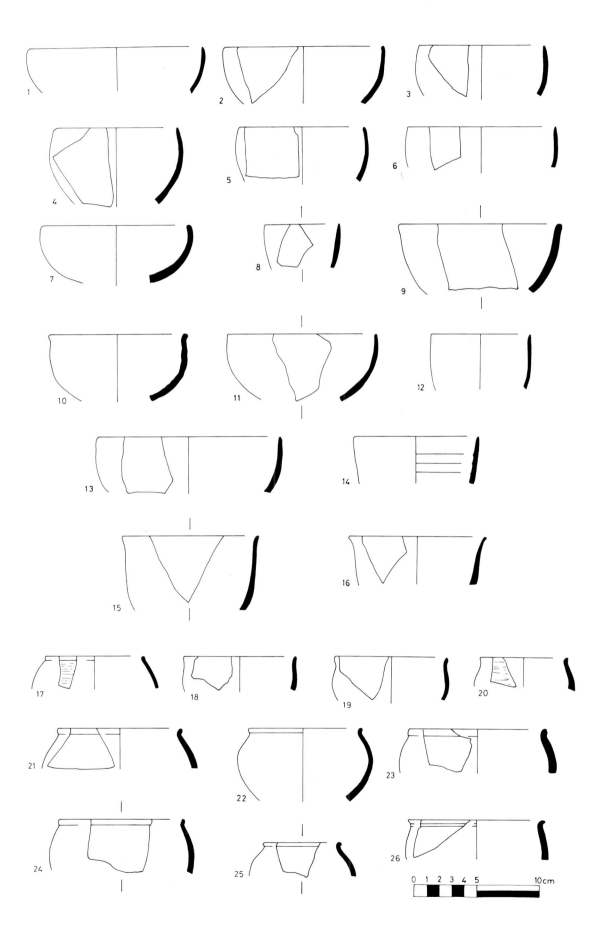

Fig. 58

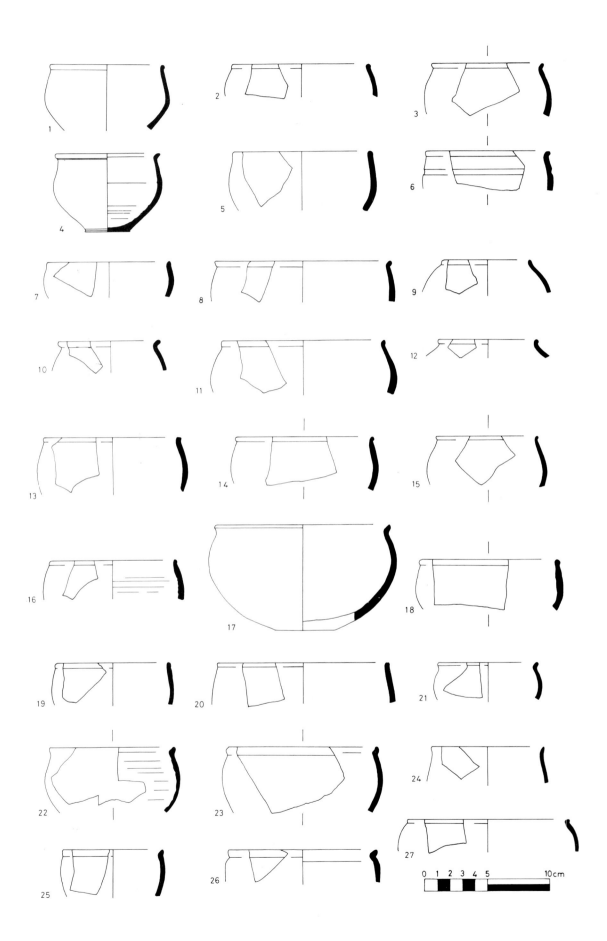

Fig. 59

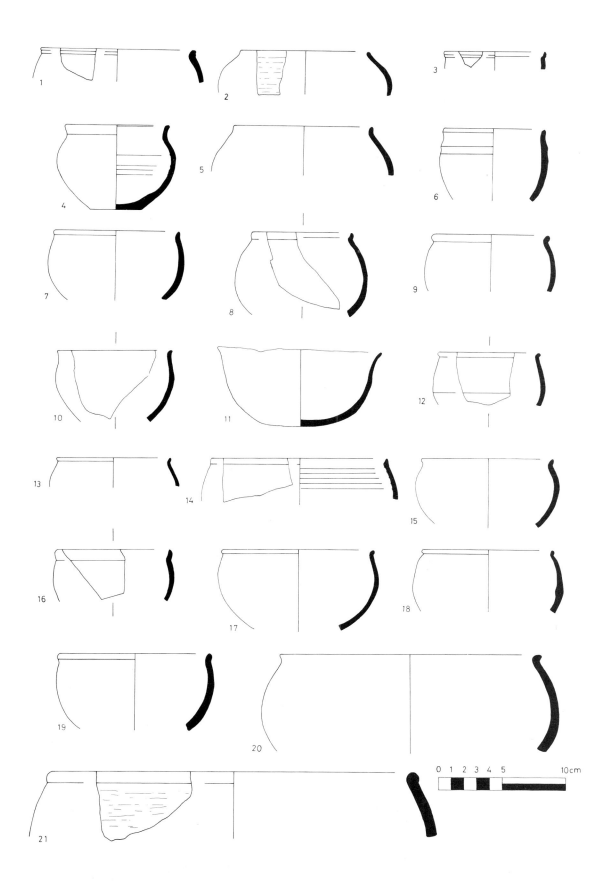

Fig. 60

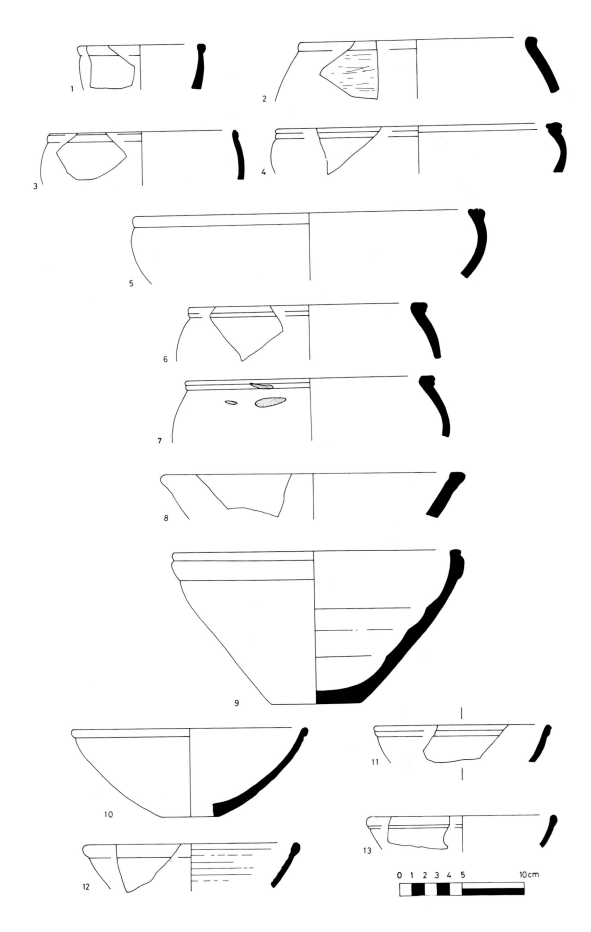

Fig. 61

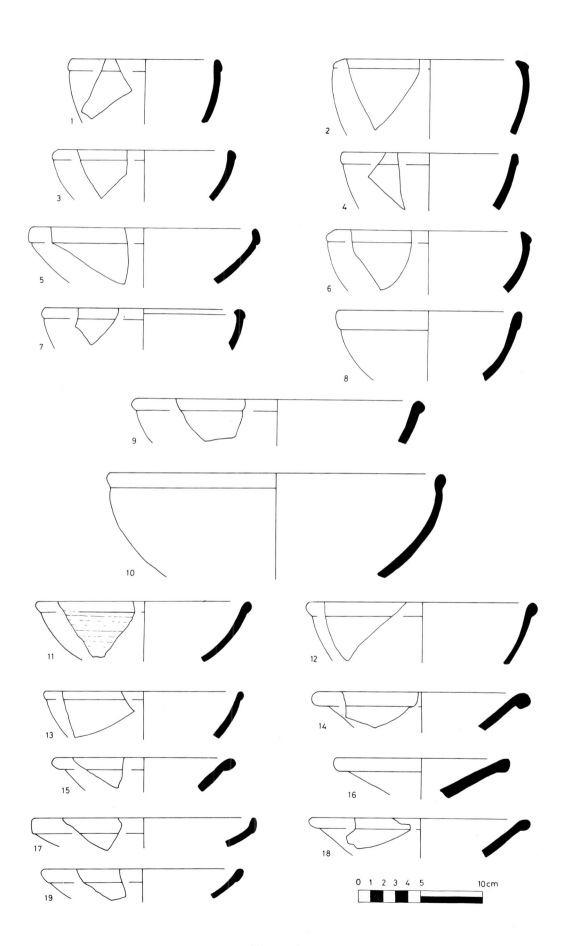

Fig. 62

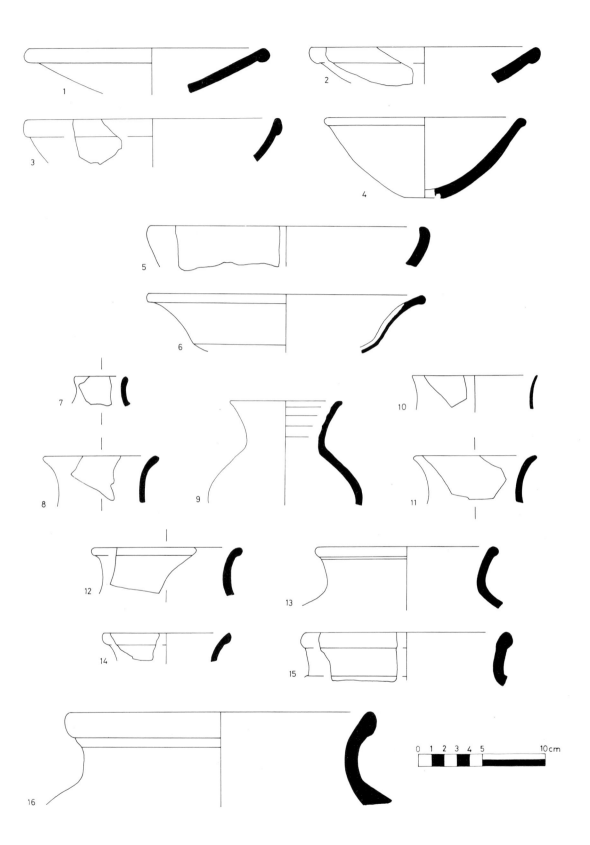

Fig. 63

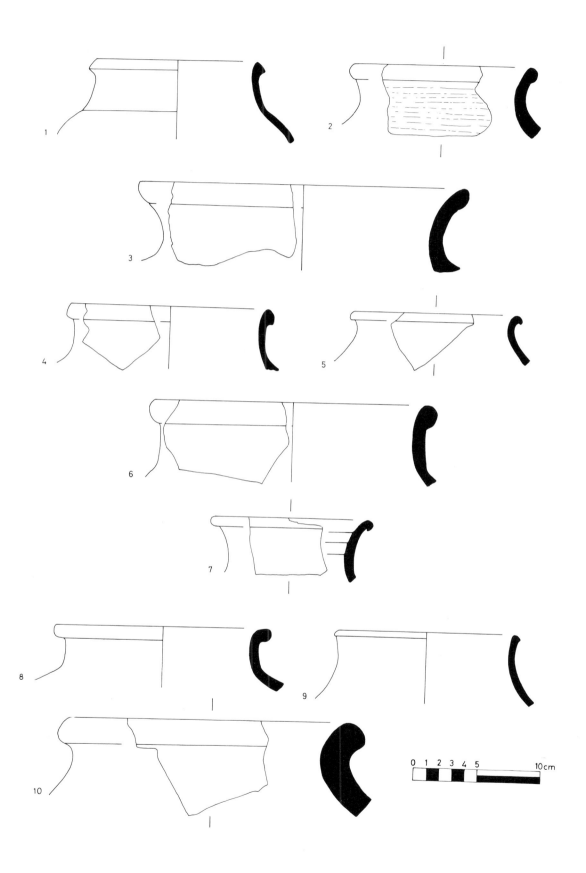

Fig. 64

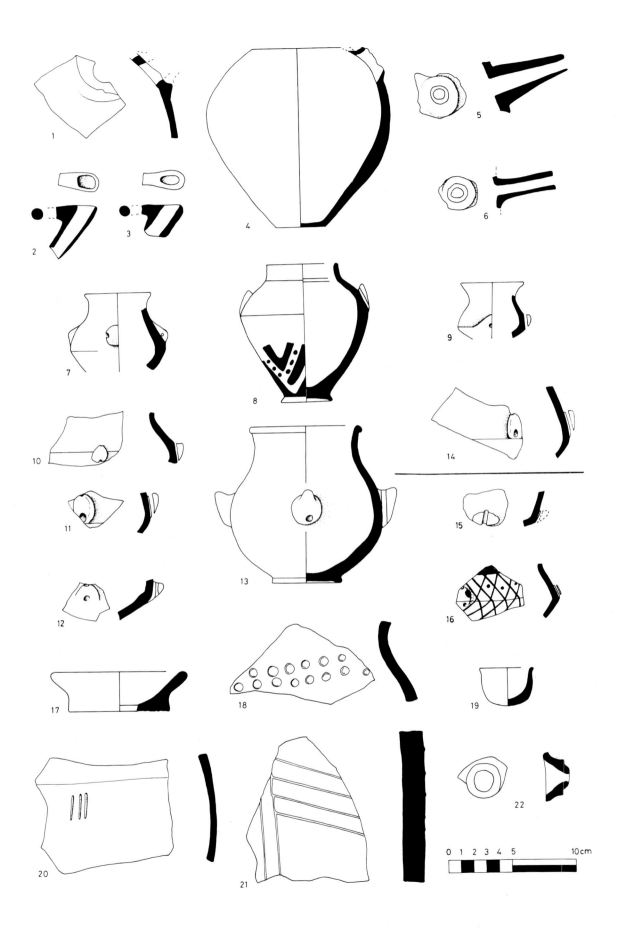

Fig. 65

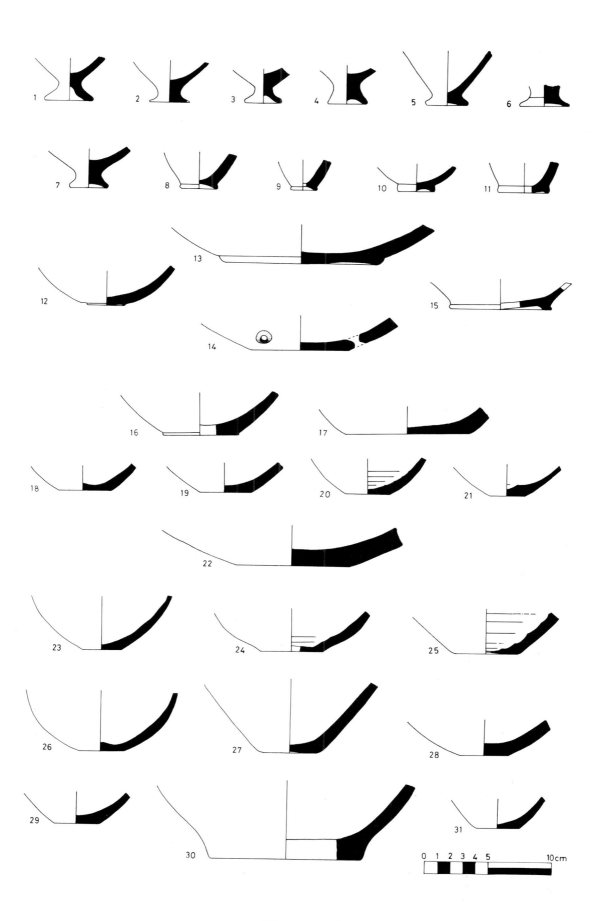

Fig. 66

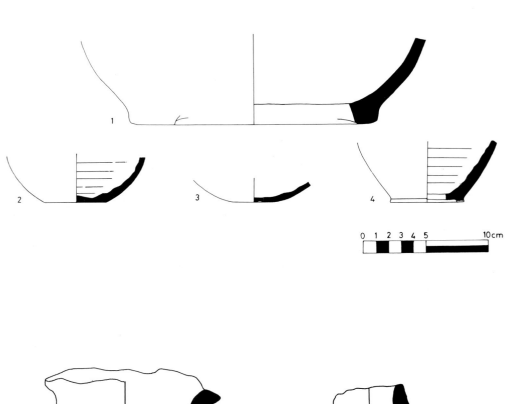

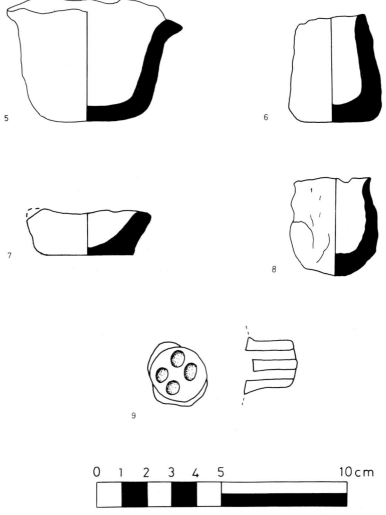

Fig. 67

CATALOGUE OF POTTERY FROM TAŞKUN MEVKİİ

Fig. 27

1. J11 501.2
   HM, tempered with medium grit and a little chaff. Pale brown burnished exterior except along the rim, which is black burnished like the interior. RD 17, H (pres.) 3.

2. J11 500.4
   HM, tempered with medium grit. Brown burnished exterior except along the rim, which is black burnished like the interior, vertical loop handle set on body. RD 14, H (pres.) 4.2.

3. J11 500.9
   HM, hard fabric tempered with chaff and medium white grit. Pale brown burnished exterior except along the rim, which is black burnished like the interior, elliptical knob set horizontally at rim. RD 16, H (pres.) 6.9.

4. J11 501.5
   HM, fine fabric tempered with medium-fine grit. Black burnished exterior and interior. RD 9, H (pres.) 4.5.

5. J11 501.20
   HM, tempered with chaff and medium grit. Black burnished interior, greyish buff smoothed exterior except along the rim, which is black smoothed. RD 14, H (pres.) 6.

6. J11 501.8
   HM, tempered with chaff and medium grit. Pale brown burnished interior except along the rim which is black burnished like the exterior. RD 20, H (pres.) 6.

7. J11 501.4
   HM, tempered with medium grit. Black burnished interior, reddish brown burnished exterior. RD 20, H (pres.) 5.4.

8. J11 501.8
   HM, tempered with medium grit and a little chaff. Black burnished interior and upper half exterior, pale brown slightly burnished lower half exterior. RD 25, H (pres.) 6.3.

9. J11 501.2
   HM, fine fabric tempered with medium-fine grit. Black burnished exterior and interior, elliptical knob set horizontally below the rim. RD 21, H (pres.) 3.6.

10. J11501.5
    HM, fine fabric tempered with medium-fine grit. Black burnished exterior and interior, three circular pellets set at the rim. RD 13, H (pres.) 2.7.

11. J11 501.23
    HM, fine fabric tempered with fine grit. Black burnished exterior and interior, elliptical knob set vertically below the rim. RD 13, H (pres.) 4.5.

12. J11 501.22
    HM, tempered with medium grit and a little chaff. Pale brown burnished exterior except along the rim, which is black burnished like the interior. RD 18, H (pres.) 4.8.

13. J11 501.12
    HM, tempered with chaff and medium grit. Pale brown slightly burnished exterior except for the rim, which is black burnished like the interior. RD 18, H (pres.) 4.5.

14. J11 501.12
    HM, tempered with medium grit and chaff. Black burnished exterior and interior. RD 16, H (pres.) 6.1.

15. J11 501.7
    HM, fine fabric tempered with medium-fine grit. Black burnished exterior and interior, three elliptical knobs set obliquely at the rim. RD 15, H (pres.) 3.3.

16. J11 501.11
    HM, tempered with medium grit and chaff. Black burnished exterior and interior. RD 17, H (pres.) 5.9.

17. J11 501.11
    HM, tempered with medium grit and a little chaff. Black burnished exterior and interior. RD 17, H (pres.) 5.5.

Fig. 28

1. J11 501.11
   HM, tempered with chaff and medium grit. Black throughout, burnished exterior and interior. RD 9, H (pres.) 4.5.

2. J11 501.22
   HM, tempered with medium grit. Pale brown burnished exterior except along the rim, which is black burnished like the interior. RD 22, H (pres.) 7.5.

3. J11 501.2
   HM, tempered with medium grit. Black throughout, burnished exterior and interior. RD 14, H (pres.) 4.7

4. J11 501.4
   HM, tempered with medium grit. Brown burnished exterior except along the rim, which is black burnished like the interior. RD 17, H (pres.) 6.3

5. J11 501.8
   HM, fine fabric tempered with medium-fine grit. Black throughout, burnished exterior and interior. RD 6, H (pres.) 15.4.

6. J11 501.4
   HM, tempered with medium grit and a little chaff. Pale brown burnished exterior except along the rim, which is black burnished like the interior. RD 12, H (pres.) 6.3.

7. J11 501.8-5
   HM, tempered with medium grit and a little chaff. Pale brown burnished exterior except along the rim, which is black burnished like the interior. RD 15, H (pres.) 6.5.

8. J11 501.8-5
   HM, tempered with medium grit and a little chaff. Mottled greyish black and pale brown burnished exterior except along the rim, which is black burnished like the interior. RD 17, H (pres.) 7.6.

9. J11 501.2
   HM, tempered with medium grit and chaff. Mottled grey to pale brown smoothed exterior, plain black interior. RD 34, H (pres.) 6.7.

10. J11 501.12
    HM, tempered with chaff and medium-coarse grit. Greyish brown streakily burnished exterior, black burnished interior. RD 30, H (pres.) 7.9.

11. J11 502.11
    HM, tempered with medium grit and a little chaff. Pale brown burnished exterior except along the rim, which is black burnished like the interior. RD 18, H (pres.) 7.1.

12. J11 501.2
    HM, fine fabric tempered with medium-fine grit. Black throughout, burnished exterior and interior. RD 14, H (pres.) 3.5.

Fig. 29

1. J11 502.4
   HM, tempered with medium grit and a little chaff. Pale grey burnished exterior except along the rim, which is black burnished like the interior. RD 14, H (pres.) 5.5.
2. J11 502.3
   HM, tempered with medium grit and a little chaff. Black throughout, burnished exterior and interior. RD 15, H (pres.) 6.8.
3. J11 502.2.9
   HM, tempered with medium grit and a little chaff. Greyish black burnished interior, buff smoothed exterior. RD 17, H (pres.) 5.7.
4. J11 502.4
   HM, tempered with chaff and medium white grit. Pale grey slightly burnished exterior except along the rim, which is black and slightly burnished, interior is black burnished. Pierced twice below the rim. RD 13, H (pres.) 2.0.
5. J11 502.1.8
   HM, fine fabric tempered with fine chaff and medium-fine grit. Brown burnished exterior except along the rim, which is black burnished like the interior. RD 13, H (pres.) 5.5.
6. J11 502.12
   HM, fine fabric tempered with medium-fine grit and a little chaff. Mottled black and greyish brown burnished exterior, black burnished interior. Decoration consists of a linear incised design of chequer-board pattern flanked by a framed vertical row of chevrons. The design is filled with a white paste. RD 18, H (pres.) 9.0.
7. J11 502.1
   HM, tempered with chaff and medium grit. Black burnished exterior, mottled brown and grey smoothed interior. RD 15, H (pres.) 9.1.
8. J11 502.1
   HM, tempered with chaff and medium grit. Black throughout, burnished exterior and interior. Elliptical knob set vertically at the rim. RD 12, H (pres.) 5.5.
9. J11 502.1
   HM, fine fabric tempered with medium-fine grit. Black throughout, burnished exterior and interior. Vertically pierced lug set at the rim. RD 8, H (pres.) 4.3.
10. J11 502.1
    HM, tempered with medium grit. Brown burnished exterior except along the rim, which is black burnished like the interior. RD 22, H (pres.) 5.5.
11. J11 502.4
    HM, fine fabric tempered with medium-fine grit. Black throughout, burnished exterior and interior. RD 11, H (pres.) 4.6.
12. J11 502.4
    HM, tempered with medium white grit and a little chaff. Pale brown burnished exterior except along the rim, which is black burnished like the interior. RD 15, H (pres.) 4.6.
13. J11 502.4
    HM, fine fabric tempered with medium-fine grit. Black throughout, burnished exterior and interior. RD 11, H (pres.) 4.6.

14. J11 505.1
    HM, tempered with chaff and medium grit. Pale brown burnished exterior except along the rim, which is black burnished like the interior. RD 31, H (pres.) 9.2.

Fig. 30

1. J11 503.15
   HM, tempered with medium grit and a little chaff. Pale brown burnished exterior except along the rim, which is black burnished like the interior. RD 16, H (pres.) 6.5.
2. J11 504.4
   HM, tempered with chaff and medium grit. Mottled black and pale brown smoothed exterior, black burnished interior. Horizontally pierced lug handle set below the rim. RD 16, H (pres.) 8.2.
3. J11 505.3
   HM, tempered with medium white grit and a little chaff. Greyish black burnished exterior, brown burnished interior. RD 19, H (pres.) 6.4.
4. J11 505.6
   HM, fine fabric tempered with medium-fine grit. Black throughout, burnished exterior and interior. Three elliptical knobs set horizontally in a row below the rim. RD 10, H (pres.) 4.1.
5. K10 101.9
   HM, tempered with medium grit. Pale brown burnished exterior except along the rim, which is black burnished like the interior. RD 13, H (pres.) 5.2.
6. K10c 101.5
   HM, tempered with medium grit and a little chaff. Grey burnished exterior and interior. RD 15, H (pres.) 3.7.
7. K10c 101.6
   HM, fine fabric tempered with medium-fine grit. Black throughout, burnished exterior and interior. Previously published (Helms 1971: Fig. 2 no. 5). RD 10, D (max.) 10.8, H 7.2.
8. K10c 101.1
   HM, fine fabric tempered with medium-fine grit. Black throughout, burnished exterior and interior. A pair of pellets set at the rim. RD 12, H (pres.) 3.5.
9. K10c 101.4
   HM, fine fabric tempered with medium-fine grit. Black throughout, burnished exterior and interior. RD 9, D (max.) 10.2, H (pres.) 6.3.
10. K10c 101.4
    HM, fine fabric tempered with medium-fine grit. Black throughout, burnished exterior and interior. A pair of conjoint pellets set at the rim. RD 12, H (pres.) 6.1.
11. K10c 101.1
    HM, fine fabric tempered with medium-fine grit. Black throughout, burnished exterior and interior. RD 18, H (pres.) 4.7.
12. K10c 101.14
    HM, fine fabric tempered with medium-fine grit. Black throughout, burnished exterior and interior. A row of elliptical knobs set obliquely below the rim. Previously published (Helms 1971: Fig. 2 no. 7). RD 12, H (pres.) 5.5.
13. K10c 101.3
    HM, tempered with medium grit and a little chaff. Black throughout, slightly burnished exterior and interior. RD 10, H (pres.) 4.5.

14. K10c 101.4
    HM, tempered with medium grit and a little chaff.
    Black throughout, burnished exterior and interior.
    RD 10, H (pres.) 5.5.
15. K10c 101.4
    HM, tempered with medium grit and a little chaff.
    Black throughout, burnished exterior and interior.
    RD 12, H (pres.) 4.7.
16. K10c 101.4
    HM, fine fabric tempered with medium-fine grit.
    Black throughout, burnished exterior and interior.
    RD 9, H (pres.) 4.5.
17. K10 101.9
    HM, fine fabric tempered with medium-fine
    grit. Black throughout, burnished exterior and
    interior. Part of a knob set below the rim. RD 15,
    H (pres.) 3.9.
18. K10c 101.4
    HM, tempered with medium-white grit and a little
    chaff. Pale grey burnished exterior, black
    burnished interior. RD 22, H (pres.) 6.5.
19. K10c 101.4
    HM, fine fabric tempered with medium-fine grit.
    Black throughout, burnished exterior and interior.
    RD 17, H (pres.) 6.6.

Fig. 31

 1. K10c 101.4
    HM, tempered with medium grit and chaff.
    Black throughout, burnished exterior and interior.
    RD 20, H (pres.) 7.8.
 2. K10c 101.4
    HM, tempered with medium grit and a little chaff.
    Black throughout, burnished exterior and interior.
    RD 15, H (pres.) 4.6.
 3. K10c 101.4
    HM, tempered with chaff and medium white grit.
    Black throughout, burnished exterior and interior.
    RD 22, H (pres.) 4.6.
 4. K10c 101.2
    HM, tempered with chaff and medium grit.
    Mottled black and grey burnished exterior, black
    slightly burnished interior. RD 17, H (pres.) 5.4.
 5. K10c 101.12
    HM, fine fabric tempered with medium-fine grit.
    Black throughout, burnished exterior and interior.
    RD 10, H (pres.) 4.3.
 6. K10c 101.4
    HM, fine fabric tempered with medium-fine grit.
    Black throughout, burnished exterior and interior.
    Three pellets set at the rim. RD 10, H (pres.) 2.7.
 7. K10c 101.4
    HM, medium grit and a little chaff. Black
    throughout, burnished exterior and interior.
    RD 10, H (pres.) 3.9.
 8. K10c 101.4
    HM, tempered with medium-coarse white grit.
    Grey smoothed exterior, black burnished interior.
    RD 22, H (pres.) 8.1.
 9. K10c 101.3
    HM, tempered with medium white grit and a little
    chaff. Reddish brown burnished exterior, black
    burnished interior. RD 16, H (pres.) 6.1.
10. K10c 101.2
    HM, tempered with medium white grit and chaff.
    Pale brown burnished exterior except along the
    rim, which is black burnished like the interior.
    RD 27, H (pres.) 10.8.

11. K10c 101.14
    HM, tempered with chaff and medium white grit.
    Pale, reddish brown burnished exterior except
    along the rim, which is black burnished like the
    interior. RD 14, H (pres.) 5.8.
12. K10c 101.4
    HM, fine fabric tempered with fine grit. Black
    throughout, burnished exterior and interior.
    RD 14, H (pres.) 7.2.
13. K10c 101.2
    HM, tempered with medium grit and a little chaff.
    Greyish brown burnished exterior except along the
    rim, which is black burnished like the interior.
    RD 21, H (pres.) 8.2.
14. K10c 101.2
    HM, fine fabric tempered with medium-fine grit.
    Black throughout, burnished exterior and interior.
    An inverted wavy pattern in relief set at the rim.
    RD 14, H (pres.) 3.1.

Fig. 32

 1. K10c 101.6
    HM, fine fabric tempered with medium-fine grit.
    Black throughout, burnished exterior and interior.
    A series of elliptical knobs set obliquely at the rim.
    RD 12, H (pres.) 3.8.
 2. K10c 101.4
    HM, tempered with chaff and medium white grit.
    Pale brown burnished exterior except along the
    rim, which is black burnished like the interior.
    RD 25, H (pres.) 8.2.
 3. K10c 101.4
    HM, tempered with medium grit. Mottled black
    and reddish brown burnished exterior, black
    burnished interior. RD 18, H (pres.) 7.6.
 4. K10c 101.4
    HM, tempered with medium-coarse grit. Pale
    grey burnished exterior, black burnished interior.
    RD 19, H (pres.) 7.7.
 5. K10c 101.6
    HM, tempered with medium grit and a little chaff.
    Black throughout, burnished exterior and interior.
    RD 14, H (pres.) 5.5.
 6. K10c 102.2.
    HM, tempered with medium grit. Brown burnished
    exterior except along the rim, which is black
    burnished like the interior. RD 18, H (pres.) 5.2.
 7. K10c 102.2
    HM, tempered with medium-coarse grit. Black
    burnished interior, greyish black burnished upper
    exterior, pale brown burnished lower exterior.
    RD 30, H (pres.) 7.4.
 8. K10 103.5
    HM, tempered with medium grit and chaff.
    Mottled pale brown and grey burnished exterior
    except along the rim, which is black burnished like
    the interior. RD 21, H (pres.) 7.0.
 9. K10c 103
    HM, tempered with medium white grit and a little
    chaff. Pale brown burnished outside except along
    the rim, which is black burnished like the interior.
    RD 22, H (pres.) 10.2.
10. K10d 126.1
    HM, fine fabric tempered with medium-fine grit.
    Black throughout, burnished exterior and interior.
    Two elliptical knobs set vertically below the rim.
    RD 12, H (pres.) 2.7.
11. K11 600.12
    HM, tempered with medium-fine grit. Black

throughout, burnished exterior and interior. A row of pellets set at the rim. RD 11, H (pres.) 4.9.

12. K11 620.2.
    HM, fine fabric tempered with medium-fine grit. Black throughout, burnished exterior and interior. Two elliptical knobs set vertically below the rim. RD 11, H (pres.) 3.7.

13. K11 610.8
    HM, fine fabric tempered with medium-fine grit. Black throughout, burnished exterior and interior. Two elliptical knobs set vertically below the rim. RD 10, H (pres.) 3.0.

14. K11 610.12
    HM, fine fabric tempered with medium-fine grit. Black throughout, burnished exterior and interior. RD 14, H (pres.) 6.6.

15. K11 610.4
    HM, fine fabric tempered with medium-fine grit. Black throughout, burnished exterior and interior. RD 11, H (pres.) 3.8.

Fig. 33

1. K11 610.1
   HM, tempered with medium grit. Black throughout, burnished exterior and interior. RD 19, H (pres.) 8.1.

2. K11 610.25
   HM, tempered with chaff and medium grit. Mottled grey and pale brown burnished exterior, black burnished interior. RD 16, H (pres.) 7.8.

3. K11 610.9
   HM, fine fabric tempered with fine grit. Black throughout, burnished exterior and interior. RD 13, H (pres.) 8.2.

4. K11 610.19
   HM, fine fabric tempered with medium-fine grit and a little chaff. Black throughout, burnished exterior and interior. RD 14, H (pres.) 5.8.

5. K11 610.22
   HM, tempered with medium white grit and chaff. Pale orange brown slightly burnished exterior except along rim, which is grey burnished, interior and top of the rim are black burnished. RD 24, H (pres.) 6.7.

6. K11 610.25
   HM, fine fabric tempered with medium-fine grit. Black throughout, burnished exterior and interior. RD 11, H (pres.) 5.1.

7. K11 610.4
   HM, tempered with medium grit and a little chaff. Pale brown burnished exterior, smoke blackened in part, interior and exterior top of rim are black burnished. RD 35, H (pres.) 12.6.

8. K11 610.22
   HM, tempered with chaff and medium-coarse white grit. Mottled grey to greyish buff burnished exterior except along rim, which is black burnished like the interior. RD 34, H (pres.) 10.8.

9. K11 610.12
   HM, tempered with chaff and medium grit. Reddish buff burnished exterior except along rim, which is black burnished like the interior. RD 30, H (pres.) 7.6.

10. K11 610.1
    HM, tempered with medium grit and a little chaff. Grey black burnished interior, brown burnished exterior. Horizontally pierced lug set below the rim. RD 9, H (pres.) 3.3.

Fig. 34

1. K11 612.2.
   HM, tempered with chaff and medium grit. Brown burnished exterior except along the rim, which is black burnished like the interior. Pierced once below the rim. RD 18, H (pres.) 5.4.

2. K11 612.2
   HM, tempered with chaff and medium grit. Greyish brown burnished exterior except along the rim, which is black burnished like the interior. Small loop handle set vertically below the rim. RD 14, H (pres.) 3.6.

3. K11 612.2.
   HM, tempered with chaff and medium white grit. Pale grey throughout, burnished exterior and interior. RD 9, H 4.4.

4. K11 613.6
   HM, tempered with medium white grit and a little chaff. Black throughout, smoothed exterior, burnished interior. Two elliptical knobs set vertically below the rim. RD 11, H (pres.) 4.3.

5. K11 620.2
   HM, tempered with medium-coarse white grit and chaff, grey core. Brown burnished interior and exterior. Decoration consists of an incised horizontal row of framed chevrons below the rim and a series of punctures over the body. RD 14, H (pres.) 4.2.

6. K11 620.2
   HM, tempered with chaff and medium white grit. Pale brown burnished exterior except along the rim, which is black burnished like the interior. RD 15, H (pres.) 6.8.

7. K11 620.2
   HM, tempered with medium grit and a little chaff. Mottled pale brown to brown burnished exterior except along the rim, which is black burnished like the interior. RD 16, H (pres.) 7.4.

8. K11 620.2
   HM, tempered with chaff and medium grit. Variable exterior ranging from pale brown through reddish brown to black, interior is black, burnished on both surfaces. RD 19, H (pres.) 5.7.

9. K11 610.6
   HM, hard fabric tempered with chaff and medium grit. Black throughout, burnished exterior and interior. Four pellets set at the rim. RD 16, H (pres.) 8.1.

10. K11 620.1
    HM, tempered with chaff and medium grit. Pale brown burnished exterior except along the rim, which is black burnished like the interior. RD 16, H (pres.) 7.2.

11. K11 620.2
    HM, fine fabric tempered with fine grit. Black throughout, burnished exterior and interior. RD 13, H (pres.) 4.6.

12. K11 620.1
    HM, fine fabric tempered with medium-fine grit. Black throughout, burnished exterior and interior. RD 14, H (pres.) 5.4.

13. K11a/c 601.8
    HM, tempered with chaff and medium grit. Pale brown burnished exterior except along the rim, which is black burnished like the interior. Previously published (Helms 1971: Fig. 2 no. 6). RD 13, H 6.7.

14. K11a/c 601.8
    HM, fine fabric tempered with medium-fine grit. Black throughout, burnished exterior and interior.

Decoration consists of a deep, wavy relief pattern pendent to the rim. RD 9, H (pres.) 3.2.

15. K11 620.2
    HM, tempered with chaff and medium-coarse grit. Exterior is burnished and ranges in colour from reddish brown through brown to black, interior is black burnished. RD 30, H (pres.) 8.9.

16. K11a/c 601.2
    HM, fine fabric tempered with medium-fine grit. Black throughout, burnished exterior and interior. A pair of pellets set at the rim. RD 10, H (pres.) 4.6.

Fig. 35

1. K11a/c 601.2
   HM, fine fabric tempered with medium-fine grit. Black throughout, slightly burnished exterior and interior. RD 9, H (pres.) 4.8.

2. K11a/c 601.12
   HM, tempered with medium-fine grit. Black throughout, burnished exterior and interior. RD 14, H (pres.) 6.1.

3. K11a/c 601.2
   HM, tempered with medium-fine grit. Black throughout, slightly burnished exterior and interior. RD 9, H (pres.) 5.5.

4. K11a/c 601.2
   HM, tempered with chaff and medium grit. Greyish brown burnished exterior except along the rim, which is black burnished like the interior. RD 18, H (pres.) 7.7.

5. K11a/c 601.9
   HM, tempered with medium grit. Black throughout, burnished exterior and interior. Decoration consists of a pair of elongated knobs pendent to the rim. RD 12, H (pres.) 5.5.

6. K11a/c 601.12
   HM, fine fabric tempered with medium-fine grit. Black throughout, burnished exterior and interior. Elliptical knob set vertically at the rim. RD 12, H (pres.) 5.1.

7. L10c/d 201.11
   HM, tempered with chaff and medium white grit. Grey throughout, burnished exterior and interior. RD 12, H (pres.) 4.5.

8. J11 501.4
   HM, tempered with medium-coarse white grit. Black burnished exterior except along the rim, which is pale brown burnished like the interior. RD 14, H (pres.) 5.9.

9. J11 501.11
   HM, tempered with medium grit and chaff. Reddish brown smoothed interior except along the rim, which is black burnished like the exterior. RD 9, H (pres.) 2.9.

10. J11 501.5
    HM, tempered with medium-fine grit. Black throughout, burnished exterior, plain interior. RD 13, H (pres.) 2.9.

11. J11 502.3
    HM, tempered with chaff and medium white grit. Plain brown exterior except along the rim, which is plain black like the interior. RD 10, H (pres.) 5.4.

12. J11 501.5
    HM, tempered with medium grit and a little chaff. Greyish black throughout, burnished exterior, smoothed interior. RD 16, H (pres.) 6.6.

13. J11 501.4
    HM, fine fabric tempered with medium-fine grit. Black throughout, burnished interior and exterior. RD 8, H (pres.) 4.2.

14. J11 501.15
    HM, fine fabric tempered with fine grit. Black burnished exterior, pale grey smoothed interior. RD 11, H (pres.) 4.8.

15. J11 501.2
    HM, tempered with chaff and medium grit. Black burnished exterior, pale greyish brown smoothed interior. RD 11, H (pres.) 6.3.

16. J11 501.21
    HM, tempered with chaff and medium grit. Black burnished exterior, brown smoothed interior. RD 14, H (pres.) 4.6.

17. J11 502.3
    HM, tempered with chaff and medium grit. Black burnished exterior except along the rim, which is pale brown burnished like the interior. RD 16, H (pres.) 8.1.

18. J11 502.9
    HM, tempered with medium grit and a little chaff. Black burnished exterior, greyish brown smoothed and patchily burnished interior. RD 13, H (pres.) 3.6.

Fig. 36

1. J11 501.17
   HM, tempered with medium white grit. Black throughout, burnished exterior, smoothed interior. RD 9, H (pres.) 4.3.

2. K11 610.20
   HM, fine fabric tempered with medium-fine grit. Black throughout, smoothed and patchily burnished interior except along the rim, which is well burnished like the exterior. RD 12, H (pres.) 4.8.

3. J11 503.15
   HM, fine fabric tempered with fine grit. Black throughout, burnished exterior, smoothed interior. RD 12, H (pres.) 3.1.

4. J11 503.9
   HM, tempered with medium grit and a little chaff. Pale grey throughout, slightly burnished exterior and interior. RD 10, H (pres.) 5.4.

5. J11 503.15
   HM, tempered with medium grit. Black throughout, burnished exterior and interior. RD 7, H (pres.) 4.7.

6. J11 505.1
   HM, tempered with medium grit and a little chaff. Black throughout, burnished exterior and interior. RD 10, H (pres.) 4.4.

7. J11 504.4
   HM, tempered with medium grit. Black burnished exterior, brown smoothed interior. RD 10, H (pres.) 6.0.

8. J11 505.9/10
   HM, tempered with medium grit. Black burnished exterior, pale brown burnished interior. RD 12, H (pres.) 3.6.

9. J11 505.8
   HM, tempered with medium grit. Pale greyish brown smoothed interior, upper exterior is greyish brown burnished, lower exterior is black burnished. RD 10, H (pres.) 3.8.

10. K10c 101.4
    HM, fine fabric tempered with medium-fine grit.

Black throughout, burnished exterior and interior. RD 10, H (pres.) 4.9.

11. K10 100.6.
HM, fine fabric tempered with medium-fine grit. Black burnished exterior, pale grey smoothed interior. Two bands in relief set obliquely on the shoulder. RD 10, H (pres.) 5.4.

12. K10c 101.14
HM, tempered with medium grit and a little chaff. Black throughout, burnished exterior and interior. RD 6, H (pres.) 4.3.

13. K10c 101.4
HM, fine fabric tempered with medium-fine grit. Black throughout, burnished exterior, smoothed interior. RD 18, H (pres.) 4.6.

14. K10c 101.23
HM, tempered with medium grit. Greyish black throughout, burnished exterior and interior. RD 11, H (pres.) 2.5.

15. K10c 101.9
HM, tempered with medium grit. Grey throughout, burnished exterior and interior. RD 12, H (pres.) 4.5.

16. K10c 101.12
HM, tempered with medium grit. Black burnished exterior, grey smoothed interior, dark grey along the rim. RD 10, H (pres.) 8.1.

17. K10c 101.14
HM, fine fabric tempered with medium-fine white grit. Black burnished exterior, greyish black smoothed interior, patchily burnished. RD 8, H (pres.) 3.9.

18. K10c 101.4
HM, fine fabric tempered with medium-fine grit. Black throughout, burnished exterior and interior. RD 8, H (pres.) 3.3.

19. K11 601.3
HM, tempered with medium white grit and a little chaff. Black burnished exterior, pale brown smoothed interior. RD 8, H (pres.) 4.8.

20. K10 105.1
HM, fine fabric tempered with medium-fine grit. Black throughout, burnished exterior and interior. RD 10, H (pres.) 2.7.

21. K10 103.6
HM, tempered with medium-coarse white grit and a little chaff. Reddish brown and grey mottled surfaces, slightly burnished exterior, smoothed interior. RD 8, H (pres.) 3.3.

22. K10c 101.4
HM, tempered with medium-coarse grit. Black throughout, burnished exterior and interior. RD 12, H (pres.) 4.3.

23. K10c 100.6
HM, tempered with medium grit. Black burnished exterior, greyish-black slightly burnished interior. RD 11, H (pres.) 3.3.

24. K11 610.2
HM, tempered with medium white grit and a little chaff. Black burnished exterior, pale brown smoothed interior. RD 11, H (pres.) 5.4.

25. K10 105.1
HM, tempered with medium-fine grit. Black throughout, burnished exterior and interior. RD 12, H (pres.) 7.5.

26. K10 103.6
HM, tempered with medium-coarse white grit and a little chaff. Reddish brown and grey mottled exterior and interior, slightly burnished exterior, smoothed interior. Knob handle set horizontally below the rim. RD 11, H (pres.) 3.9.

Fig. 37

1. K11 610.25
HM, fine fabric tempered with medium-fine grit. Black throughout, burnished exterior, smoothed interior. RD 9, H (pres.) 4.3.

2. K11 613.9
HM, fine fabric tempered with medium-fine grit. Grey burnished exterior, pale grey smoothed interior. RD 10, H (pres.) 4.3.

3. K11 610.18
HM, tempered with medium grit and chaff. Black burnished exterior except along the rim, which is reddish brown burnished, like the interior. RD 13, H (pres.) 8.6.

4. K11 610.1
HM, fine fabric tempered with medium-fine grit. Black throughout, burnished exterior and interior RD 9, H (pres.) 4.2.

5. K11 620.2
HM, fine fabric tempered with fine grit. Black throughout, burnished exterior, smoothed interior. RD 8, H (pres.) 3.0.

6. K11 620.2
HM, tempered with medium grit and a little chaff. Black burnished exterior except along the rim, which is brown burnished like the interior. RD 11, H (pres.) 3.6.

7. K11 620.1
HM, tempered with medium white grit and a little chaff. Pale greyish brown slightly burnished exterior except along the rim, which is black burnished like the interior. RD 11, H (pres.) 3.6.

8. K11 620.2
HM, fine fabric tempered with medium-fine grit. Black throughout, burnished exterior and interior. RD 13, H (pres.) 7.5.

9. K11 620.2
HM, fine fabric tempered with medium-fine grit. Black throughout, burnished exterior and interior. RD 10, H (pres.) 8.5.

10. K11 620.12
HM, tempered with medium white grit and a little chaff. Lower half of exterior is reddish brown burnished, upper half of exterior and interior are black burnished. RD 9, H (pres.) 6.6.

11. K11 620.2
HM, fine fabric tempered with medium-fine grit. Black burnished exterior and along top of rim, greyish buff smoothed interior. RD 8, H (pres.) 5.5.

12. K11 620.2
HM, fine fabric tempered with medium-fine grit. Greyish brown throughout, burnished exterior and interior. RD 12, H (pres.) 4.2.

13. K11a/c 601.12
HM fine fabric tempered with medium-fine grit. Black throughout, burnished exterior and interior. RD 7, H (pres.) 6.0.

14. L10c/d 201.6
HM, fine fabric tempered with fine grit and mica additives. Greyish brown highly burnished exterior, smoke blackened patch, pale brown smoothed interior. RD 13, H (pres.) 5.1.

15. L10c/d 201.7
HM, fine fabric tempered with fine grit. Black to brown highly burnished exterior, lustrous appearance, greyish pale brown smoothed interior.

RD 8, H (pres.) 4.2.

16. J11 501.6
HM, tempered with medium-coarse grit. Black burnished exterior except along the rim, which is pale brown burnished, reddish brown burnished interior. RD 7, H (pres.) 3.9.

17. L10c/d 201.7
HM, fine fabric tempered with fine grit. Black to brown highly burnished exterior, greyish buff slightly burnished interior. RD 7, H (pres.) 6.6.

18. J11 501.6
HM, tempered with medium-coarse grit. Black burnished exterior except along the rim, which is pale brown burnished, reddish brown burnished interior. RD 20, H (pres.) 9.0.

19. K11 611.1
HM, tempered with medium grit and a little chaff. Greyish brown burnished exterior except along the rim, which is black burnished like the interior. RD 14, H (pres.) 3.3.

Fig. 38

1. J11 501.6
HM, tempered with medium grit and chaff. Grey burnished exterior, pale greyish brown smoothed interior. RD 26, H (pres.) 10.2.

2. J11 501.11
HM, tempered with medium grit and chaff. Black burnished exterior, pale brown smoothed interior. RD 28, H (pres.) 11.1.

3. J11 502.3
HM, coarse fabric tempered with medium-coarse grit and chaff. Black burnished exterior except along the rim which is brown burnished, black plain interior. Triangular ledge handle set horizontally at the rim. RD 21, H (pres.) 6.0.

4. J11 502.3
HM, tempered with medium grit and chaff. Black burnished exterior, greyish black smoothed interior. RD 16, H (pres.) 6.9.

5. K10 103.1
HM, tempered with medium grit and a little chaff. Black slightly burnished exterior, grey smoothed interior. RD 12, H (pres.) 6.6.

6. K11a/c 601.1
HM, tempered with medium grit. Black throughout, burnished exterior, smoothed interior. RD 14, H (pres.) 5.4.

7. J11 501.14
HM, tempered with medium grit and a little chaff. Black burnished exterior, pale greyish brown smoothed interior. RD 39, H (pres.) 11.4.

8. J11 501.4
HM, coarse fabric tempered with medium-coarse white grit. Reddish brown throughout, burnished exterior, smoothed interior. Triangular ledge handle set horizontally at the rim. RD 20, H (pres.) 8.1.

Fig. 39

1. J11 501.8
HM, tempered with medium grit and chaff. Black burnished exterior, reddish brown smoothed interior. RD 13, H (pres.) 10.2.

2. J11 501.6
HM, tempered with medium grit and chaff. Black burnished exterior, pale greyish brown smoothed interior, patchily burnished. RD 18, H (pres.) 14.4.

3. J11 501.5
HM, tempered with medium white grit and a little chaff. Mottled black and brown burnished exterior, pale grey smoothed interior. Triangular ledge handle set horizontally at the rim. RD 16, H (pres.) 6.3.

4. J11 501.4
HM, tempered with medium grit. Black and greyish brown mottled burnished exterior, pale brown smoothed interior. RD 17, H (pres.) 6.3.

5. J11 501.2
HM, tempered with medium white grit and chaff. Pale grey throughout, burnished exterior, smoothed interior. RD 21, H (pres.) 8.1.

6. K11 601.7. (Burial)
HM, tempered with medium grit. Plain fabric, mottled brownish black on the exterior, smoke blackened in parts. RD 10, W (max.) 13.1, H 12.7.

7. J11 501.11
HM, tempered with medium grit. Black burnished exterior, brown burnished along the rim, pale brown smoothed interior. RD 14, H (pres.) 4.5.

8. J11 501.4
HM, tempered with medium grit and a little chaff. Black burnished exterior, pale orange brown smoothed interior. RD 17, H (pres.) 3.3.

9. J11 501.12
HM, tempered with medium grit and chaff. Black burnished exterior except along the rim, which is pale brown burnished like the interior. RD 13, H (pres.) 6.0.

10. J11 501.4
HM, tempered with medium grit and a little chaff. Black burnished exterior, pale orange brown smoothed interior. RD 23, H (pres.) 8.4.

11. J11 501.12
HM, tempered with chaff and medium grit. Black burnished exterior except along the rim, which is pale brown smoothed like the interior. RD 23, H (pres.) 11.1.

Fig. 40

1. J11 501.15
HM, tempered with chaff and medium white grit. Black burnished exterior, pale greyish brown smoothed interior. Part of a relief pattern survives. RD 22, H (pres.) 15.3.

2. J11 501.8
HM, coarse fabric tempered with chaff and medium-coarse grit, dark grey core. Reddish brown burnished exterior, greyish brown smoothed interior. RD 16, H (pres.) 6.0.

3. J11 501.8
HM, tempered with chaff and medium grit. Black burnished exterior except along the rim, which is pale greyish brown and slightly burnished like the interior. RD 15, H (pres.) 7.2.

4. J11 501.8
HM, coarse fabric tempered with chaff and medium-coarse white grit. Black burnished exterior except along the rim, which is pale brown smoothed like the interior. Triangular ledge handle set horizontally at the rim. RD 20, H (pres.) 13.8.

5. J11 502.1
HM, coarse fabric tempered with medium-coarse grit. Black and greyish brown mottled patchily burnished exterior, reddish brown plain interior. Triangular ledge handle set horizontally at the rim.

RD 17, H (pres.) 7.5.

6. J11 501.12

HM, tempered with chaff and medium grit. Black and pale brown mottled and burnished exterior, pale brown smoothed and patchily burnished interior. RD 16, H (pres.) 6.9.

7. J11 501.16

HM, tempered with medium grit and a little chaff. Black burnished exterior, reddish brown smoothed interior. RD 29, H (pres.) 8.7.

8. J11 501.16

HM, tempered with chaff and medium grit. Black and brown streakily burnished exterior, pale grey smoothed interior. RD 24, H (pres.) 7.5.

Fig. 41

1. J11 502.1

HM, coarse fabric tempered with chaff and medium-coarse white grit, grey core. Pale brown burnished exterior and interior. RD 21, H (pres.) 10.8.

2. J11 502.1

HM, coarse fabric tempered with chaff and medium-coarse grit. Black burnished exterior except below the rim, which is pale greyish brown burnished, reddish brown to buff smoothed interior. RD 23, H (pres.) 2.5.

3. J11 502.1

HM, tempered with chaff and medium grit. Black burnished exterior except along the rim, which is pale greyish brown burnished, brown smoothed interior. Part of a triangular ledge handle set at the rim survives. RD 14, H (pres.) 4.8.

4. J11 502.5

HM, tempered with medium white grit, dark grey core. Dirty pale greyish brown plain exterior and interior. Part of a knob handle set horizontally below the rim survives. RD 17, H (pres.) 4.5.

5. J11 503.3

HM, tempered with chaff and medium white grit. Exterior and interior colour varies from dirty dark brown to black, both surfaces are smoothed. Triangular ledge handle set at the rim. RD 21, H (pres.) 5.7.

6. J11 505.3

HM, tempered with medium white grit. Black burnished exterior, pale grey smoothed interior except along rim which is black smoothed. RD 24, H (pres.) 7.5.

7. J11 503.7

HM, fine fabric tempered with medium-fine grit. Black lightly burnished exterior, reddish brown burnished interior. RD 21, H (pres.) 7.2.

8. J11 503.3

HM, tempered with chaff and medium white grit. Exterior and interior colour varies from grey to pale greyish brown, both surfaces are patchily smoothed. RD 16, H (pres.) 9.0.

9. J11 505.5

HM, tempered with medium grit. Greyish black and pale grey mottled exterior, greyish black and pale greyish brown mottled interior. Burnished exterior, smoothed interior. Triangular ledge handle set at rim. RD 15, H (pres.) 9.6.

10. J11 505.3

HM, tempered with medium grit and a little chaff. Black burnished exterior, black slightly burnished interior. RD 22, H (pres.) 9.0.

Fig. 42

1. J11 505.8

HM, tempered with medium grit and a little chaff. Black burnished exterior, brown slightly burnished interior. RD 15, H (pres.) 15.3.

2. J11 505.5

HM, tempered with medium grit and a little chaff. Grey black burnished exterior, brown and grey mottled smoothed interior. RD 16, H (pres.) 9.0.

3. J11 505.3

HM, tempered with medium white grit and a little chaff. Black burnished lower exterior, pale grey burnished upper exterior, pale greyish brown burnished interior. RD 10, H (pres.) 4.5.

4. K10c 101.8

HM, tempered with chaff and medium grit. Black and reddish brown streakily burnished exterior, greyish black smoothed interior. RD 15, H (pres.) 7.5.

5. K10c 101.4

HM, tempered with medium grit. Black burnished exterior, reddish brown smoothed interior. RD 19, H (pres.) 5.7.

6. K10c 101.12

HM, tempered with chaff and medium grit. Black burnished exterior, pale brown smoothed interior. RD 24, H (pres.) 5.1.

7. K10c 101.13

HM, tempered with medium grit. Black burnished exterior, reddish brown burnished interior. RD 18, H (pres.) 5.1.

8. K10c 101.4

HM, tempered with medium grit. Black slightly burnished exterior and interior. RD 15, H (pres.) 6.0.

9. K10c 101.1

HM, tempered with chaff and medium grit. Black burnished lower exterior, greyish brown burnished upper exterior, greyish brown smoothed interior. RD 14, H (pres.) 8.7.

10. K10c 101.4

HM, tempered with chaff and medium grit. Black burnished exterior except along the rim, which is reddish brown burnished like the interior. Triangular ledge handle set at the rim. RD 14, H (pres.) 8.7.

11. K10c 101.2

HM, tempered with medium grit and a little chaff. Black burnished exterior, black smoothed interior. Two pellets decorate the shoulder. RD 14, H (pres.) 10.2.

12. K10c 101.4

HM, tempered with medium white grit. Black burnished exterior, except along the rim, which is greyish brown streakily burnished, grey smoothed interior. RD 18, H (pres.) 5.1.

Fig. 43

1. K10c 101.23

HM, tempered with medium grit. Black burnished exterior, black smoothed interior. Previously published (Helms 1971: Fig. 2 no. 9). RD 12, H (pres.) 15.0.

2. K10c 101.4

HM, tempered with chaff and a little grit. Black to brownish beige slightly burnished exterior, reddish brown to black smoothed interior. Previously published (Helms 1971: Fig. 2 no. 1). RD 22, H (pres.) 10.2.

3. K10c 101.11
HM, coarse fabric tempered with chaff and coarse white grit. Dirty black burnished exterior, buff-cream plain interior. A knob handle set below the rim survives. RD 32, H (pres.) 6.0.

4. K10 103.5
HM, tempered with medium grit and a little chaff. Black burnished exterior, beige slightly burnished interior. RD 20, H (pres.) 12.0.

5. K10 103.7
HM, tempered with medium white grit and a little chaff, grey core. Beige buff exterior and interior, smoothed in parts. RD 25, H (pres.) 2.7.

6. K10c 101.8
HM, tempered with medium grit and a little chaff. Black burnished exterior except along the rim, which is brownish beige burnished, reddish brown burnished interior. RD 22, H (pres.) 9.3.

Fig. 44

1. K10c 101.2
HM, tempered with medium grit and chaff. Black slightly burnished exterior, beige smoothed interior. Part of a triangular ledge handle set at the rim survives. RD 14, H (pres.) 7.5.

2. K10c 101.1
HM, tempered with medium white grit and a little chaff. Pale brownish beige smoothed exterior, except along the rim, which is black burnished like the interior. Part of a triangular ledge handle set at the rim survives. RD 14, H (pres.) 5.7.

3. K10c 101.4
HM, tempered with medium grit and a little chaff. Black slightly burnished exterior, brownish beige smoothed interior. RD 30, H (pres.) 12.6.

4. K10c 101.4
HM, coarse fabric tempered with medium-coarse white grit. Black burnished exterior, pale brown smoothed interior. RD 20, H (pres.) 11.1.

5. K10c 101.4
HM, tempered with medium grit. Black burnished exterior, beige smoothed interior. RD 28, H (pres.) 13.5.

6. K10c 101.1
HM, tempered with medium white grit and a little chaff. Greyish black burnished exterior, dirty brownish beige smoothed interior. RD 18, H (pres.) 6.0.

7. K10c 101.4
HM, tempered with medium grit. Black burnished exterior, reddish brown smoothed interior. Triangular ledge handle set at the rim. RD 17, H (pres.) 8.4.

8. K10c 101.12
HM, tempered with medium grit and a little chaff. Black burnished exterior, brown slightly burnished interior. Part of a triangular ledge handle set at the rim. RD 20, H (pres.) 3.9.

Fig. 45

1. K10c 101.4
HM, coarse fabric tempered with medium-coarse white grit. Black burnished exterior except along the rim, which is reddish brown and slightly burnished like the interior. Part of a triangular ledge handle set at the rim. Previously published (Helms 1971: Fig. 2 no. 2). RD 20, H (pres.) 8.7.

2. K10c 101.2
HM, tempered with medium grit and a little chaff. Black and brown mottled exterior, smoothed in parts, plain brown interior. RD 19, H (pres.) 9.0.

3. K11 610.22 (Pit 2)
HM, tempered with medium white grit and a little chaff. Greyish black burnished exterior, beige smoothed interior. Part of a triangular ledge handle set at the rim survives. RD 14, H (pres.) 5.7.

4. K11 610.17 (Pit 1)
HM, tempered with medium grit and a little chaff. Black to buff burnished exterior, buff streakily burnished interior. RD 24, H (pres.) 6.9.

5. K11 620.1
HM, tempered with medium grit and a little chaff. Black burnished exterior, brownish beige smoothed interior except along the rim, which is burnished. Triangular ledge handle set at the rim. RD 19, H (pres.) 23.1.

6. K11 613.2 (Pit 3)
HM, tempered with medium grit and a little chaff. Black burnished exterior, greyish black stroke burnished interior. RD 15, H (pres.) 9.6.

7. K11 613.8
HM, tempered with medium white grit and a little chaff. Black burnished exterior, reddish brown smoothed interior. RD 18, H (pres.) 9.3.

Fig. 46

1. J11 501.16 (Pit 1)
HM, tempered with chaff and medium grit. Black burnished exterior, reddish brown smoothed interior. RD 40, H (pres.) 13.2.

2. J11 501.8
HM, coarse fabric tempered with medium-coarse grit and chaff. Black burnished exterior except along the rim, which is beige-brown burnished, pale brown smoothed interior. RD 35, H (pres.) 8.7.

Fig. 47

1. K11 610.9
HM, tempered with medium grit and chaff. Black burnished exterior, buff smoothed interior. Triangular ledge handle set at the rim. RD 16, H (pres.) 14.1.

2. K11 620.1
HM, tempered with medium grit. Black to brown plain exterior, red plain interior. RD 16, H (pres.) 14.7.

3. K11 620.1
HM, coarse fabric tempered with chaff. Black burnished exterior, pale brown smoothed interior. Part of a triangular ledge handle set at the rim survives. RD 17, H (pres.) 16.5.

4. K11a/c 601.9
HM, tempered with medium grit. Pale brown to beige throughout, burnished exterior, smoothed interior. RD 18, H (pres.) 7.2.

5. K11a/c 601.8
HM, tempered with medium grit and a little chaff. Grey burnished exterior except along the rim, which is black burnished like the interior. RD 10, H (pres.) 6.9.

6. K11a/c 601.12
HM, tempered with medium grit. Black burnished exterior, beige smoothed interior. RD 18, H (pres.) 17.7.

7. K11a/c 601.12
HM, tempered with medium grit. Black burnished exterior, beige smoothed interior. RD 15, H (pres.) 9.9.

8. K11a/c 601.8
HM, tempered with medium grit and chaff. Reddish brown plain exterior and interior, burnt throughout. Part of a triangular ledge handle set at the rim survives. RD 12, H (pres.) 2.8.

Fig. 48

1. K10c 101.1
HM, tempered with chaff and a little medium grit greyish black burnished exterior, grey smoothed interior. RD 12, H (pres.) 6.9.

2. K10c 101.18
HM, tempered with medium grit. Black burnished exterior, beige smoothed interior. RD 12, H (pres.) 5.4.

3. K11a/c 601.9
HM, tempered with medium grit. Black burnished exterior, reddish brown smoothed interior. RD 13, H (pres.) 6.3.

4. L10c/d 201.11
HM, tempered with chaff and medium grit. Black burnished exterior, pale brown burnished interior. RD 12, H (pres.) 3.6.

5. J11 503.16
HM, coarse fabric tempered with chaff and coarse grit. Black burnished exterior, smoothed orange brown interior. RD 29, H (pres.) 14.7.

6. J11 504.2
HM, tempered with medium white grit and a little chaff. Black burnished exterior, pinkish buff smoothed interior. RD 21, H (pres.) 12.0.

7. K10c 101.23
HM, coarse fabric tempered with medium-coarse grit. Dirty reddish brown throughout, smoothed in parts. RD 26, H (pres.) 17.4.

8. J11 501.8
HM, tempered with medium grit and chaff. Black burnished exterior, pale brown smoothed interior. RD 13, H (pres.) 8.4.

9. K10c 101.3
HM, tempered with medium grit. Black burnished exterior, beige smoothed interior. RD 12, H (pres.) 3.6.

10. K10c 101.1
HM, tempered with medium grit and chaff. Grey burnished exterior, pale brown smoothed interior. RD 14, H (pres.) 5.4.

11. J11 505.3 (Pit 2)
HM, tempered with medium white grit. Black burnished exterior except along the rim, which is beige burnished, pinkish buff smoothed interior. RD 16, H (pres.) 6.0.

12. K10c 101.15
HM, tempered with medium grit and a little chaff. Black burnished exterior, greyish black burnished interior. RD 8, H (pres.) 2.4.

Fig. 49

1. K10c 101.6
HM, tempered with medium white grit. Black burnished exterior except along the rim, which is beige burnished, beige rough interior. RD 20, H (pres.) 8.7.

2. K10c 101.11
HM, tempered with medium grit. Pale brown to beige burnished exterior, grey and pale brown mottled interior. Decoration consists of a row of incised triangles filled with punctures. Previously published (Helms 1971: Fig. 2 no. 22). RD 18, H (pres.) 2.4.

3. K10c 101.11
HM, tempered with chaff and medium grit. Dirty brownish-black plain exterior, dirty pale brown interior. RD 18, H (pres.) 6.3.

4. K10c 101.21
HM, tempered with medium-coarse grit. Black burnished exterior, greyish black plain interior, brownish brown patches along the rim. Previously published (Helms 1971: Fig. 2 no. 8). RD 8, H (pres.) 8.7.

5. K10c 101.17
HM, fine fabric tempered with fine grit. Black burnished exterior, black smoothed interior. RD 8, H (pres.) 4.2.

6. K10c 101.23
HM, tempered with medium grit. Black burnished exterior, greyish black smoothed interior. RD 6, H (pres.) 4.2.

7. K11 610.17 (Pit 1)
HM, fine fabric tempered with fine grit. Black burnished exterior, pale brown smoothed interior. Part of a tiny ledge handle set at the rim survives. RD 7, H (pres.) 4.2.

8. K11 611.5
HM, fine fabric tempered with fine grit. Black burnished exterior except along the rim, which is grey burnished like the interior. Decoration consists of a pair of solid knobs set at the shoulder. RD 6, H (pres.) 5.1.

9. K11 620.2
HM, tempered with medium grit and chaff. Black burnished exterior, pale brown to beige stroked burnished interior. RD 13, H (pres.) 7.5.

10. K11 620.2
HM, tempered with medium grits and a little chaff. Black burnished exterior, brown smoothed inside. RD — not applicable. H (pres.) 6.0.

11. K11 613.4
HM, tempered with medium grit and a little chaff. Black burnished exterior, brownish beige smoothed interior. RD 39, H (pres.) 12.6.

12. J11 503.4
HM, tempered with medium grit and a little chaff. Reddish brown smoothed exterior, black burnished interior. RD 11, H (pres.) 4.2.

13. K11 613.6
HM, tempered with medium grit and a little chaff, dark grey core. Beige to brown burnished exterior, grey smoothed interior. RD 18, H (pres.) 11.7.

14. K10c 102.5
HM, tempered with medium-coarse white grit. Black burnished exterior, beige slightly burnished interior. RD 20, H (pres.) 4.8.

15. K11 620.1
HM, fine fabric tempered with fine grit. Black highly burnished exterior, grey smoothed interior. RD 9, H (pres.) 4.5.

Fig. 50

1. L10c/d 201.5
HM, tempered with medium-fine grit. Greyish brown to black burnished exterior, pale brownish

beige smoothed interior except around the rim, which is burnished. RD 7, H (pres.) 5.1.

2. L10c/d 201.11
HM, fine fabric tempered with fine grit. Black burnished exterior and along the interior of rim, rest of the interior is beige and smoothed. RD 8, H (pres.) 2.4.

3. K11a/c 601.12
HM, tempered with medium grit. Black burnished exterior, beige smoothed interior. Single loop handle links rim to shoulder. Previously published (Helms 1971: Fig. 2 no. 4). RD 8, H (pres.) 10.5.

4. K11 610.20
HM, coarse fabric tempered with chaff and medium-coarse white grit. Black burnished exterior, grey smoothed interior. RD — not applicable. H (pres.) 9.5.

5. L10c/d 201.1
HM, tempered with medium grit. Black burnished exterior, grey smoothed interior. RD 30, H (pres.) 7.2.

6. J11 500.6
HM, tempered with medium-fine grit. Black throughout, burnished exterior and interior. BD 3, H (pres.) 0.6.

7. J11 500.10. section cleaning
HM, tempered with medium-fine grit. Black throughout, burnished exterior and interior. BD 3, H (pres.) 0.9.

8. J11 501.11
HM, tempered with medium grit. Black throughout, burnished interior, smoothed exterior. BD 3, H (pres.) 2.7.

9. J11 503.7
HM, tempered with medium-fine grit. Black throughout, burnished exterior, smoothed interior. BD 3, H (pres.) 2.1.

10. J11 500.5. section cleaning
HM, tempered with chaff and medium white grit. Black burnished exterior, black and beige mottled inside. BD 18, H (pres.) 3.0.

11. J11 501.22
HM, tempered with medium white grit and a little chaff. Beige throughout, smoothed exterior, rough interior. BD 8, H (pres.) 2.4.

12. J11 503.6 (Pit 3)
HM, tempered with chaff and a little medium grit. Dirty black to beige exterior, reddish-buff plain interior. BD 14, H (pres.) 5.7.

13. J11 503.7
HM, tempered with chaff and medium grit, pale brown core. Black burnished exterior, pale brown smoothed interior. BD 22, H (pres.) 7.8.

14. J11 503.15
HM, tempered with medium grit and a little chaff. Black burnished exterior, beige smoothed interior. BD 16, H (pres.) 8.4.

15. K10c 101.2
HM, tempered with chaff and medium white grit. Beige brown slightly burnished exterior, black slightly burnished interior. BD 12, H (pres.) 2.7.

Fig. 51

1. J11 503.15
HM, tempered with medium grit. Black burnished exterior, pinkish-buff plain interior. BD 18, H (pres.) 5.4.

2. K10c 101.4
HM, tempered with medium grit and a little chaff, dark grey core. Greyish black slightly burnished exterior, pale brown smoothed interior. BD 18, H (pres.) 7.5.

3. L10c/d 201.11
HM, tempered with chaff and medium grit. Black to brown slightly burnished exterior, black smoothed interior. Pierced once in the lower body. BD 2.5, H (pres.) 3.6.

4. K10 103.5
HM, tempered with chaff and medium white grit. Black plain exterior, reddish-buff plain interior. BD 12, H (pres.) 3.3.

5. K10c Locus not specified
HM, tempered with chaff and medium grit. Dirty brown throughout, plain grey around base on the exterior. BD 22, H (pres.) 13.5.

6. K10c 101.24
HM, tempered with chaff and medium grit. Black throughout, smoothed exterior and interior. BD 3, H (pres.) 1.3.

7. J11 504.4
HM, tempered with chaff and medium grit, grey core. Pale grey plain exterior, beige brown plain interior. BD 14, H (pres.) 3.3.

8. J11 501.2
HM, tempered with medium grit. Pale brown to beige smoothed exterior, black plain interior. BD 8, H (pres.) 1.8.

9. J11 501.11
HM, tempered with medium-coarse grit. Reddish brown smoothed exterior, black burnished interior. BD 4, H (pres.) 1.8.

10. J11 502.3
HM, tempered with chaff and medium white grit. Greyish black burnished exterior, black smoothed interior. BD 16, H (pres.) 1.8.

11. K10c 101.24
HM, tempered with chaff and medium grit. Pale grey to brown smoothed exterior, black burnished interior. BD 8, H (pres.) 1.2.

12. J11 505.3 (Pit 2)
HM, tempered with medium-fine grit. Pale grey burnished exterior, black burnished interior. BD 3, H (pres.) 1.5.

13. J11 505.3 (Pit 2)
HM, tempered with medium white grit. Pale grey slightly burnished exterior, black plain interior. BD 13, H (pres.) 1.5.

14. K10c 100.2
HM, tempered with medium-fine grit. Black throughout, burnished exterior and interior. BD 2, H (pres.) 0.6.

15. L10c/d 201.11
HM, tempered with medium-fine grit. Black throughout, burnished exterior, smoothed interior. BD 4.5, H (pres.) 2.7.

16. J11 505.3
HM, coarse fabric tempered with medium-coarse white grit. Beige throughout, burnished exterior, rough interior. BD 5, H (pres.) 2.4.

17. K10c 101.6
HM, tempered with medium grit. Black burnished exterior, beige smoothed interior. BD base 6, H (pres.) 2.1.

Fig. 52

1. K10c 101.18
   HM, tempered with medium grit. Beige burnished top and bottom. D 16, H (pres.) 6.0.
2. K10c 101.5
   HM, tempered with chaff and medium grit. Beige burnished top, black plain bottom. D 20, H (pres.) 1.5.
3. J11 501.8
   HM, tempered with chaff and medium white grit. Beige buff smoothed top, grey and brown mottled slightly burnished bottom. D 8.5, H (pres.) 3.6.
4. J11 501.8
   HM, tempered with chaff and a little medium grit. Beige burnished top, greyish black to beige burnished bottom. D 19, H (pres.) 1.5.
5. J11 501.2
   HM, tempered with chaff and medium grit. Grey and pale brown mottled top and bottom, smoothed on both surfaces. D 18, H (pres.) 2.4.
6. K11 620.1
   HM, tempered with medium grit and a little chaff. Beige buff smoothed top and bottom. D 19, H (pres.) 1.5.
7. J11 505.3
   HM, tempered with medium grit and a little chaff. Beige throughout, burnished top, plain bottom. D 16, H (pres.) 3.3.
8. J11 501.12
   HM, tempered with chaff and medium grit. Beige throughout, burnished top and bottom. D 13, H (pres.) 3.9.

Fig. 53

1. J11 501.14
   HM, tempered with chaff and a little grit, dark grey core. Beige buff smoothed top, grey smoothed around the edge, greyish black and brown mottled bottom. A pair of holes pierce the lid on opposite sides of the handle. D 19, H (pres.) 2.4.
2. J11 501.23
   HM, coarse fabric tempered with coarse grit and chaff. Buff burnished top, brown burnished bottom. D 15.5, H (pres.) 2.9.
3. J11 502.5
   HM, tempered with chaff and medium white grit, dark grey core. Beige burnished top except along the edge, which is grey burnished like the bottom. D 16, H (pres.) 2.1.
4. J11 503.3
   HM, tempered with chaff and medium-coarse grit. Grey and beige brown mottled top, beige brown bottom, smoothed in parts on both surfaces. D 20, H (pres.) 2.7.
5. J11 503.7
   HM, tempered with medium grit and a little chaff. Beige buff smoothed top and bottom. D 24, H (pres.) 1.2.
6. J11 503.7
   HM, tempered with chaff and medium grit, dark grey core. Beige to pale brown throughout, slightly burnished top and bottom. D 15, H (pres.) 0.9.
7. K10c 101.3.2
   HM, tempered with chaff and medium grit. Beige burnished top, black plain bottom. D 20, H (pres.) 1.5.
8. K10c 101.18
   HM, tempered with medium grit. Beige burnished

top, black plain bottom. Part of an incised pattern survives around the edge. D 14, H (pres.) 1.3.

Fig. 54

1. J11 501.22
   HM, tempered with chaff and medium-coarse white grit. Plain pinkish buff throughout. H (pres.) 1.2.
2. K10 103.5
   HM, tempered with chaff and a little medium white grit. Black slightly burnished exterior, dirty beige, black and reddish brown mottled plain interior. H (pres.) 9.0.
3. J11 501.16
   HM, tempered with chaff and medium grit. Black burnished exterior, beige buff smoothed interior. Decoration consists of a pair of solid knobs. H (pres.) 4.8.
4. J11 501.16 (Pit 1)
   HM, tempered with chaff and medium grit. Black burnished exterior, greyish brown smoothed interior. Decoration consists of a pair of solid knobs. H (pres.) 9.3.
5. K11 613.9
   HM, tempered with medium grit. Black burnished exterior, grey smoothed interior. Part of a relief pattern survives.
6. J11 502.3
   HM, tempered with medium grit and a little chaff. Black burnished exterior, beige brown smoothed interior. Decoration consists of a pair of solid knobs. H (pres.) 5.1.
7. J11 501.10
   HM, tempered with medium-fine grit. Black throughout, burnished exterior, smoothed interior. Part of a relief pattern survives. H (pres.) 5.1.
8. J11 502.9
   HM, tempered with chaff and medium grit. Black burnished exterior, beige brown smoothed interior. Part of a relief pattern survives. H (pres.) 7.5.
9. J11 501.4
   HM, tempered with medium-coarse white grit. Black burnished exterior, beige buff rough interior. Part of a relief pattern survives. H (pres.) 4.5.
10. J11 501.4
    HM, coarse fabric tempered with medium-coarse white grit. Black burnished exterior, pinkish buff rough interior. Decoration consists of a relief design of three vertical lines and a knob. H (pres.) 9.3.
11. K10c 101.6
    HM, tempered with medium grit. Black to pale brown burnished exterior, greyish black smoothed interior. Decoration consists of incised lines and punctures. H (pres.) 1.8.
12. K11 613.5 (Pit 3)
    HM, tempered with medium grit. Black throughout, burnished exterior, smoothed interior. Part of an incised pattern, with fugitive traces of white fill. H (pres.) 5.1.
13. K11 620.2
    HM, tempered with chaff and medium grit. Black throughout, burnished exterior and interior. Decoration consists of an incised pattern filled with white paste. H (pres.) 3.0.
14. K11 620.2
    HM, tempered with chaff and medium white grit, black core. Black burnished interior, reddish

brown to grey smoothed interior. Part of an incised pattern survives. H (pres.) 5.7.

15. J11 502.1
HM, tempered with medium grit. Pinkish buff throughout, plain exterior and interior. Two rows of a punctured design survives. H (pres.) 3.6.

16. J11 503.7
HM, tempered with chaff and medium white grit. Reddish brown throughout, smoothed exterior, plain interior. Two rows of a punctured design survives. H (pres.) 3.9.

17. J11 501.4
HM, tempered with medium grit. Greenish cream throughout, smoothed exterior, plain interior. Decoration, in dark brown, consists of part of a wavy line. H (pres.) 3.6.

18. K11a/c 601.1
HM, tempered with medium grit. Cream throughout, smoothed exterior, plain interior. Decoration, in orange-red, consists of a wavy line and part of a row of framed hatched triangles. Previously published (Helms 1971: Fig. 2 no. 20). H (pres.) 3.6.

19. K10c 101.4
HM, fine fabric tempered with fine grit. Cream throughout, smoothed exterior, plain interior. Decoration, in brown, consists of part of a hatched triangle design. Previously published (Helms 1971: Fig. 2 no. 21). H (pres.) 3.0.

20. K11 620.1
WM, tempered with medium-fine grit. Beige brown fabric, cream beige slipped exterior. Part of a geometric decoration, in reddish brown, survives. H (pres.) 5.1.

21. K11 620.1
WM, tempered with medium-fine grit. Beige brown fabric, cream-beige slipped exterior. Part of a geometric decoration, in reddish brown, survives. H (pres.) 4.5.

22. K11 620.1
WM, tempered with medium-fine grit. Beige brown fabric, cream beige slipped exterior. Decoration, in reddish brown, consists of a bold geometric pattern. H (pres.) 6.9.

23. K11 620.1
WM, tempered with medium-fine grit. Beige brown fabric, cream beige slipped exterior. Decoration, in reddish brown, consists of a bold geometric pattern. H (pres.) 6.0.

24. K11 620.1
WM, tempered with medium-fine grit. Beige brown fabric, cream beige slipped exterior. Decoration, in reddish brown, consists of part of a geometric pattern. H (pres.) 5.4.

25. K11 620.2
WM, tempered with fine grit. Beige brown fabric, cream beige slipped exterior. Decoration, in reddish brown, consists of part of a geometric pattern. H (pres.) 4.8.

Fig. 55

1. J11 502.4
WM, tempered with medium-fine grit and a little chaff. Reddish brown fabric and slip, slightly burnished exterior and interior. RD 21, H (pres.) 1.8.

2. K11 613.9
WM, tempered with medium-fine grit, some mica additives and a little chaff. Red fabric and slip, burnished exterior and interior. RD 19, H (pres.) 5.4.

3. J11 501.23
WM, tempered with medium grit and a little mica. Pale brown fabric slipped reddish brown throughout, slightly burnished exterior, smoothed interior. RD 15, H (pres.) 4.5.

4. K11 620.2
WM, tempered with medium-fine grit. Reddish buff fabric slipped red throughout, plain exterior and interior. RD 14, H (pres.) 6.0.

5. J11 503.4
WM, tempered with medium-fine grit and a little mica, grey core in parts. Pinkish buff throughout, plain exterior and interior. RD 17, H (pres.) 4.8.

6. K11 613.4
WM, tempered with medium white grit. Orange buff fabric slipped reddish brown throughout, burnished exterior and interior. RD 13, H (pres.) 3.9.

7. K11 610.4
WM, tempered with medium-fine grit. Pinkish buff throughout, plain exterior and interior. RD 11, H (pres.) 3.3.

8. J11 503.12
WM, tempered with medium-fine grit. Pale brown fabric slipped red throughout, plain exterior and interior. RD 16, H (pres.) 7.2.

9. J11 503.15
WM, tempered with medium-fine grit. Reddish brown fabric throughout, plain exterior and interior. RD 17, H (pres.) 5.4.

10. J11 501.5
WM, tempered with medium grit. Pale brown fabric, red slipped and smoothed exterior. H (pres.) 4.6.

11. K11 620.2
WM, tempered with medium-fine grit, grey core in parts. Orange buff fabric, red slipped plain exterior. H (pres.) 4.8.

12. J11 502.4
WM, tempered with medium grit and chaff. Reddish buff throughout, plain exterior. H (pres.) 9.9.

13. J11 503.3
WM, tempered with medium-fine grit, beige core. Pale brown to orange throughout, smoothed exterior. H (pres.) 7.5.

14. J11 503.9
HM, tempered with medium grit and a little chaff. Black fabric, black burnished interior of bowl, pale brown smoothed exterior, plain beige underneath the stand. H (pres.) 6.0.

15. K11 620.2
WM, tempered with medium-fine grit. Beige buff fabric slipped pale reddish brown, plain exterior. H (pres.) 7.2.

16. J11 501.8
WM, fine orange fabric tempered with fine grit. Reddish brown slipped and burnished exterior. BD 13, H (pres.) 6.0.

17. K11 613.8
WM, tempered with medium grit and a little chaff. Cream throughout, dirty creamish buff exterior. BD 11, H (pres.) 5.7.

18. J11 503.3
HM, tempered with chaff and medium grit. Pale brown smoothed exterior, beige to pale brown plain underneath. BD 8, H (pres.) 4.8.

Fig. 56

1. J11 501.6
   WM, hard fabric tempered with medium grit, reddish brown throughout. Exterior has a pale creamy brown reserved slip. Previously published (Helms 1973: Fig. 9). RD 21, W max 51, H 55.2.
2. J11 503.14
   WM, tempered with medium grit and a little chaff, reddish brown throughout. Exterior has a cream reserved slip. RD 18.5., H (pres.) 7.4.
3. K11 613.2
   WM, tempered with medium-fine grit, pale orange brown throughout. Exterior has a cream reserved slip. RD 17.5, H (pres.) 7.7.
4. J11 503.15
   WM, tempered with medium grit and a little chaff. Interior is pale orange brown, exterior is pale brown, with a greenish cream reserved slip. H (pres.) 11.1.
5. K11a/c 601.9
   WM, tempered with medium grit, reddish brown throughout. Exterior has a pale creamy brown reserved slip. H (pres.) 1.9.
6. J11 501.4
   WM, fine fabric tempered with medium-fine grit, pale pinkish brown throughout. Exterior has a cream reserved slip. H (pres.) 7.8.
7. K10c 101.9
   WM, tempered with medium-fine grit. Interior in pale orange brown, exterior is pale beige brown, with a creamy white reserved slip. H (pres.) 6.3.
8. K11a/c 601.8
   WM, tempered with medium-fine grit, pale grey throughout. Exterior has a creamy beige reserved slip. H (pres.) 3.9.
9. J11 502.1
   WM, tempered with medium grit, reddish brown throughout. Exterior has a pale creamy brown reserved slip. H (pres.) 6.0.
10. K10c 101.14
    WM, tempered with medium grit. Interior is pale pinkish brown, exterior is beige brown, with a creamy white reserved slip. H (pres.) 3.6.
11. K10c 101.6
    WM, tempered with medium-fine grit, pale orange brown throughout. Exterior has a creamy white reserved slip. H (pres.) 5.0.
12. J11 502.1
    WM, tempered with medium grit, reddish brown fabric erring towards brown on exterior, reserved slip pale cream brown. H (pres.) 3.0.
13. K10c 101.1
    WM, fine fabric tempered with medium-fine grit, beige buff throughout. Exterior has a creamy white reserved slip. H (pres.) 5.1.

Fig. 57

1. K10c 101.1
   WM, tempered with medium grit, reddish buff throughout. Exterior has an off-white reserved slip. RD 10, H (pres.) 5.1.
2. K10c 101.1
   WM, tempered with medium-fine grit, pale beige brown throughout. Reserved slip on exterior is off-white tinged with pink. RD 12, H (pres.) 2.7.
3. K10c 101.7
   WM, fine fabric tempered with medium-fine white grit, pale pinkish brown throughout. Exterior has a creamy white reserved slip. Previously published

(Helms 1971: Fig. 2 no. 14). RD 10, H (pres.) 6.3.

4. K10c 101.4
   WM, tempered with medium grit, pale brown throughout. Exterior has a creamy pink reserved slip. RD 12, H (pres.) 3.3.
5. K10c 101.3
   WM, tempered with medium-fine grit. Interior is pinkish cream, exterior is pale brown, with a cream reserved slip. RD 12, H (pres.) 4.2.
6. K10c 101.14
   WM, tempered with medium grit, pale brown throughout. Exterior has a pale buff reserved slip. RD 28, H (pres.) 5.1.
7. K10c 101.14
   WM, tempered with medium-fine grit, pale beige brown throughout. Exterior has a creamy buff reserved slip. Previously published (Helms 1971: Fig. 2 no. 11). RD — not applicable. H (pres.) 4.0.
8. J11 501.2
   WM, tempered with medium to fine grit. Interior is pale orange brown, exterior is beige brown, with a pale cream brown reserved slip. RD 21, H (pres.) 3.4.
9. J11 501.16
   WM, tempered with medium grit, pale reddish brown throughout. Exterior has a pale brown reserved slip. RD 11, H (pres.) 11.2.
10. K11 610.2
    WM, tempered with medium-fine grit, pale orange brown fabric, with buff core. Smoothed exterior has a creamy white reserved slip. RD 14, H (pres.) 9.0.
11. K11 613.9
    WM, tempered with chaff and medium-fine grit, dull beige brown throughout. Exterior has a creamy beige reserved slip and two rows of punctures along the shoulder. RD 17, H (pres.) 12.6.
12. J11 503.13
    WM, tempered with medium grit. Interior is reddish buff, exterior is beige buff, with a cream reserved slip. H (pres.) 8.4.

Fig. 58

1. J11 503.4
   WM, tempered with medium-fine grit and a little mica, pale pinkish brown throughout. RD 14, H (pres.) 3.6.
2. J11 501.16
   WM, fine fabric tempered with fine grit, very pale brown exterior, pale reddish brown interior. RD 13, H (pres.) 4.6.
3. K10c 101.4
   WM, fine fabric tempered with fine grit, pale greenish cream throughout. RD 10, H (pres.) 3.9.
4. K10c 101.8
   WM, tempered with medium-fine grit, pale greenish cream throughout. Previously published (Helms 1971: Fig. 2 no. 12). RD 10, H (pres.) 6.3.
5. K10c 101.9
   WM, fine fabric tempered with fine-very fine grit. Cream fabric with a greenish cream slurry. RD 10.3, H (pres.) 4.2.
6. K10c 101.12
   WM, fine fabric tempered with very fine grit, pale greenish cream throughout. RD 12, H (pres.) 3.6.
7. K10c 101.14
   WM, tempered with medium grit and a little mica, pale pinkish brown throughout. RD 12,

H (pres.) 4.6.

8. K10c 101.3
WM, fine hard fabric tempered with fine grit, pale greenish cream throughout. RD 6, H (pres.) 3.4.

9. K10 103.7
WM, tempered with medium grit, pale pinkish brown throughout. RD 13, H (pres.) 5.4.

10. K10c 101.2
WM, fine hard fabric tempered with fine grit, pale pinkish orange throughout. RD 11, H (pres.) 5.4.

11. K11 610.8
WM, very fine hard fabric tempered with very fine grit, greenish cream throughout. Smoothed exterior and interior. RD 12, H (pres.) 1.8.

12. K11 610.17
WM, very fine hard fabric tempered with very fine grit, creamy white throughout. Smoothed exterior and interior. RD 8, H (pres.) 4.5.

13. K11 610.4
WM, tempered with medium-fine grit and a little mica, pale creamy brown throughout. RD 15, H (pres.) 4.5.

14. K11 610.17
WM, very fine hard fabric tempered with very fine grit, pale pinkish orange throughout. RD 10, H (pres.) 3.9.

15. J11 502.2
WM, very fine hard fabric tempered with very fine grit, greenish cream throughout. RD 11, H (pres.) 5.4.

16. K11 610.1
WM, very fine hard fabric tempered with very fine grit, greenish cream throughout. Smoothed exterior and interior. RD 11, H (pres.) 3.9.

17. J11 500.10
WM, fine fabric tempered with fine grit, pale greenish cream throughout. RD 8, H (pres.) 2.7.

18. J11 501.12
WM, very fine fabric tempered with very fine grit, very pale creamy brown throughout. RD 9, H (pres.) 2.7.

19. J11 501.12
WM, very fine fabric tempered with very fine grit, pale pinkish brown throughout. RD 9, H (pres.) 3.3.

20. J11 501.1
WM, tempered with medium-fine white grit, pale orange brown throughout. RD 7, H (pres.) 2.4.

21. J11 501.27
WM, fine fabric tempered with fine grit. Pale brown exterior, pale reddish brown interior. RD 10, H (pres.) 3.3.

22. J11 501.7
WM, fine fabric tempered with fine grit, pale creamy brown throughout. RD 9, H (pres.) 5.9.

23. J11 501.8
WM, tempered with medium-fine grit, pale brown throughout, pale reddish brown core. RD 11, H (pres.) 3.5.

24. J11 501.14
WM, fine fabric tempered with fine grit, cream throughout. RD 10, H (pres.) 4.2.

25. J11 501.8
WM, tempered with medium-fine grit, pale pinkish brown throughout. RD 6, H (pres.) 3.0.

26. J11 501.6
WM, fine fabric tempered with fine grit, pale pinkish brown throughout. RD 11, H (pres.) 2.9.

Fig. 59

1. J11 501.6
WM, fine fabric tempered with fine grit, pale orange brown throughout. RD 9, H (pres.) 5.1.

2. J11 501.2
WM, tempered with medium-fine grit, pale pinkish brown throughout. RD 11, H (pres.) 3.0.

3. J11 501.17
WM, fine fabric tempered with fine grit, cream throughout. RD 9, H (pres.) 4.2.

4. J11 501.17
WM, tempered with medium-fine grit, red throughout. Wheel striations on the interior. RD 7, H 6.4.

5. J11 502.2
WM, tempered with medium-fine grit, pale orange brown throughout. RD 11, H (pres.) 4.6.

6. J11 501.5
WM, tempered with medium-fine grit, pale cream brown throughout. Horizontal groove around the shoulder. RD 10, H (pres.) 3.3.

7. J11 502.1
WM, fine fabric tempered with fine grit, pale orange brown throughout. RD 10, H (pres.) 2.6.

8. J11 502.9
WM, fine fabric tempered with fine grit. Pale pinkish cream exterior, pale greenish cream interior. RD 8, H (pres.) 3.2.

9. Trench 73 500.10
WM, fine fabric tempered with fine-very fine grit, pale greenish cream throughout. RD 9, H (pres.) 2.7.

10. J11 502.1
WM, fine fabric tempered with fine grit, pale pinkish brown throughout. RD 8, H (pres.) 2.7.

11. J11 505.9
WM, fine fabric tempered with fine grit, pale creamy brown throughout. RD 9, H (pres.) 4.4.

12. J11 502.3
WM, fine fabric tempered with fine grit, pale creamy brown throughout. RD 8, H (pres.) 1.5.

13. J11 505.3
WM, tempered with medium-fine grit and a little mica, pale pink brown throughout. RD 11, H (pres.) 4.4.

14. J11 503.8
WM, tempered with medium-fine grit, pale pinkish brown throughout. RD 11, H (pres.) 3.9.

15. J11 503.4
WM, fine fabric tempered with fine grit and a little mica, pale creamy brown throughout. RD 8, H (pres.) 4.0.

16. J11 503.11
WM, fine fabric tempered with fine grit, pale orange brown throughout. Marked wheel striations on the interior. RD 10, H (pres.) 2.9.

17. K10c 101.2
WM, tempered with medium grit, pale pinkish brown throughout. RD 14, H (pres.) 8.0.

18. K10c 101.4
WM, tempered with medium-fine grit, pale creamy brown throughout. RD 11, H (pres.) 4.1.

19. K10c 101.2
WM, fine fabric tempered with fine grit, pale pinkish brown throughout. RD 9, H (pres.) 3.2.

20. K10c 101.2
WM, tempered with medium-fine grit and a little mica, pale pinkish brown throughout. RD 14, H (pres.) 3.6.

21. K10c 101.5
WM, tempered with medium-fine grit, pinkish cream throughout RD 8, H (pres.) 2.9.
22. K10c 101.4
WM, fine fabric tempered with fine grit, pale orange to pink throughout. RD 10, H (pres.) 4.7.
23. K10c 101.7
WM, tempered with medium-fine grit, pale pinkish brown throughout. RD 12, H (pres.) 5.2.
24. K10c 101.1
WM, fine fabric tempered with very fine grit, greenish cream throughout. RD 8, H (pres.) 2.7.
25. K10c 101.1
WM, fine fabric tempered with fine grit, pale pinkish brown throughout. RD 8, H (pres.) 3.6.
26. K10c 101.12
WM, tempered with medium-fine grit, pale pinkish brown throughout. RD 12, H (pres.) 2.6.
27. K10c 101.2
WM, fine fabric tempered with fine grit, pale pinkish brown throughout. Smoothed exterior and interior. RD 13, H (pres.) 2.7.

Fig. 60

1. K10 103.5
WM, fine fabric tempered with fine grit, greenish cream throughout. RD 12, H (pres.) 2.4.
2. K10 103.3
WM, fine fabric tempered with fine grit, pale pinkish brown throughout. RD 10, H (pres.) 3.5.
3. K10c 101.1
WM, very fine fabric tempered with very fine grit, creamy pink throughout. RD 8, H (pres.) 1.1.
4. K11 610.2
WM, tempered with medium grit, pinkish brown throughout, dark grey core. Smoke blackened on one side. Wheel striations on the interior. RD 8, H 6.4.
5. K11 610.11
WM, fine fabric tempered with fine grit, pale creamy brown throughout. RD 9, H (pres.) 3.9.
6. K11 610.17
WM, tempered with medium white grit, pale brown throughout. Groove around shoulder. RD 8, H (pres.) 5.7.
7. K11 610.17
WM, very fine fabric tempered with very fine grit, pale orange brown throughout. RD 10, H (pres.) 5.4.
8. K11 610.9
WM, fine fabric tempered with fine grit, pale pinkish brown throughout. RD 8, H (pres.) 6.6.
9. K11 610.17
WM, tempered with fine grit and the occasional medium stone grit, cream throughout. RD 9, H (pres.) 4.5.
10. K11 613.2
WM, tempered with medium-fine grit, pale orange brown throughout. RD 9, H (pres.) 5.7.
11. K11 610.7
WM, fine fabric tempered with fine grit, pale greenish cream throughout. Lumpy interior. RD 13, H (pres.) 6.3.
12. K11 613.2
WM, tempered with medium-fine grit, creamy pink throughout. RD 8, H (pres.) 4.2.
13. K11 613.4
WM, fine fabric tempered with fine grit, cream throughout. RD 9, H (pres.) 2.4.

14. K11 613.2
WM, tempered with medium fine grit, pink throughout. Wheel striations on the interior. RD 14, H (pres.) 3.3.
15. K11a/c 601.12
WM, tempered with medium-fine grit, pale pink throughout. Previously published (Helms 1971: Fig. 2 no. 13). RD 10.5, H (pres.) 5.7.
16. K11a/c 601.9
WM, tempered with medium-fine grit, cream throughout. RD 9, H (pres.) 4.2.
17. K11a/c 601.10
WM, tempered with medium-fine grit and a little mica, pale pinkish brown throughout. RD 12, H (pres.) 6.4.
18. K11 620.1
WM, tempered with medium-fine grit, pale creamy brown throughout. RD 10, H (pres.) 5.1.
19. K11 610.2
WM, tempered with medium-fine grit speckled with mica additives, pale creamy grey throughout. RD 12, H (pres.) 6.1.
20. K11 620.2
WM, tempered with medium-fine grit, pale greyish brown throughout. RD 20.5, H (pres.) 7.8.
21. J11 502.3
WM, tempered with medium grit, pale orange brown throughout. RD 29, H (pres.) 5.1.

Fig. 61

1. J11 501.13
WM, tempered with medium-fine grit, pale creamy brown throughout. RD 10, H (pres.) 3.6.
2. J11 502.3
WM, tempered with medium grit, orange throughout. RD 19, H (pres.) 4.6.
3. J11 505.1
WM, tempered with medium-fine grit, pale pinkish brown throughout. RD 15, H (pres.) 4.2.
4. J11 505.9/10
WM, tempered with medium-fine grit, pale reddish brown throughout. RD 23, H (pres.) 3.9.
5. J11 503.12
WM, tempered with medium grit, pale orange brown throughout. RD 28, H (pres.) 5.7.
6. K11 610.1
WM, tempered with medium-fine grit, pale pinkish brown throughout. RD 19, H (pres.) 4.5.
7. K11 620.2
WM, tempered with medium-fine grit, pinkish cream throughout. Smoothed exterior and interior. Traces of red paint on the shoulder and rim. RD 18, H (pres.) 5.1.
8. K10c 101.17
WM, tempered with medium fine grit, pale cream throughout. RD 24, H (pres.) 3.6.
9. K11 610.12
WM, tempered with medium grit, pinkish brown throughout. Smoke blackened patch on the base and interior. RD 24, H (pres.) 12.6.
10. K11a/c 602.1
WM, tempered with medium grit, pale orange brown throughout. RD 19, H (pres.) 7.2.
11. J11 501.4
WM, tempered with medium-fine grit, pale pinkish brown throughout. RD 14, H (pres.) 3.0.
12. J11 502.1
WM, fine fabric tempered with fine grit, pale orange brown throughout. RD 17, H (pres.) 3.6.

13. K10c 101.5
    WM, tempered with medium-fine grit, pale creamy brown throughout. RD 15, H (pres.) 2.7.

Fig. 62

1. J11 501.6
   WM, tempered with medium-fine grit, orange throughout. RD 12, H (pres.) 5.1.
2. K10 103.3
   WM, tempered with medium-fine grit, beige smoothed throughout. RD 14, H (pres.) 9.0.
3. K10c 101.9
   WM, tempered with medium-fine grit, pale pinkish brown throughout. RD 14, H (pres.) 4.2.
4. K10c 101.1
   WM, tempered with medium-fine grit, pale pinkish brown throughout. RD 14, H (pres.) 4.5.
5. K10c 101.14
   WM, tempered with medium-fine grit, pale pinkish brown throughout. RD 18, H (pres.) 1.5.
6. K10c 101.12
   WM, tempered with medium-fine grit, pale greyish brown throughout. Previously published (Helms 1971: Fig. 2 no.18). RD 15, H (pres.) 4.9.
7. K10c 101.1
   WM, tempered with medium-fine grit, pale dirty greenish brown. RD 16, H (pres.) 3.3.
8. K11 620.2
   WM, tempered with medium-fine grit, pale reddish brown throughout, smoke blackened patches on the interior. RD 15, H (pres.) 5.7.
9. J11 501.4
   WM, tempered with medium grit, pale creamy brown throughout. RD 23, H (pres.) 3.6.
10. K11 613.2
    WM, fine fabric tempered with fine grit, orange throughout. RD 27, H (pres.) 8.1.
11. J11 502.1
    WM, tempered with medium-fine grit, pale orange brown throughout. RD 17, H (pres.) 4.9.
12. K11 613.2
    WM, tempered with medium-fine grit, pink throughout. RD 18, H (pres.) 5.1.
13. K10c 101.1
    WM, tempered with medium-fine grit, pale pinkish brown throughout. RD 16, H (pres.) 3.8.
14. J11 500.10
    WM, tempered with medium grit. Reddish brown smoothed exterior, pale reddish brown interior, pale brown core. RD 18, H (pres.) 3.0.
15. J11 502.9
    WM, tempered with medium grit. Reddish brown burnished exterior, pale brown interior. RD 14, H (pres.) 2.7.
16. K11 610.1
    WM, tempered with medium grit and a little mica, pale brown throughout. RD 14, H (pres.) 3.8.
17. K10c 101.2
    WM, fine fabric tempered with fine grit, pale pinkish brown throughout. RD 18, H (pres.) 2.4.
18. K10c 101.14
    WM, tempered with medium-fine grit, beige throughout, burnished exterior, plain interior. RD 14, H (pres.) 3.0.
19. K10c 101.1
    WM, tempered with medium-fine grit, creamy pink throughout. RD 16, H (pres.) 2.4.

Fig. 63

1. K11 620.2
   WM, tempered with medium-fine grit, pale creamy brown throughout. Smoothed exterior and interior. RD 18, H (pres.) 3.6.
2. K11 610.8
   WM, tempered with medium grit. Reddish brown slipped slightly burnished exterior, pale brown interior, pale brown core. RD 18, H (pres.) 3.0.
3. K10c 101.19
   WM, tempered with medium grit and a little coarse grit, pale creamy brown throughout. RD 20, H (pres.) 3.6.
4. K11 610.1
   WM, tempered with medium grit, pale pinkish brown throughout. RD 16, H (pres.) 6.3.
5. J11 500.4
   WM, tempered with medium grit, greenish cream, pale brown core. RD 22, H (pres.) 3.1.
6. K11 610.17
   WM, tempered with medium black grit, pale brown fabric, red slipped exterior and interior. Large part of interior surface is badly abraded. RD 22, H (pres.) 4.8.
7. J11 501.8
   WM, tempered with medium grit, pale reddish brown throughout. RD 4, H (pres.) 2.4.
8. J11 502.2
   WM, tempered with medium white grit, orange throughout. RD 9, H (pres.) 3.7.
9. K11a/c 601.2
   WM, tempered with medium-fine grit, pale beige brown fabric fired orange buff in parts around rim, patches of dark grey from smoke. Previously published (Helms 1971: Fig. 2 no.15). RD 9, H (pres.) 8.4.
10. K10c 101.1
    WM, very fine fabric tempered with very fine grit, greenish cream throughout. Previously published (Helms 1971: Fig. 2 no. 16). RD 10, H (pres.) 2.7.
11. K10c 101.18
    WM, tempered with medium-fine grit, pale yellowish cream throughout. RD 9.5, H (pres.) 3.9.
12. K10c 101.1
    WM, tempered with medium-fine grit, pale cream brown throughout. RD 12, H (pres.) 3.9.
13. J11 501.9
    WM, tempered with medium-fine grit, pale pinkish brown throughout. Smoothed exterior and interior. RD 15, H (pres.) 5.1.
14. K10c 101.6
    WM, tempered with medium grit, pale pinkish brown throughout. RD 10, H (pres.) 2.4.
15. J11 501.22
    WM, tempered with medium grit temper, reddish brown throughout. RD 16, H (pres.) 4.5.
16. J11 501.8
    WM, tempered with medium grit, pale pinkish brown throughout. RD 24, H (pres.) 7.5.

Fig. 64

1. J11 502.12
WM, tempered with medium-fine grit and a little chaff. Brown slightly burnished exterior, brown plain interior, with patches of grey to black. RD 13, H (pres.) 6.6.

2. J11 505.1
WM, tempered with medium grit, pale pinkish orange throughout. RD 14, H (pres.) 8.7.

3. J11 501.8
WM, tempered with medium grit, pale brown throughout. Smoothed exterior and interior. RD 26, H (pres.) 6.9.

4. K11 610.4
WM, tempered with medium-fine grit, pale pinkish brown throughout. RD 16, H (pres.) 4.8.

5. K11 611.1
WM, tempered with medium-fine grit. Pale reddish brown fabric, with pale beige brown slipped exterior. RD 13, H (pres.) 4.2.

6. K11 610.1
WM, tempered with medium-fine grit, pale pinkish brown throughout. RD 22, H (pres.) 6.6.

7. K11a/c 601.10
WM, tempered with medium-fine grit, pink throughout. RD 12, H (pres.) 5.1.

8. K11 613.1
WM, tempered with medium-fine grit, pale beige brown throughout, stroke burnished exterior, smoothed interior. RD 17, H (pres.) 5.1.

9. K11a/c 602.2
WM, fine fabric tempered with fine grit, pale reddish brown throughout. RD 14, H (pres.) 5.7.

10. K11a/c 601.1
WM, tempered with medium grit, pale creamy brown, with a cream slurry on the exterior. Previously published (Helms 1971: Fig. 2 no. 10). RD 22, H (pres.) 7.5.

Fig. 65

1. K10c 101.14
WM, tempered with medium-fine grit, cream throughout. H (pres.) 6.6.

2. J11 501.23
HM, fine black fabric tempered with fine grit, highly burnished exterior. H (pres.) 4.2.

3. J11 503.15
HM, fine black fabric tempered with fine grit, highly burnished exterior. H (pres.) 2.4.

4. J11 503.17
WM, tempered with medium grit, creamy pink throughout. Spout is broken. H (pres.) 14.1.

5. K11 620.12
WM, tempered with medium-fine grit, pale orange brown throughout. H (pres.) 3.9.

6. K11 613.2
WM, tempered with medium grit, pale orange brown throughout. H (pres.) 2.4.

7. J11 502.2
WM, tempered with medium grit, pale orange brown throughout. Horizontally pierced lug handle set at the shoulder. H (pres.) 4.8.

8. J11 501.16
WM, fine fabric tempered with fine grit, pink throughout. Vertically pierced lug set at the shoulder. Decoration, in reddish brown, consists of a geometric pattern. H (pres.) 11.1.

9. J11 505.8
WM, fine fabric tempered with fine-very fine grit, pale greenish cream throughout. Vertically pierced lug set at the shoulder. H (pres.) 3.3.

10. K11 620.1
WM, tempered with medium-fine grit, greenish cream throughout. Vertically pierced lug set at the shoulder. H (pres.) 4.2.

11. K11 611.7
WM, fine fabric tempered with fine grit, creamy white throughout. Vertically pierced lug set at the shoulder. H (pres.) 3.3.

12. K10c 101.6.5
WM, tempered with medium grit, pale pinkish brown throughout. Vertically pierced lug set at the shoulder. H (pres.) 3.3.

13. K11 610.4
WM, tempered with medium-fine grit, pinkish brown throughout, smoke blackened patch around the bottom. Two vertically pierced lugs set at the shoulder are preserved. H (pres.) 12.6.

14. K11a/c 601.7
WM, very fine fabric tempered with very fine grit, creamy white throughout. Vertically pierced lug set at the shoulder; finger strokes around edge of the lug. H (pres.) 5.7.

15. K10c 101.14
WM, fine fabric tempered with fine grit, cream throughout. Vertically pierced lug set at the shoulder. H (pres.) 2.7.

16. K11 610.20
WM, fine fabric tempered with fine grit, pale brown throughout. Vertically pierced lug set at the shoulder. Decoration, in red, consists of a net pattern and dots. H (pres.) 4.3.

17. J11 501.22
WM, tempered with medium grit, pale brown throughout, smoke blackened in parts. H (pres.) 3.0.

18. K10d 126.3
WM, tempered with medium-fine grit, pale creamy brown plain interior, pale beige brown burnished exterior. Decoration consists of two horizontal rows of incised circles around the shoulder. H (pres.) 6.6.

19. K11 613.4
HM, tempered with chaff and occasional medium grit, pale grey throughout, grey core. H (pres.) 3.0.

20. J11 501.15
WM, tempered with medium grit, pale orange brown, grey core. Three vertical incisions decorate the body. H (pres.) 8.7.

21. J11 503.15
HM, tempered with medium grit, greenish cream throughout. Part of a geometric relief pattern decorates the sherd. H (pres.) 12.0.

22. K10c 101.5. Possible base
HM, tempered with medium grit and a little chaff, pale brown throughout. H (pres.) 1.8.

Fig. 66

1. J11 505.8
   WM, fine fabric tempered with fine grit, cream throughout. BD 4, H (pres.) 3.4.
2. J11 501.8
   WM, fine fabric tempered with very fine grit, greenish cream throughout. BD 13, H (pres.) 3.4.
3. J11 501.5
   WM, fine fabric tempered with very fine grit, cream throughout, smoothed exterior and interior. BD 3, H (pres.) 2.7.
4. K10c 101.2
   WM, fine fabric tempered with fine grit, pale creamy brown throughout, smoothed exterior and interior. BD 3.6, H (pres.) 2.7.
5. K11 610.4
   WM, fine fabric tempered with very fine grit, creamy white throughout, smoothed exterior and interior. BD 3.3, H (pres.) 4.2.
6. K11 600.15
   WM, fine fabric tempered with very fine grit, creamy white throughout, smoothed exterior and interior. BD 4, H (pres.) 2.0.
7. K11 610.2
   WM, fine fabric tempered with fine grit, greenish cream throughout. BD 3, H (pres.) 3.3.
8. J11 501.20
   WM, tempered with medium-fine grit, cream throughout, smoothed exterior, plain interior. BD 3, H (pres.) 2.7.
9. J11 501.2
   WM, fine fabric tempered with fine grit, cream throughout, smoothed exterior and interior. BD 2.2, H (pres.) 2.4.
10. J11 501.23
    WM, fine fabric tempered with fine grit, pale greenish cream throughout, smoothed exterior and interior. BD 2.8, H (pres.) 2.1.
11. J11 501.3
    WM, fine fabric tempered with fine grit, pale creamy brown throughout. BD 4, H (pres.) 2.4.
12. J11 501.4
    WM, fine fabric tempered with fine grit, pale brown smoothed exterior, pale orange brown smoothed interior. BD 3, H (pres.) 3.0.
13. J11 503.7
    WM, tempered with medium-fine grit, pale pinkish brown throughout. BD 6, H (pres.) 3.1.
14. J11 501.9
    WM, tempered with medium-fine grit, beige throughout, smoothed exterior, plain interior. Pierced at the base. BD 8, H (pres.) 2.4.
15. J11 501.1
    WM, tempered with medium-fine grit, pale pinkish brown, smoothed exterior, plain interior. BD 8, H (pres.) 1.8.
16. J11 501.3
    WM, tempered with medium-fine grit, pale pinkish brown throughout, smoothed exterior and interior. BD 3, H pres.
17. J11 501.3
    WM, tempered with medium-fine grit, pink throughout. BD 10, H (pres.) 2.1.
18. J11 500.10
    WM, tempered with medium-fine grit, pale pinkish brown throughout. BD 3, H (pres.) 2.1.
19. J11 502.8
    WM, tempered with medium-fine grit, pale brown exterior, beige interior. BD 5, H (pres.) 2.4.
20. J11 503.4
    WM, tempered with medium-fine grit, pale pinkish brown throughout. Wheel striations on the interior. BD 7, H (pres.) 2.9.
21. J11 505.9
    WM, fine fabric tempered with fine grit, pale brown exterior, pale orange brown interior. BD 3, H (pres.) 2.1.
22. J11 503.15
    WM, tempered with medium grit, pale pinkish brown throughout, smoothed exterior. BD 9, H (pres.) 3.1.
23. K10c 101.8
    WM, tempered with medium-fine grit, creamy white throughout. Wheel striations on the interior. BD 3, H (pres.) 4.4.
24. K10c 101
    WM, tempered with medium-fine grit, pale pinkish buff throughout. Wheel striations on the interior. BD 5, H (pres.) 3.3.
25. K10c 101.14
    WM, tempered with medium grit, cream throughout. Marked wheel striations on the interior. BD 5, H (pres.) 3.3.
26. K10c 101.14
    WM, tempered with medium-fine grit, pale pinkish brown throughout. BD 3.5, H (pres.) 4.8.
27. K10c 101.14
    WM, tempered with medium grit and a little mica, pale creamy brown throughout. BD 5, H (pres.) 5.7.
28. K10c 101.2
    WM, fine fabric tempered with fine grit, pale orange brown throughout. BD 4, H (pres.) 2.7.
29. K11 610.17
    WM, fine fabric tempered with fine grit, pale brown throughout. BD 3.5, H (pres.) 2.5.
30. K11a/c 601.1
    WM, tempered with medium grit, pale creamy brown throughout, smoothed exterior, plain interior. BD 12, H (pres.) 6.3.
31. K11 610.17
    WM, fine fabric tempered with fine grit, pale brown throughout. BD 3.4, H (pres.) 2.7.

Fig. 67

1. K11a/c 601.1
   WM, tempered with medium grit, cream throughout. BD 20, H (pres.) 6.6.
2. K11a/c 601.1
   WM, tempered with medium-fine grit, creamy red throughout. Marked wheel striations on the interior. BD 5, H (pres.) 3.6.
3. K11a/c 601.1
   WM, tempered with medium-fine grit, creamy red throughout. Marked wheel striations on the interior. BD 3.5, H (pres.) 1.5.
4. L10c/d 201.1
   WM, tempered with medium-fine grit, pale greenish cream throughout. BD 6, H (pres.) 4.8.
5. K11 613.2
   HM, coarse fabric tempered with chaff and coarse grit. Greyish black fabric mottled brown in parts. Two crude lugs set opposite each other on the rim. H (pres.) 5.1, W (max.) 7.1.
6. J11 504.3
   HM, tempered with medium-coarse grit, yellowish throughout. H (pres.) 8.4, W (max.) 3.8.

7. J11 501.4
   HM, tempered with medium grit and occasional
   chaff. Plain grey fabric. BD 3.5, H (max. pres.)
   1.9.
8. K11 613.5
   HM, crudely made small cup, tempered with chaff
   and coarse grit, brown throughout. H (pres.) 4.1,
   W (max.) 3.5.
9. J11 501.8
   HM, tempered with medium grit and a little chaff,
   pale beige brown throughout. L 2.1, W (max.
   pres.) 2.4.

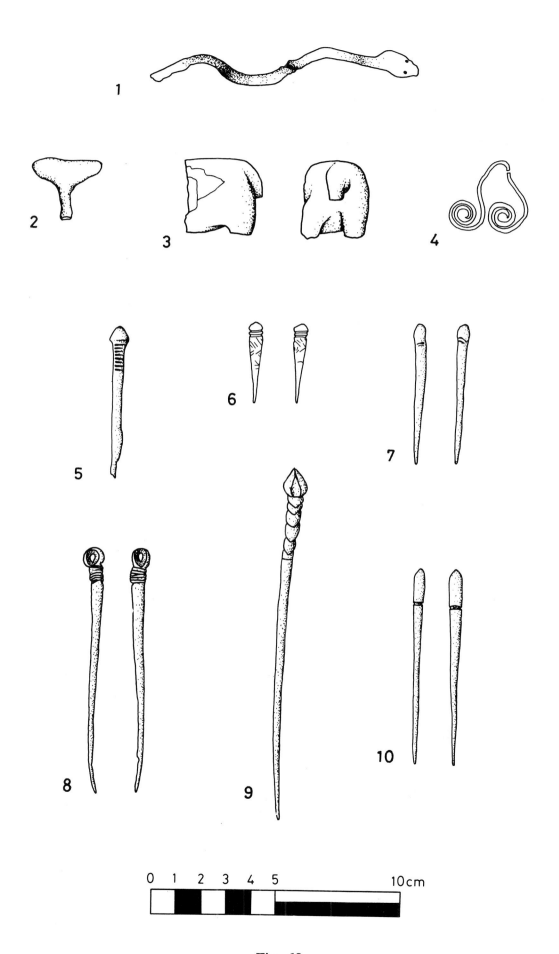

Fig. 68

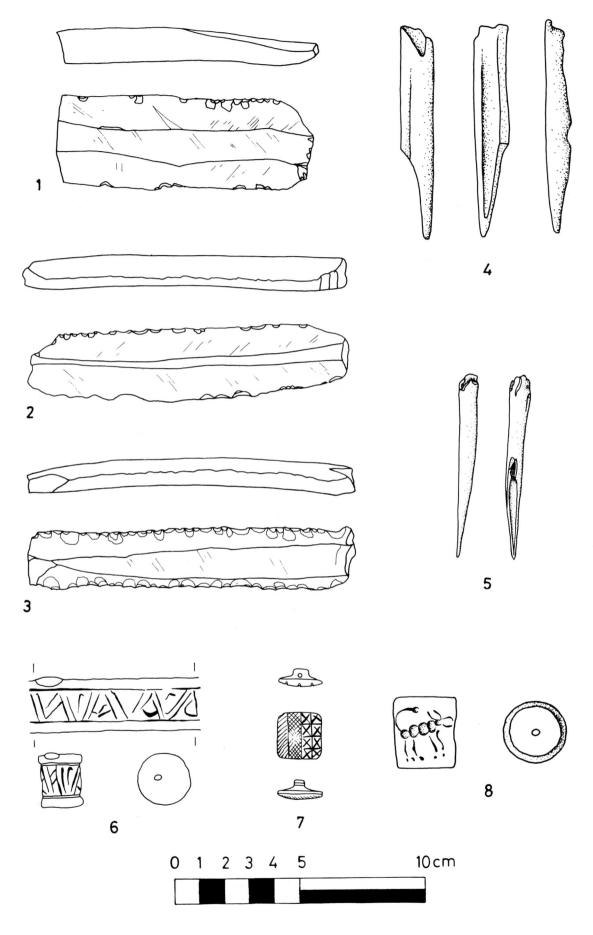

Fig. 69

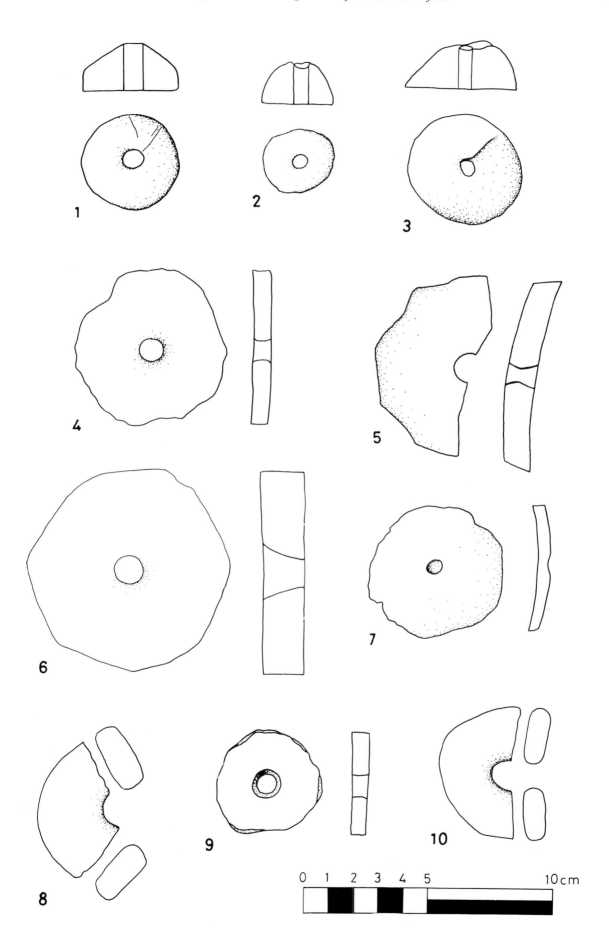

Fig. 70

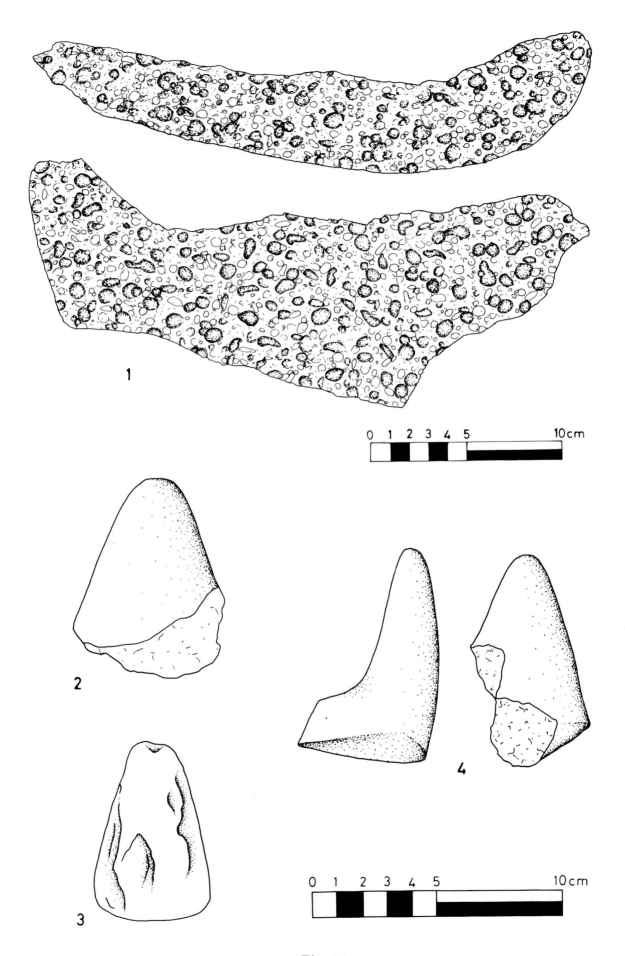

Fig. 71

CATALOGUE OF OBJECTS FROM TAŞKUN MEVKİİ

Fig. 68

1. K11 613.4
   Snake made from a ribbon of copper(?), two perforations at the head. Previously published (Helms 1973: Fig. 10 no. 71/20). L 10.8, W (max.) 1.06.

2. L10c/d 201.5
   Fragment of bone pin, head and partial shaft. Head roughly triangular, the shaft round in section. Roughly worked and polished. Previously published (Helms 1971: Fig. 2 no. 28). H (pres.) 2.4, W (max. pres.) 2.4.

3. K10c 101.1
   Back half of an animal (quadruped) figurine in reddish brown clay. End of both legs and tail are broken off. Previously published (Helms 1971: Fig. 2 no. 25; Helms 1973: Fig. 10 no. 70/7). H (pres.) 3.1, W (pres.) 2.9, Th 3.0.

4. K10c 101.12
   Bronze(?) ornament, with two drooping spiral tendrils. In two pieces, broken near the neck. Previously published (Helms 1971: Fig. 2 no. 27; Helms 1973: Fig. 10 no. 70/4). L 3.7, W (max. pres.) 3.2.

5. K11 613.5
   Copper pin with a conical head. Decorated with eight horizontal incisions below the head. Previously published (Helms 1973: Fig. 10 no. 71/19). L (pres.) 6.3, W (max.) 0.8.

6. K10 103.7
   Worked bone point. Two horizontal grooves around the head and a series of incisions along the shank. Previously published (Helms 1973: Fig. 10 no. 71/25). L 3.3, W (max.) 0.6.

7. J11 502.2
   Bone point with two incisions on the broad end. L 5.7, W (max.) 0.4.

8. Locus not known
   Copper(?) pin with pierced head and incised upper shank immediately below the head. Previously published (Helms 1973: Fig. 10 no. 71/17). L 9.9, W (max.) 0.7.

9. K11a/c 601.8
   Bronze(?) pin with head marked off by a deep incised line. Four incised lines on head converge at the tip, incised chevron decoration below the head. L 14.3, W (max.) 0.9. Previously published (Helms 1971: Fig. 2 no. 26; Helms 1973: Fig. 10 no. 70/6).

10. J11 505.10
    Bone point with horizontal groove around the broad end. L 8, W (max.) 0.6.

Fig. 69

1. L10c/d 201.7
   Parallel sided blade in reddish grey chert, perhaps intentionally snapped off at one end. Poor nibbling retouch on both edges, much less on the ventral side. Parallel spines. Bulb of percussion present. L (max.) 10.4, W (max.) 3.8, Th (max.) 1.9.

2. K10c 101.14
   Parallel sided blade of poor quality flint, with many chert inclusions. Unifacially worked on dorsal side, some intrusive retouch. Bulb of percussion obscured. Some slight sheen on the spine. L (max.) 13.1, W (max.) 3.2, Th (max.) 1.6.

3. L10c/d 201.11
   Curved, unifacially worked, parallel sided blade of good honey flint with a few chert inclusions. Definite sickle-sheen on one blade edge. Bulb of percussion present. L (max.) 13.1, W (max.) 2.9, Th (max.) 1.6.

4. K11a/c 601.9
   Fragment of polished bone point, tip broken. L (pres.) 8.9, W (max. pres.) 1.5.

5. J11 502.3
   Worked bone point. L (pres.) 7.5, W (max. pres.) 0.9.

6. Locus not specified
   Cylinder seal in grey clay incised with a framed zig-zag pattern, short strokes used as filling. D 2.1, H 2.3. Previously published (Helms 1973: Fig. 10 no. 71/27).

7. K11 610.8
   Square stamp seal in brownish black stone with a pierced boss. Slightly curved face is incised with a geometric pattern comprising a row of oblique lines and net design, and two rows of squares filled with crosses. W (max.) 1.8, L (max.) 1.7, H 0.8. Previously published (Helms 1973: Fig. 10 no. 71/16).

8. L10c/d 201.5
   Cylinder seal in grey clay, vertically perforated. Scene comprises three animals (scorpions?) represented in paratactic style. D 2.6, H 2.9. Previously published (Helms 1971: Fig. 2 no. 23; Helms 1973: Fig. 10 no. 70/3).

Fig. 70

1. K11a/c 600.1
   Spindle whorl in black burnished clay. Conical, flat-based and centrally perforated. Previously published (Helms 1971: Fig. 2 no. 24). D (max.) 3.9, Th 1.95.

2. K11 611.2
   Spindle whorl in bone. Conical, flat-based and centrally perforated. D (max.) 2.9, Th 1.6.

3. J11 503.17
   Spindle whorl in bone. Conical, irregularly shaped, flat-based and centrally perforated. D (max.) 4.6, Th 2.0.

4. K11a/c 601.12
   HM, circular perforated sherd, possibly a loomweight, tempered with medium grit. Black throughout, burnished exterior, smoothed interior. D (max. pres.) 6.3, Th (max.) 0.75.

5. L10c/d 201.2
   HM, fragment of circular perforated sherd, possibly a loomweight. Coarse fabric tempered with coarse grit, grey burnished exterior, pale brown burnished interior. Perforation countersunk on both sides. D (max. pres.) 7.4, Th (max.) 1.2.

6. K10c 101.9
   HM, circular perforated sherd, possibly loomweight. Coarse fabric tempered with coarse grit, black burnished exterior, brown plain interior. Perforation countersunk on interior side. D (max. pres.) 8.7, Th (max.) 1.7.

7. K11 610.4
   HM, circular perforated sherd, possibly loomweight, tempered with medium grit and a little chaff. Black throughout, burnished exterior, plain interior. D (max. pres.) 5.4, Th (max.) 0.45.

8. J11 501.4
   HM, part of a circular perforated sherd, possibly loomweight, tempered with medium white grit and a little chaff. Black burnished exterior, pale greyish brown smoothed interior. W (max. pres.) 5.4, Th (max.) 1.2.

9. K10c 120.2
   HM, circular perforated sherd, possibly loomweight, tempered with medium grit. Black burnished exterior, pale greyish brown smoothed interior. D (max. pres.) 4.2, Th (max.) 0.75.

10. K11 610.2
    HM, half of a circular perforated sherd, possibly loomweight, tempered with medium white grit and chaff. Black burnished exterior, pale greyish brown plain interior. D (max.) 5.4, Th (max.) 0.9.

Fig. 71

1. K10c 101.9
   Fragment of a saddle-shaped stone mortar in grey, pitted basalt. L (max.) 22.7, W (max.) 7.8, Th (max.) 3.8.

2. J11 501.22
   Cone, possibly the horn of a hearth, in plain mottled beige and black fabric tempered with coarse white grit and some chaff, dark grey core. L 8.2, W (max.) 6.1.

3. K11 620.8
   Edge ground, greenish black stone axe. L 7.2, W (max.) 4.6.

4. K11 610.9
   Cone, possibly the horn of a hearth, in friable brown clay tempered with chaff and coarse grit. Brown burnished. L 8.7, W (max. pres.) 5.4.

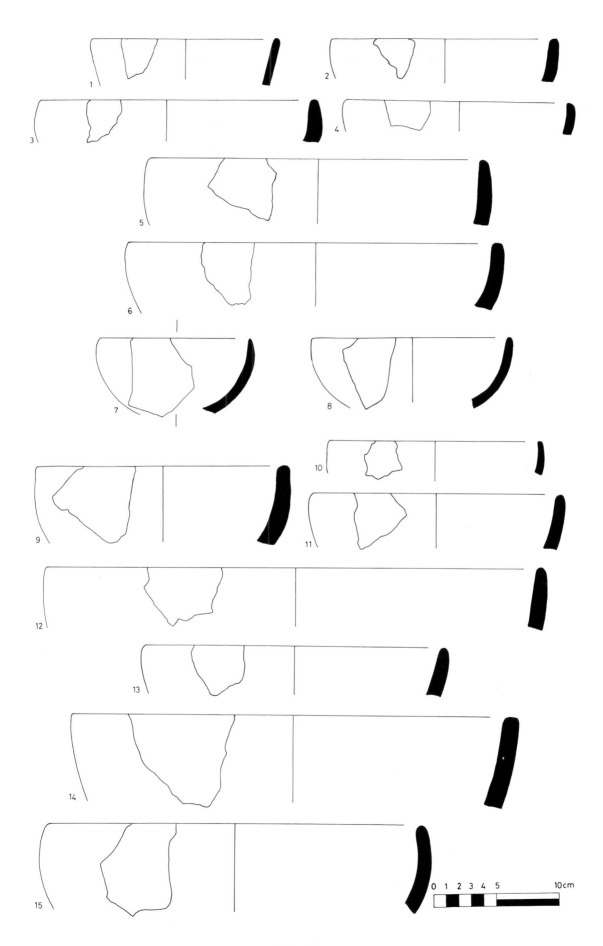

Fig. 72

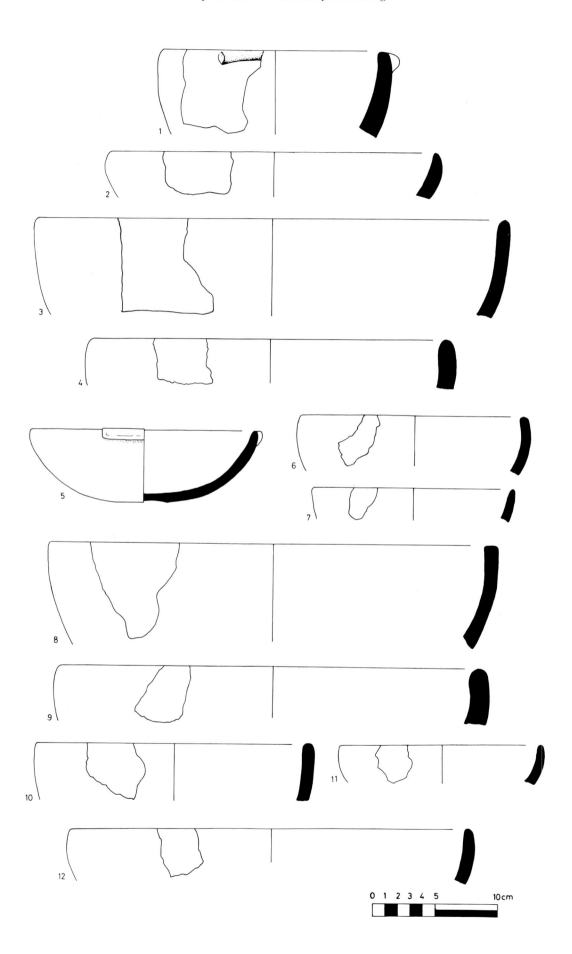

Fig. 73

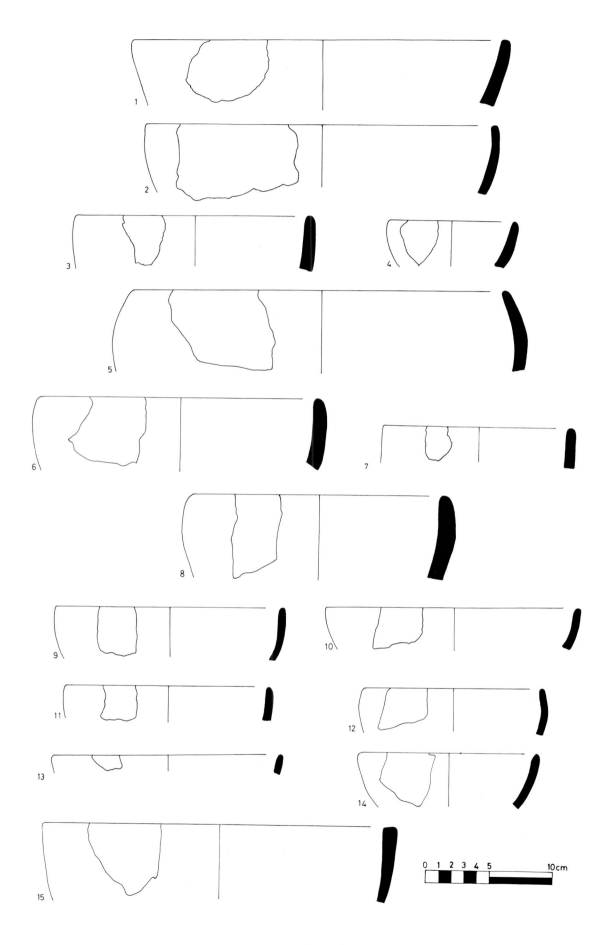

Fig. 74

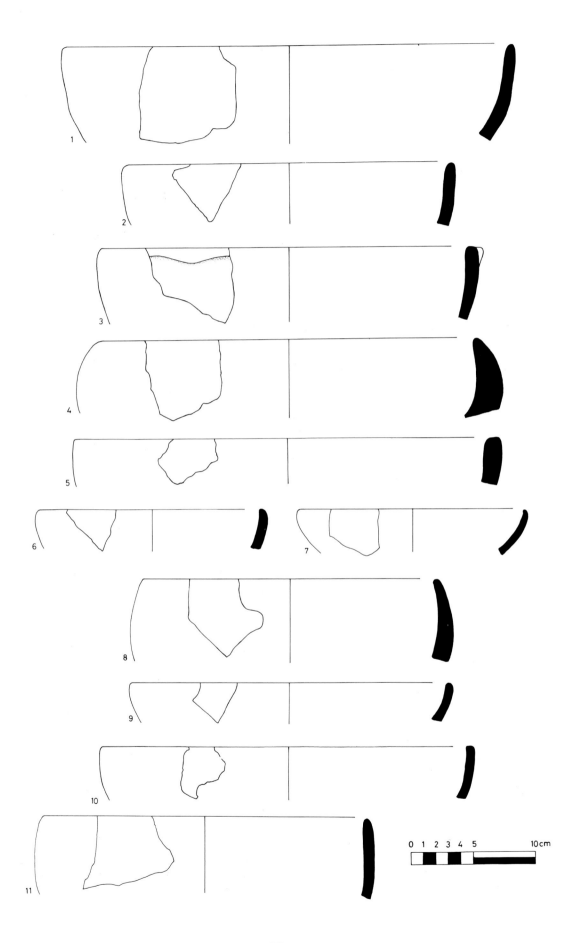

Fig. 75

Fig. 76

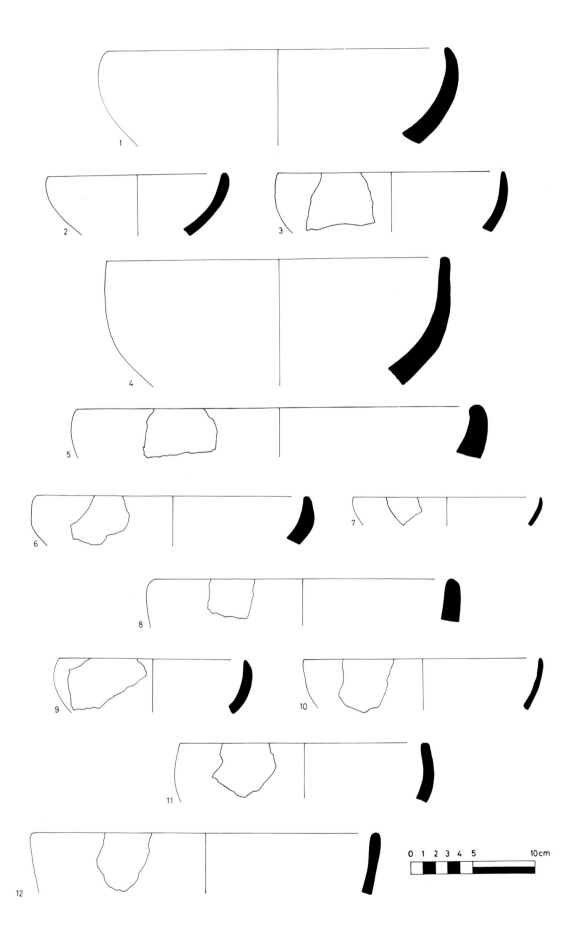

Fig. 77

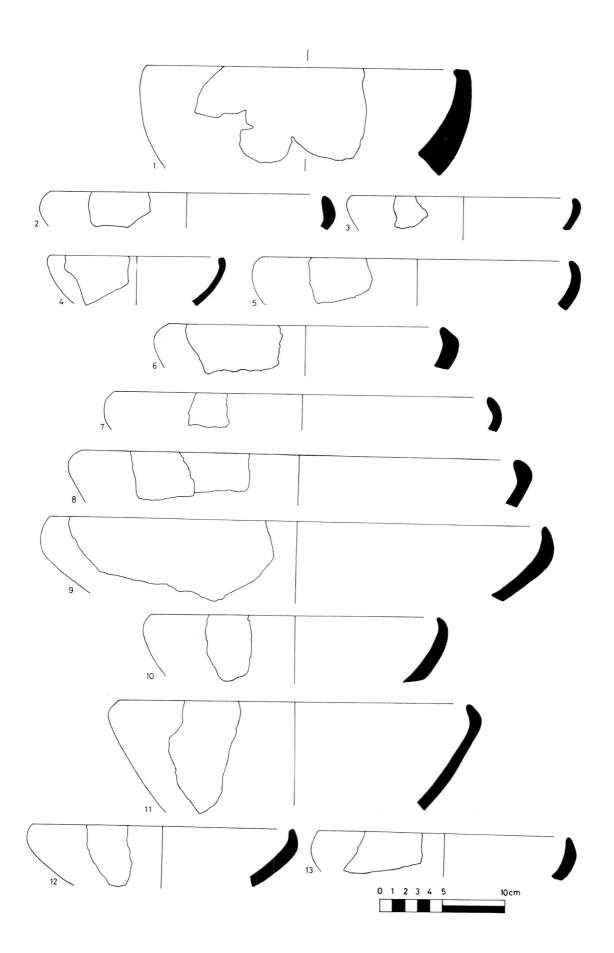

Fig. 78

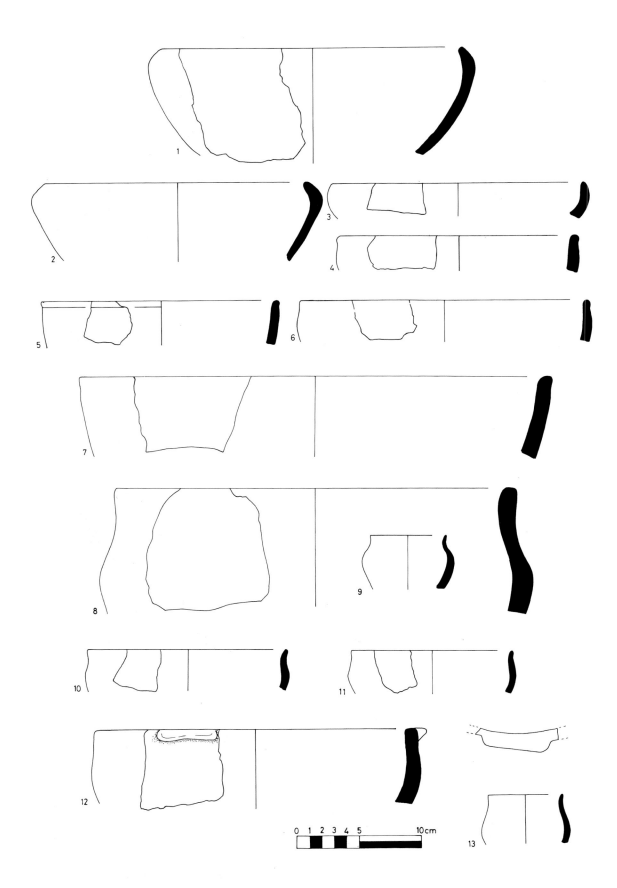

Fig.79

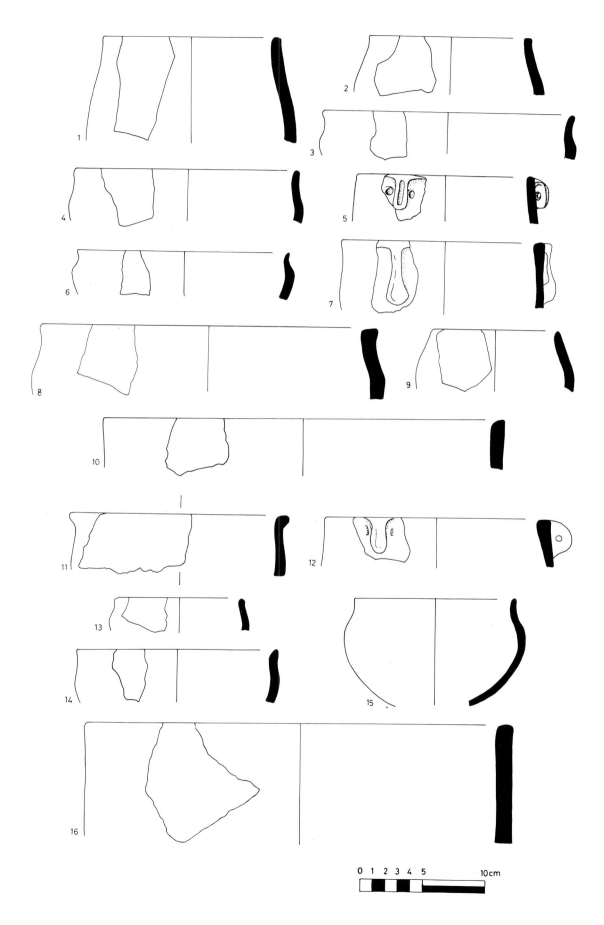

Fig. 80

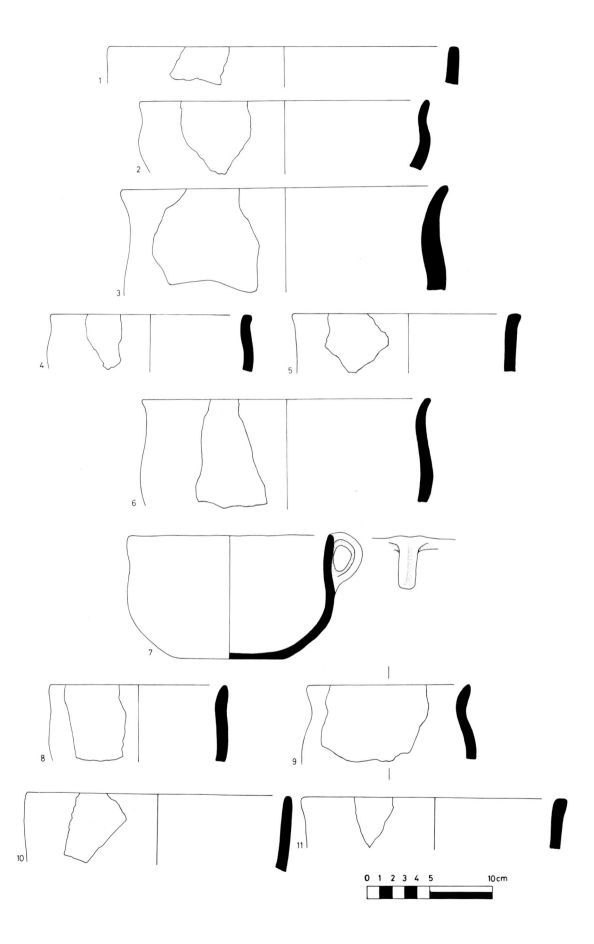

Fig. 81

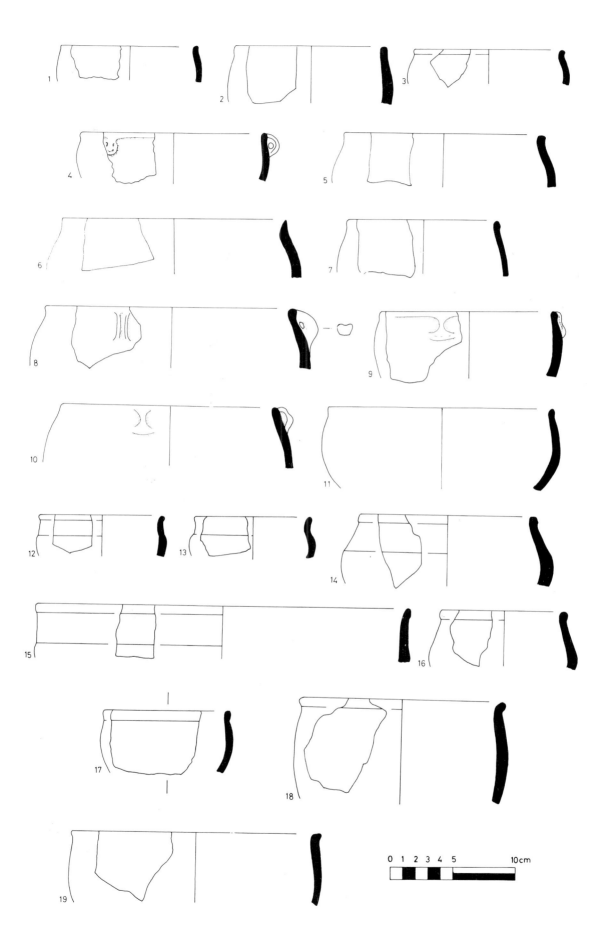

Fig. 82

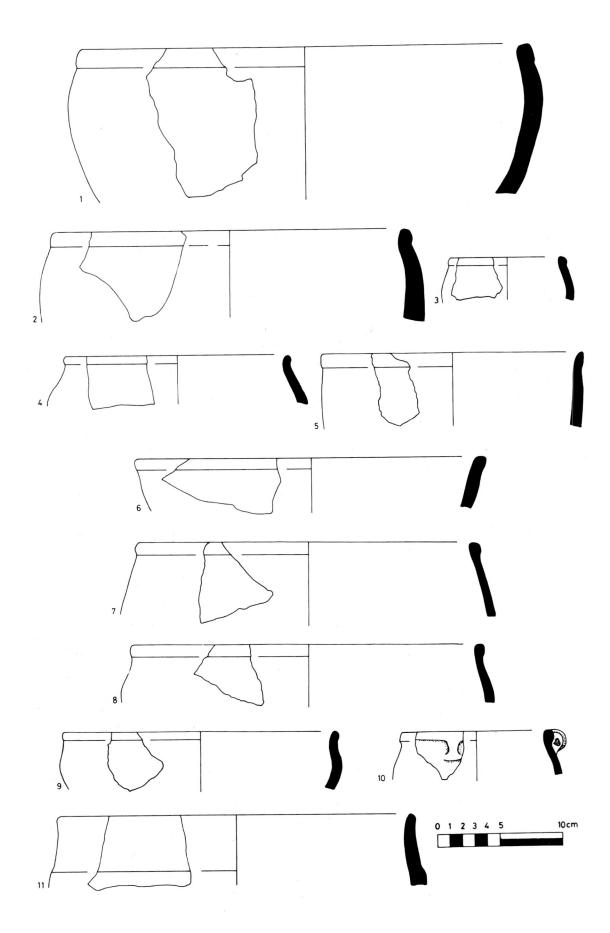

Fig. 83

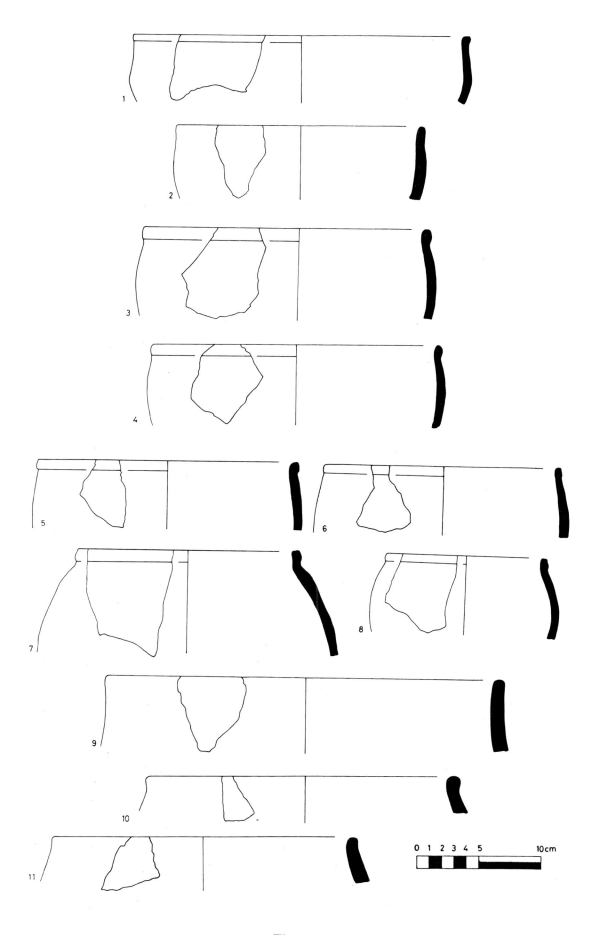

Fig. 84

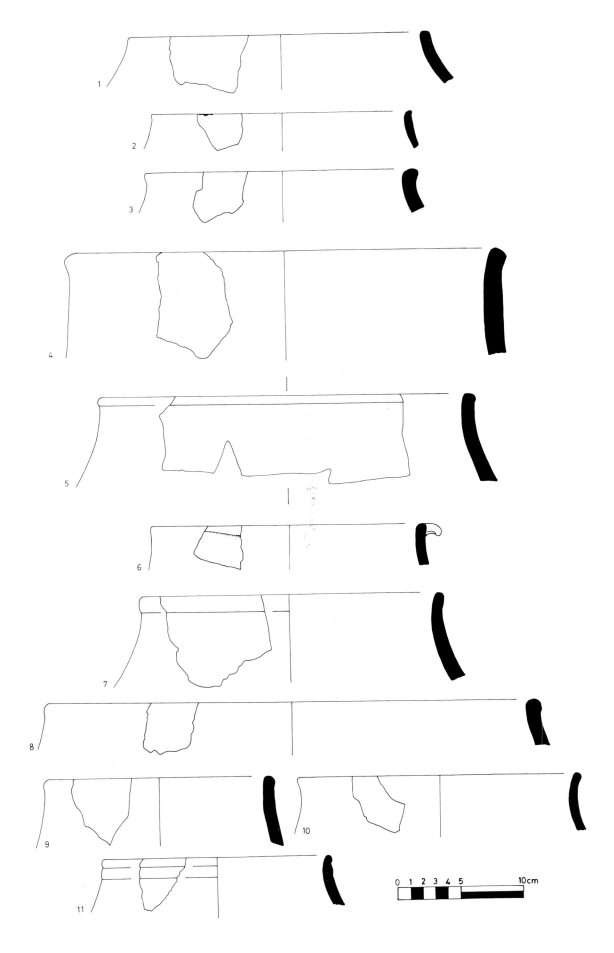

Fig. 85

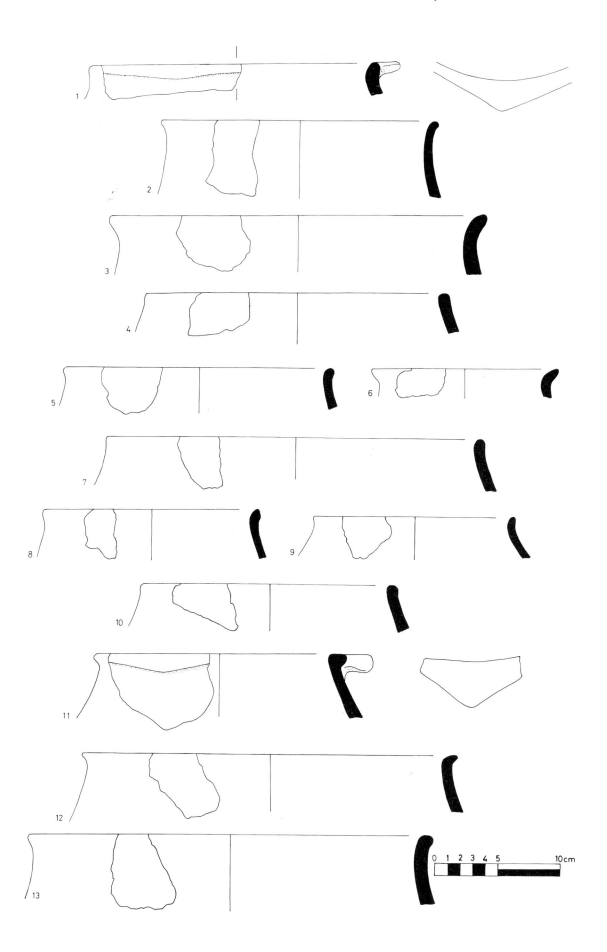

Fig. 86

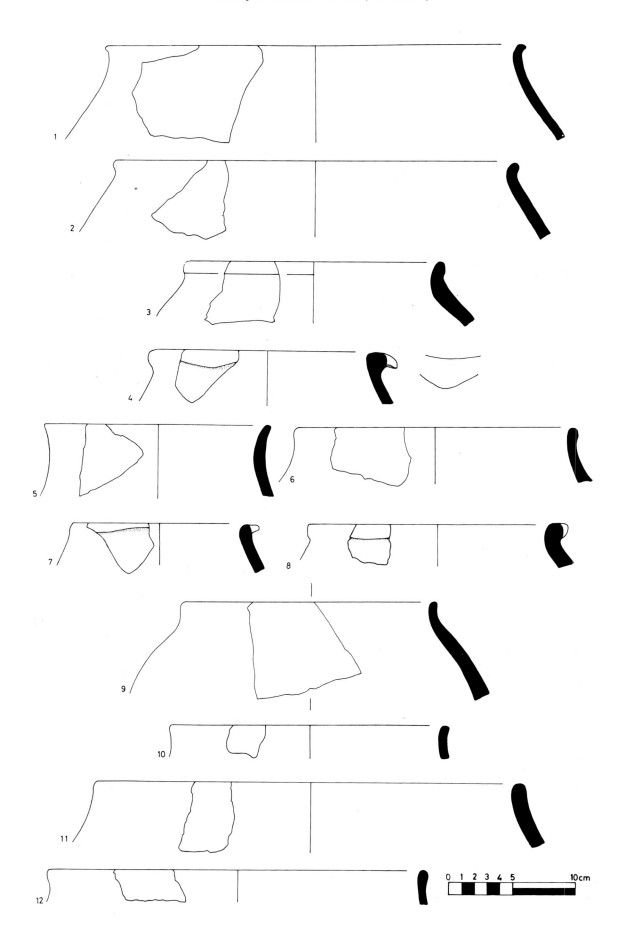

Fig. 87

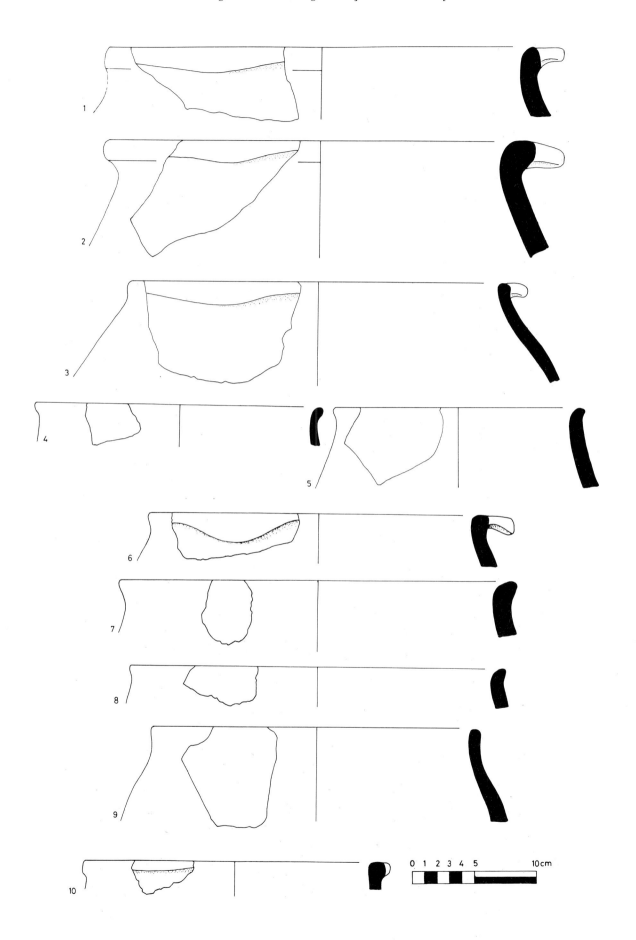

Fig. 88

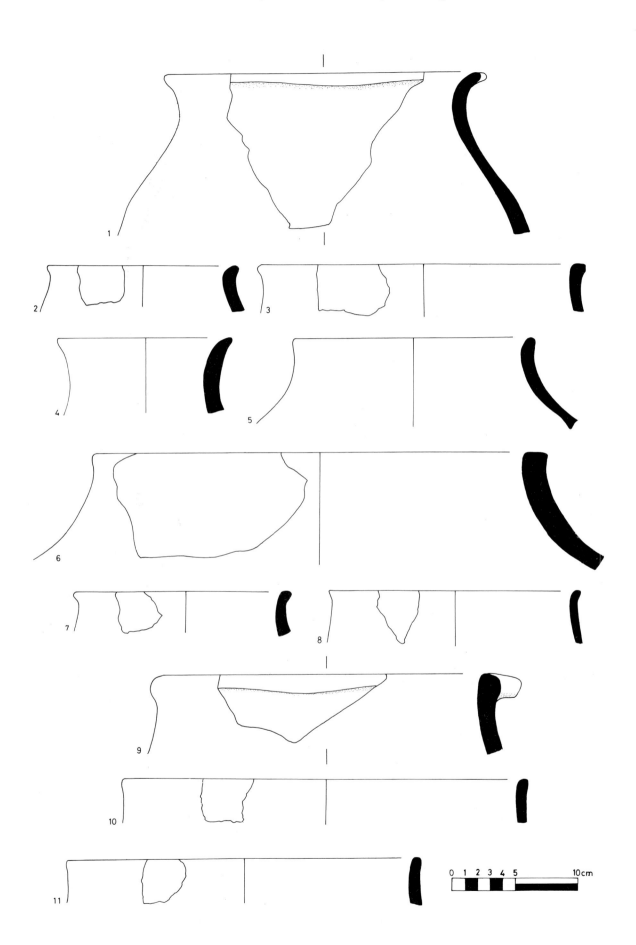

Fig. 89

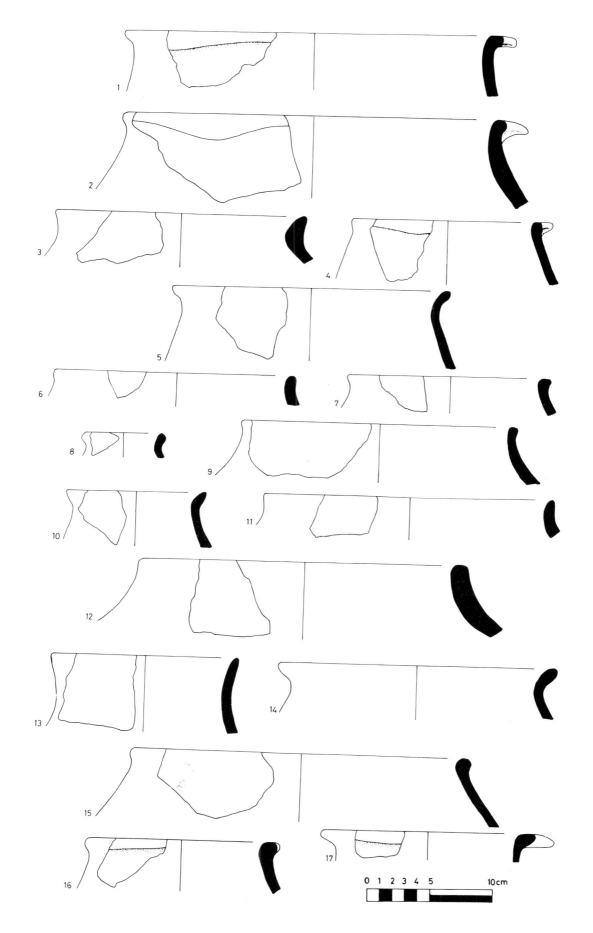

Fig. 90

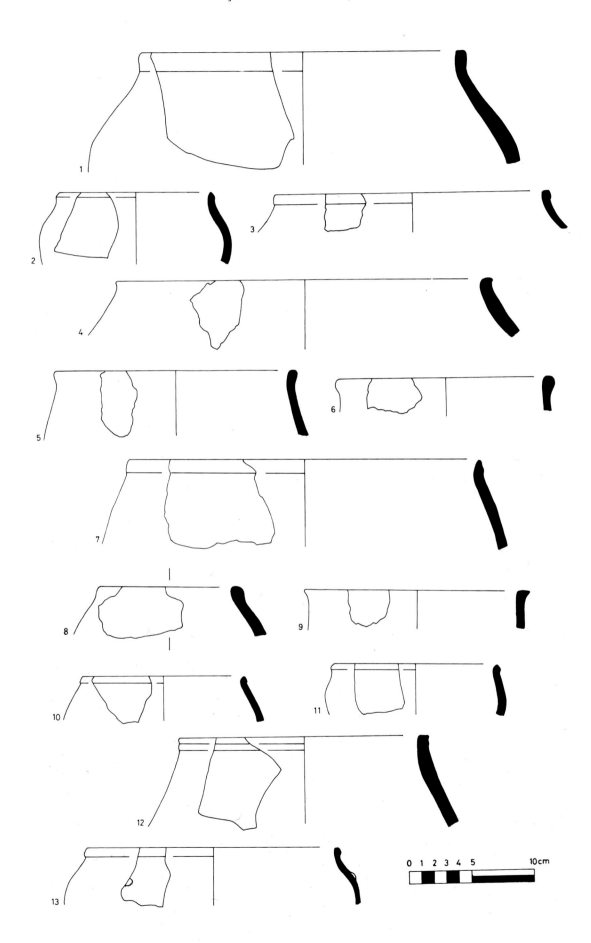

Fig. 91

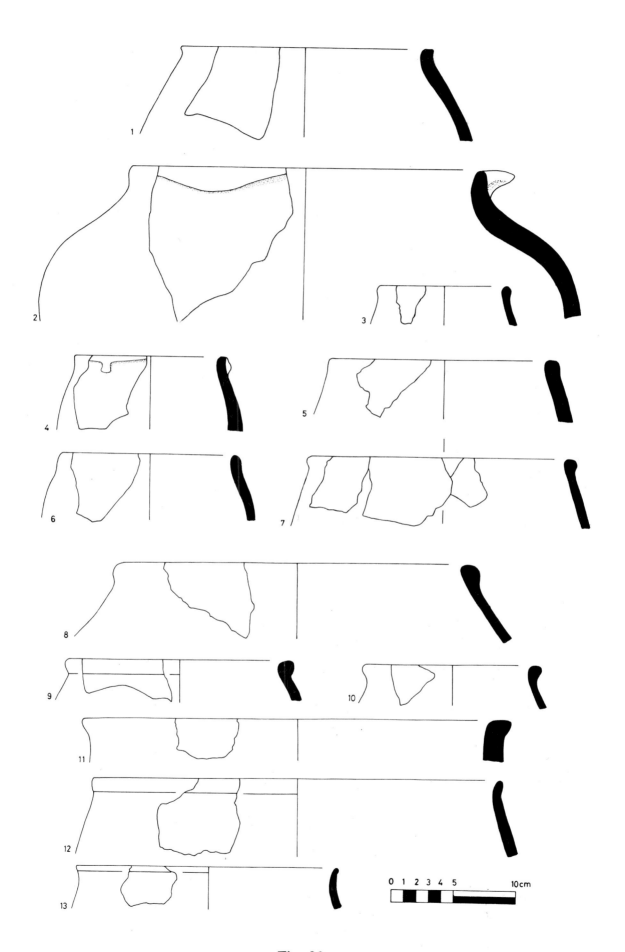

Fig. 92

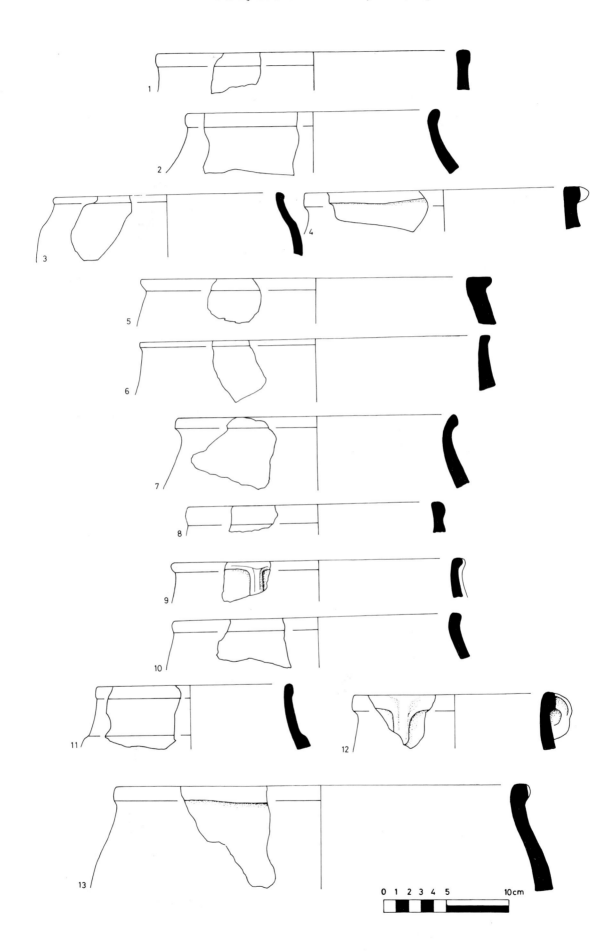

Fig. 93

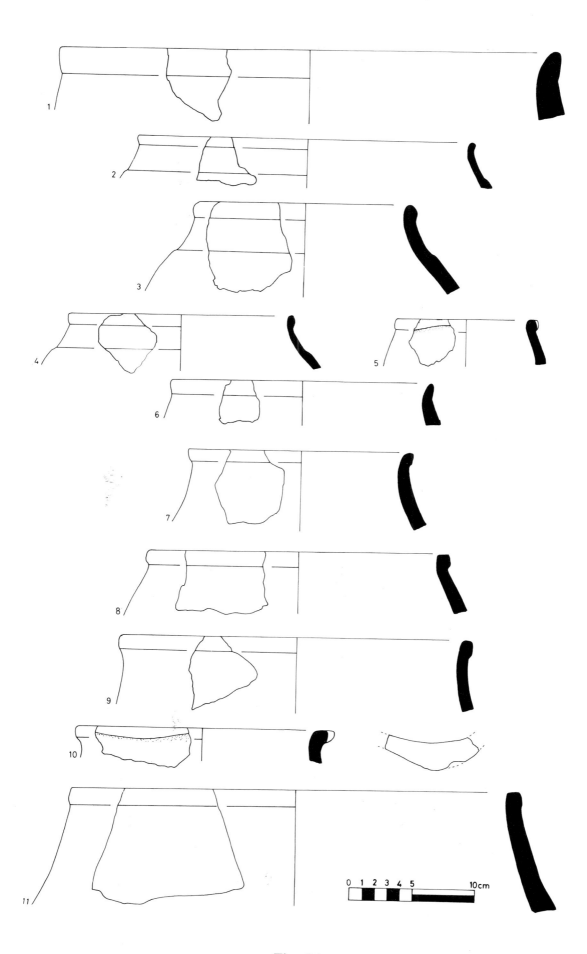

Fig. 94

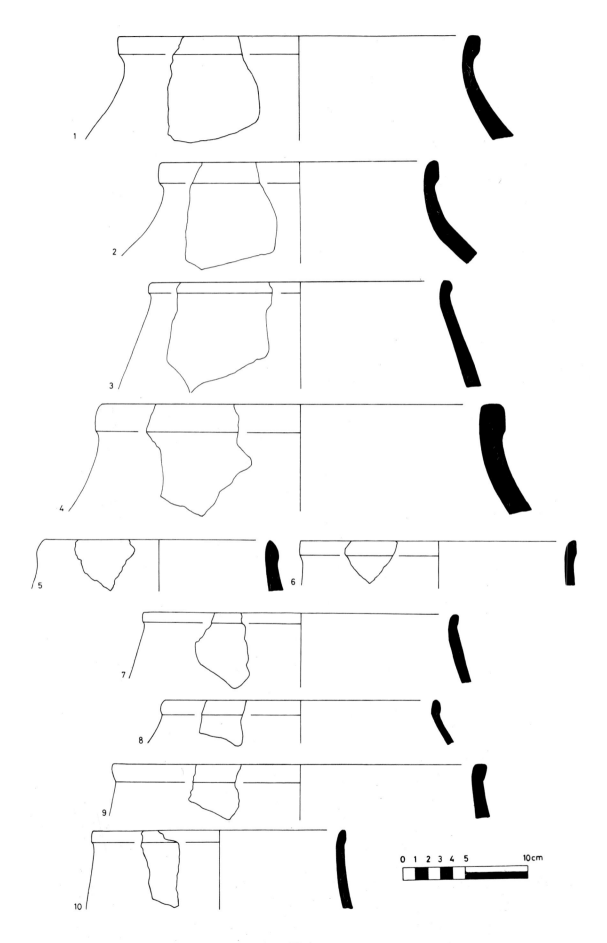

Fig. 95

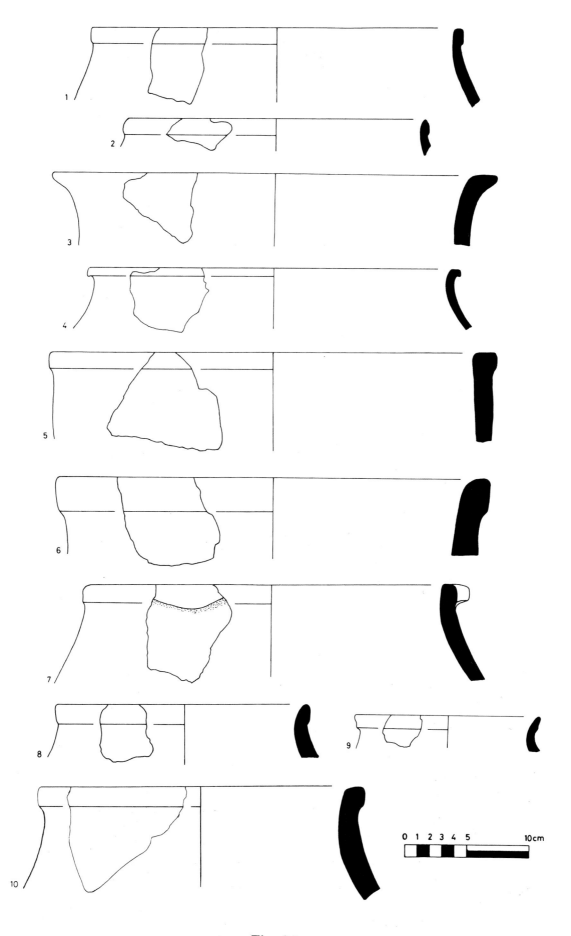

Fig. 96

Fig. 97

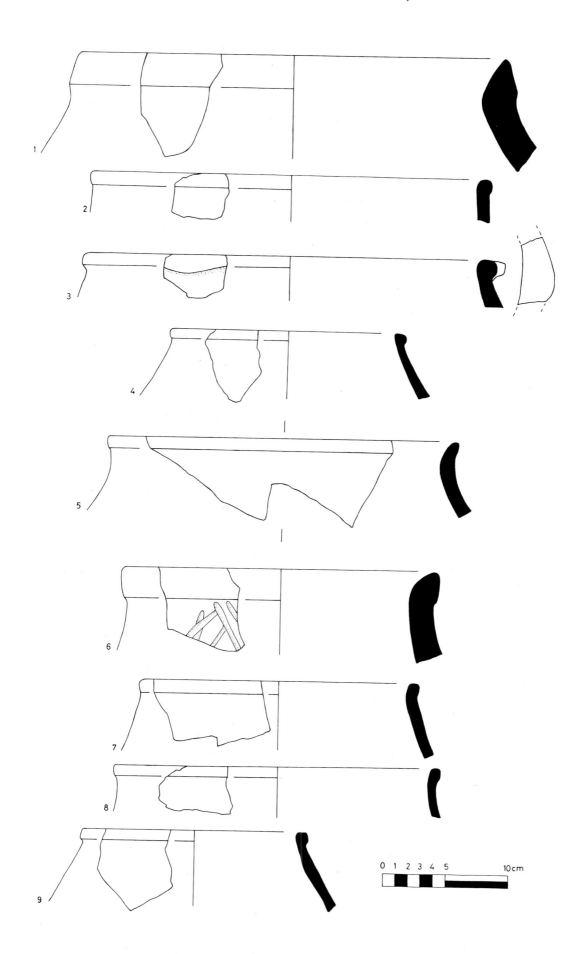

Fig. 98

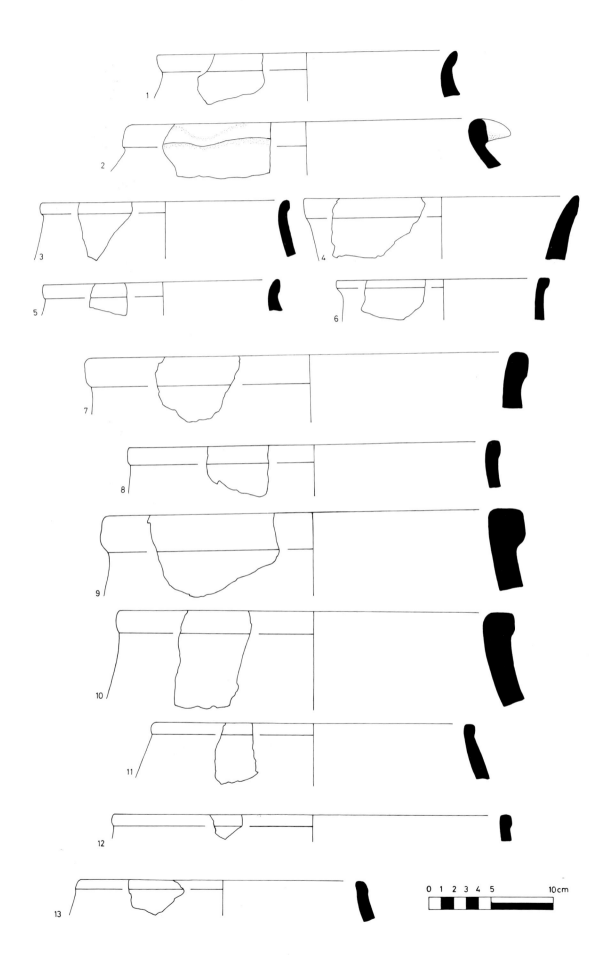

Fig. 99

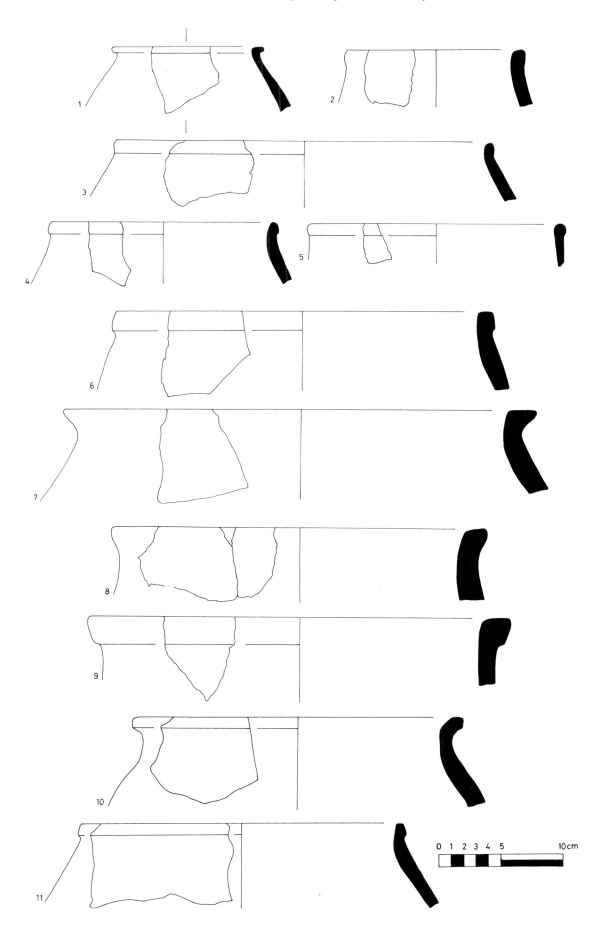

Fig. 100

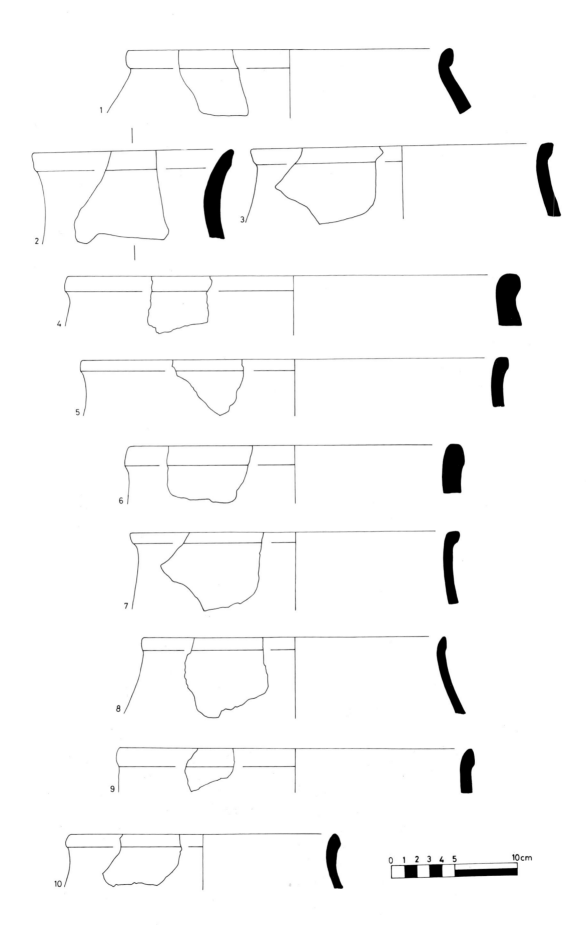

Fig. 101

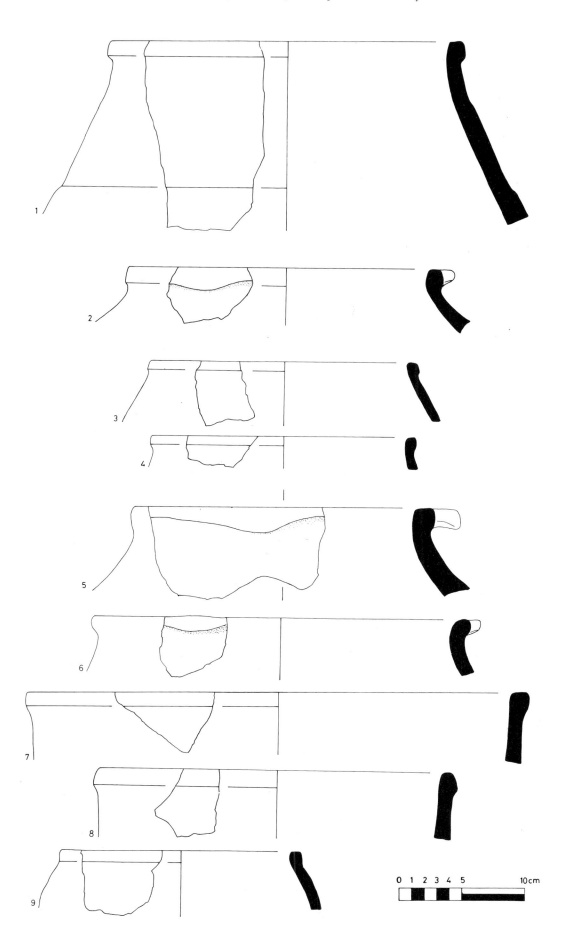

Fig. 102

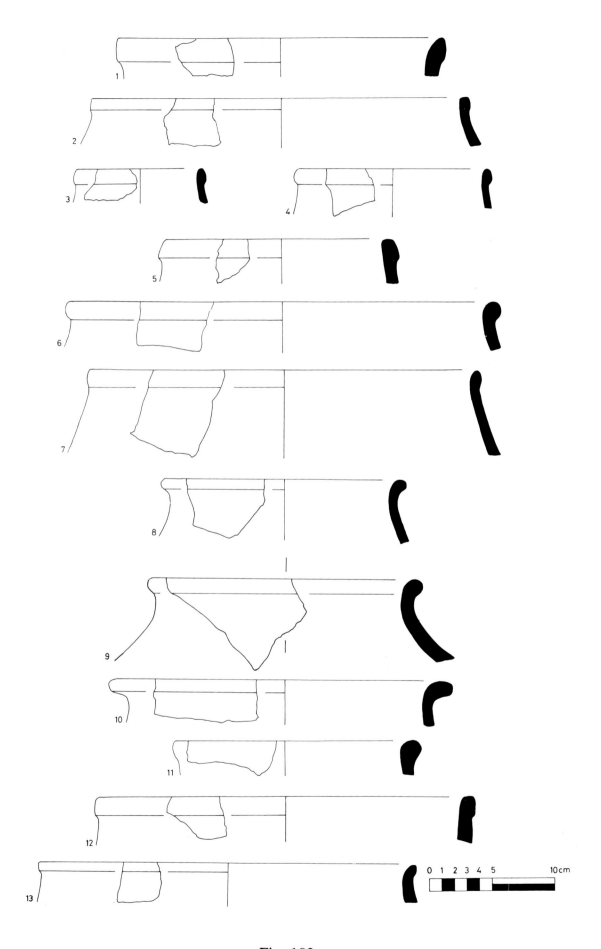

Fig. 103

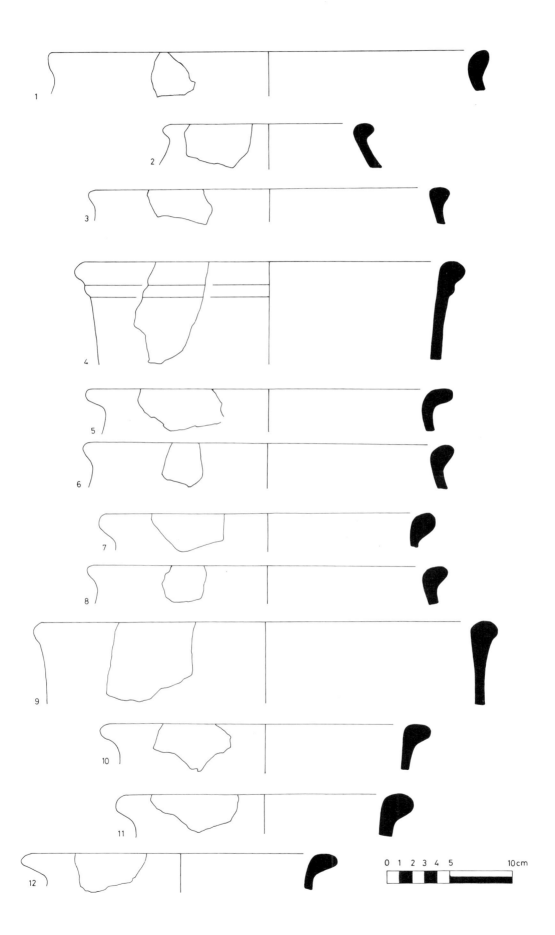

Fig. 104

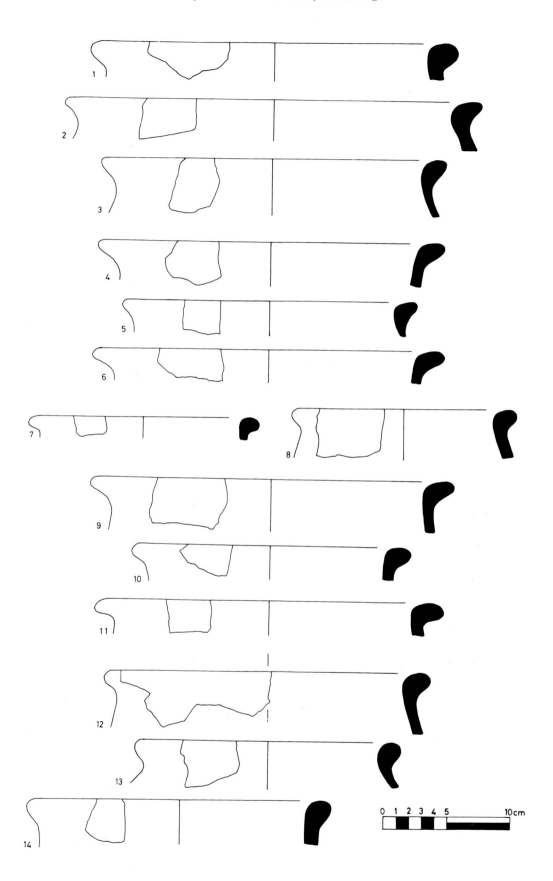

Fig. 105

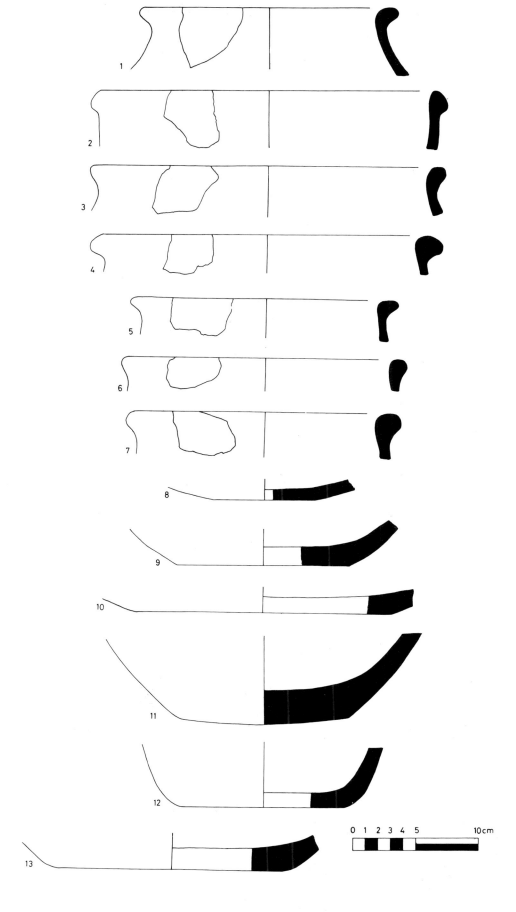

Fig. 106

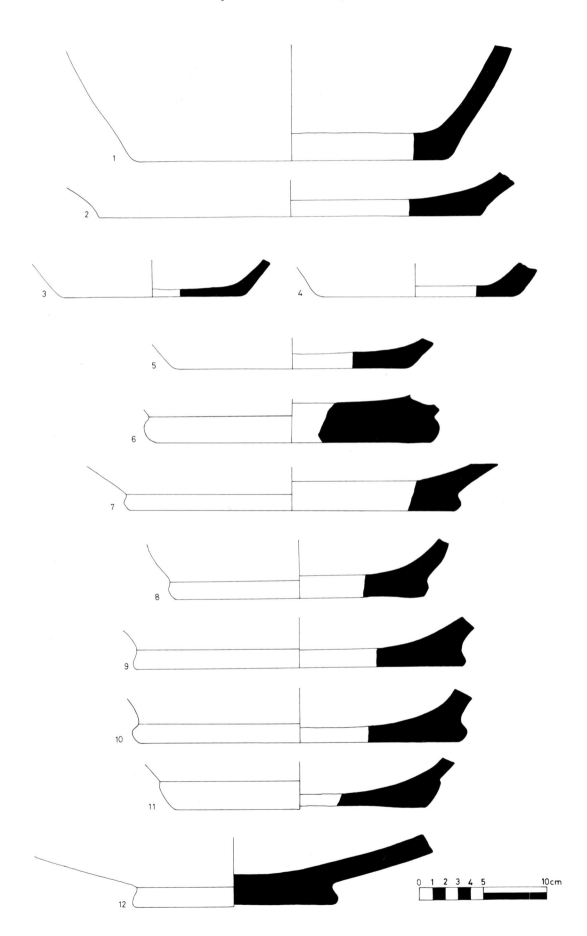

Fig. 107

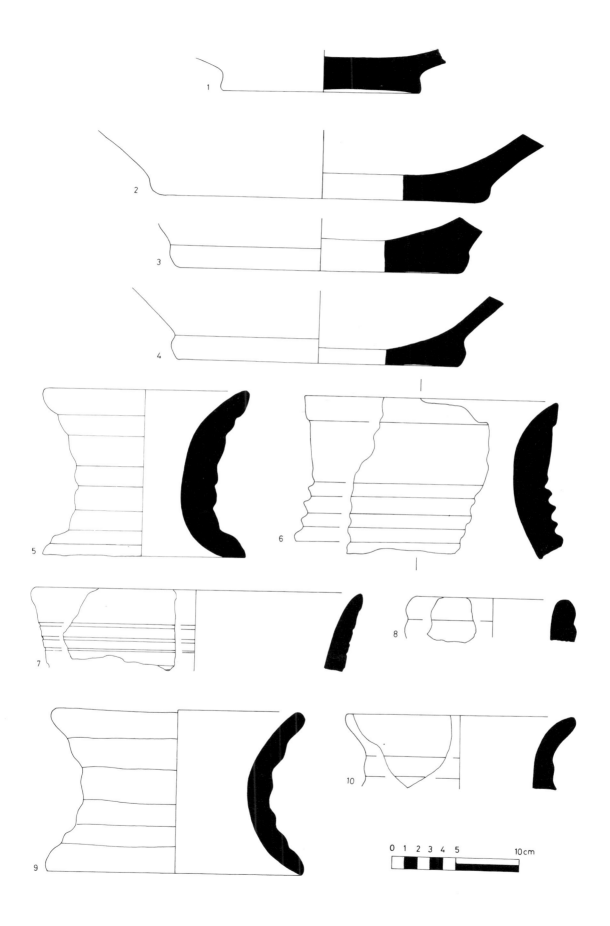

Fig. 108

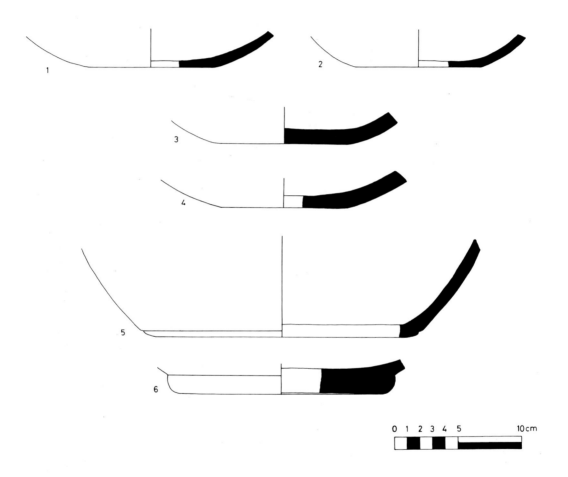

Fig. 109

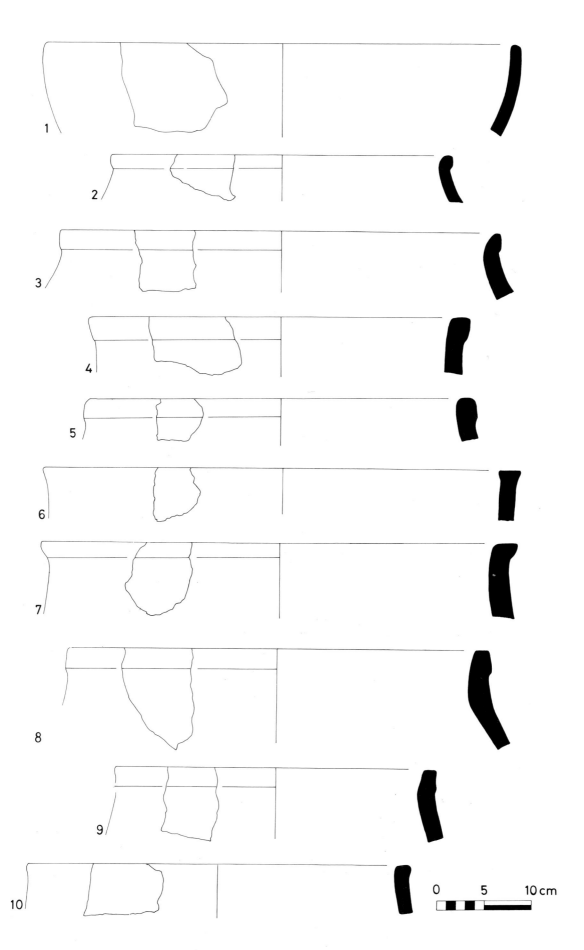

Fig. 110

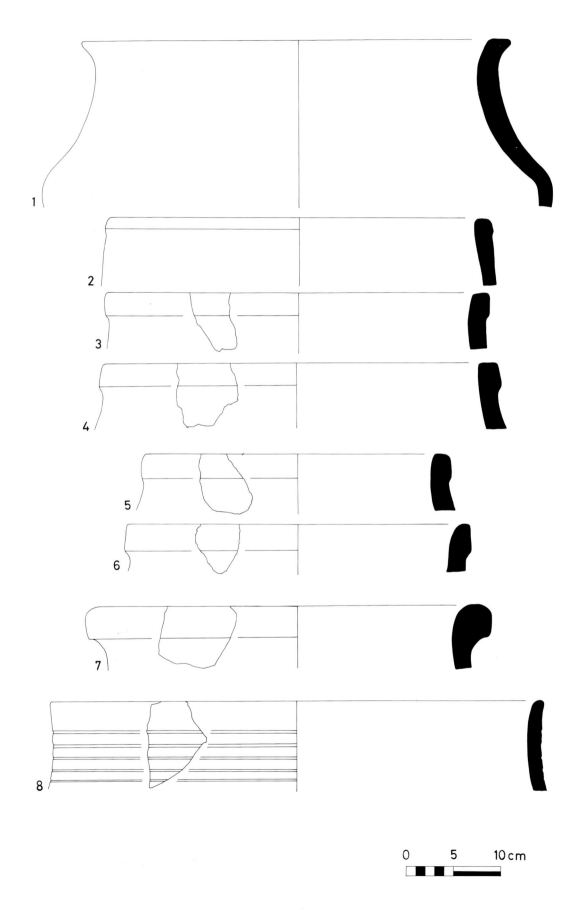

Fig. 111

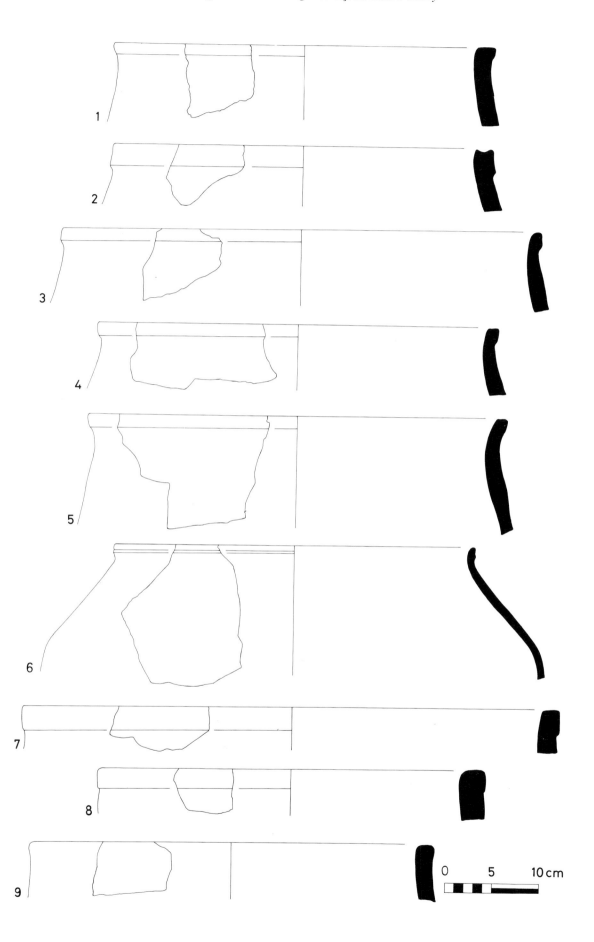

Fig. 112

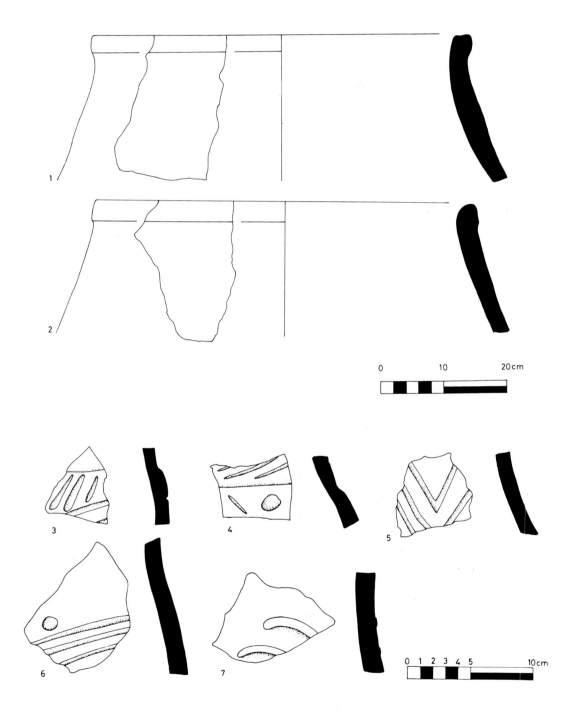

Fig. 113

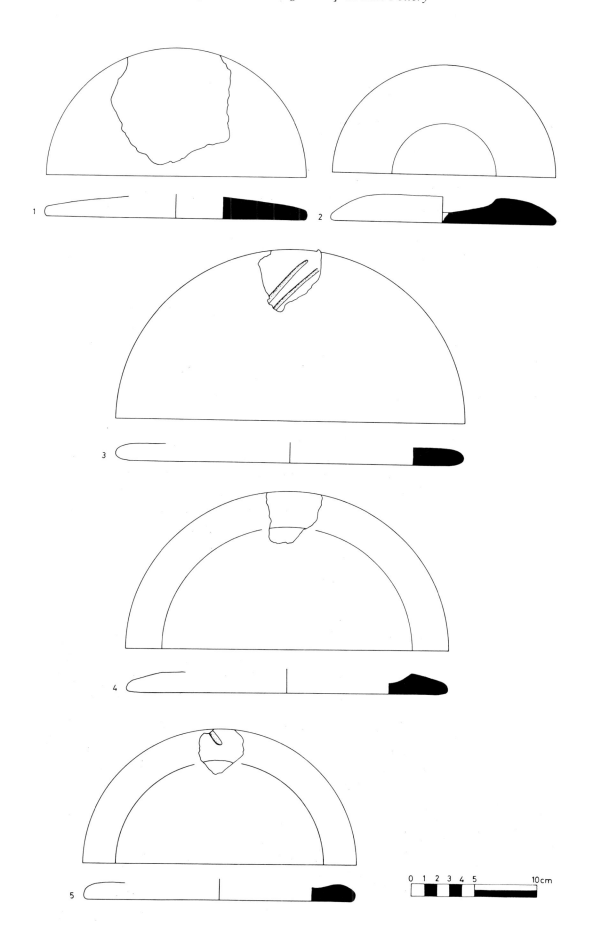

Fig. 114

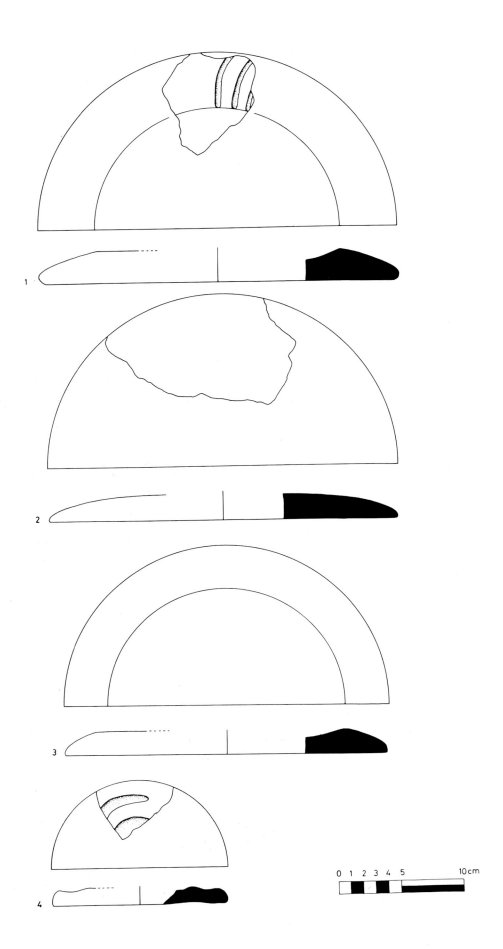

Fig. 115

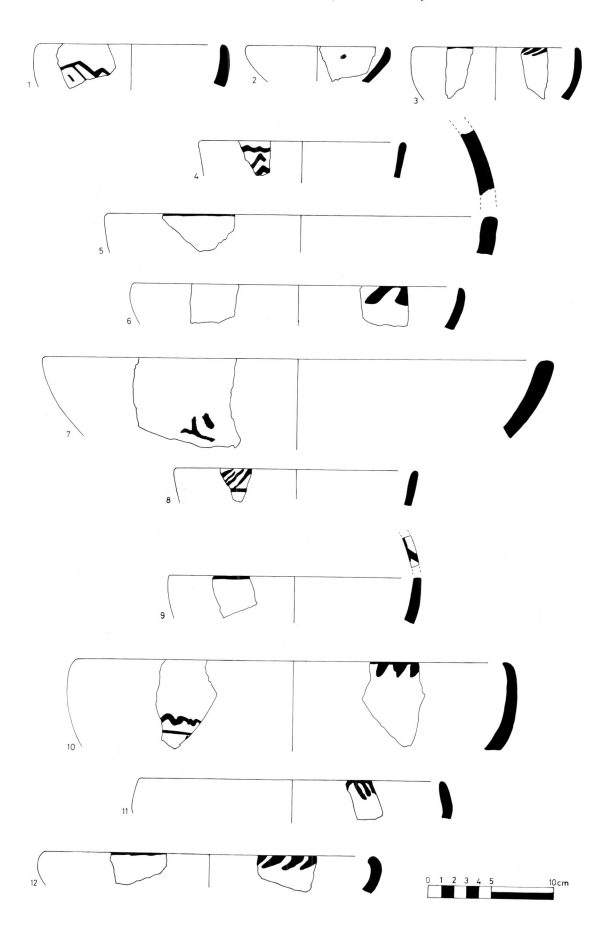

Fig. 116

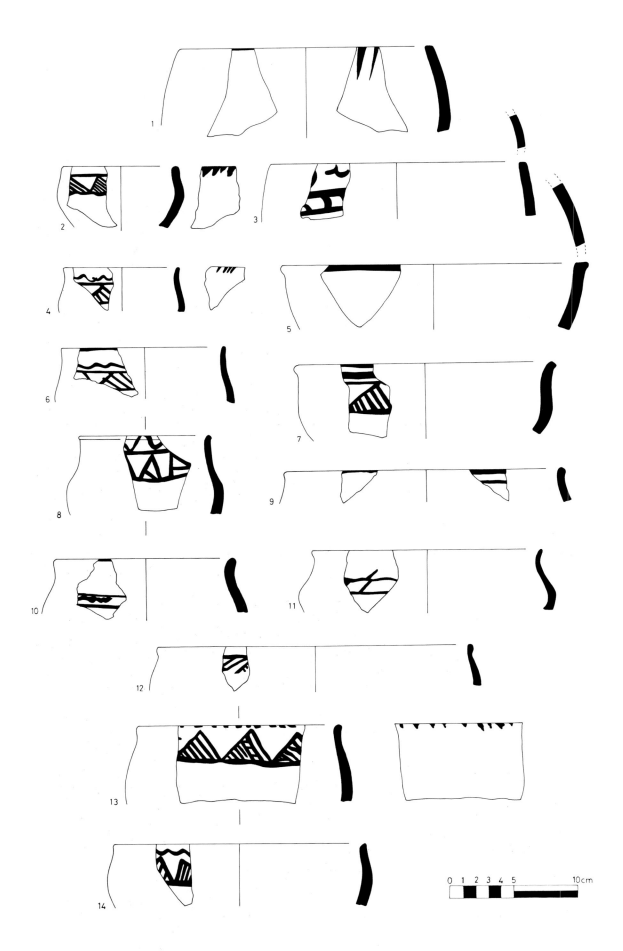

Fig. 117

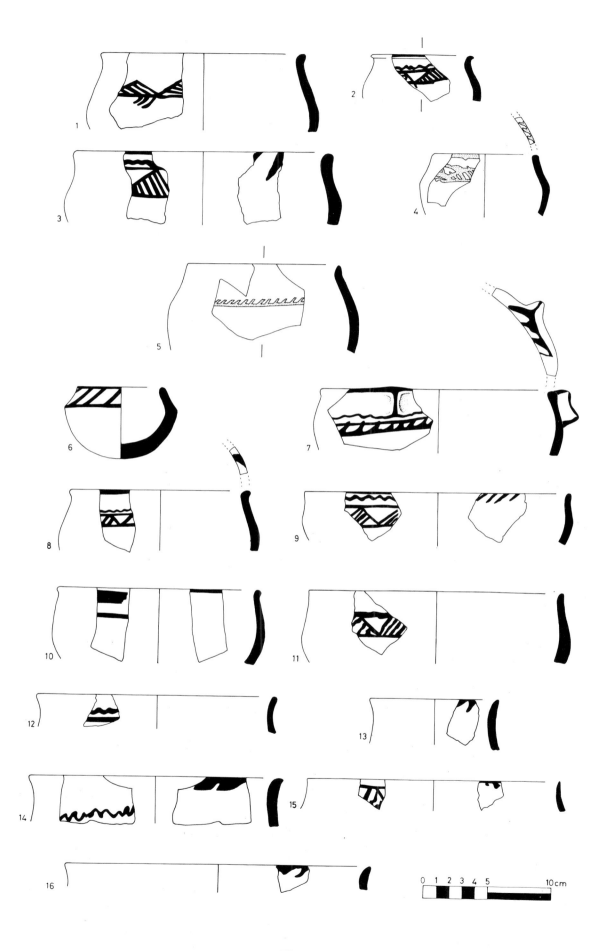

Fig. 118

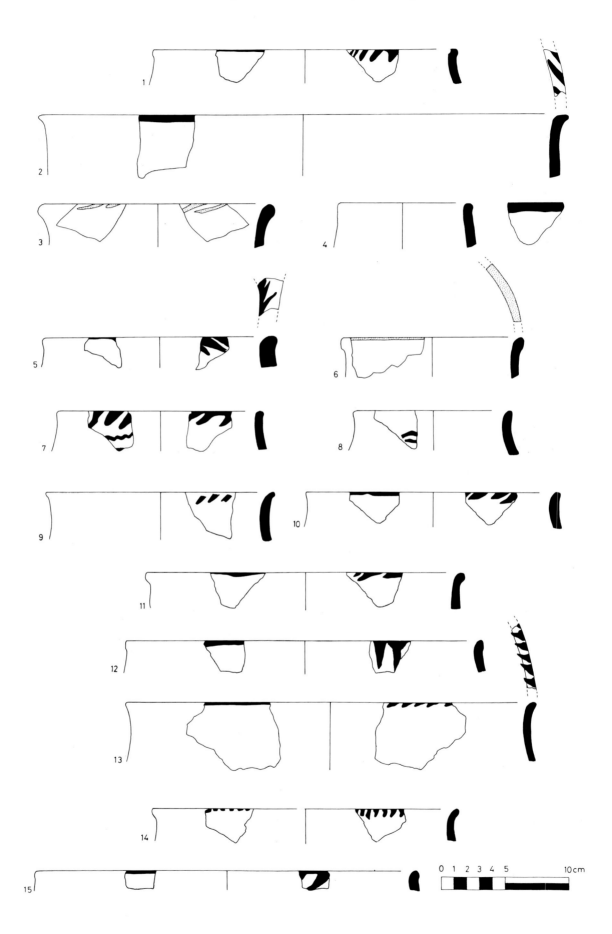

Fig. 119

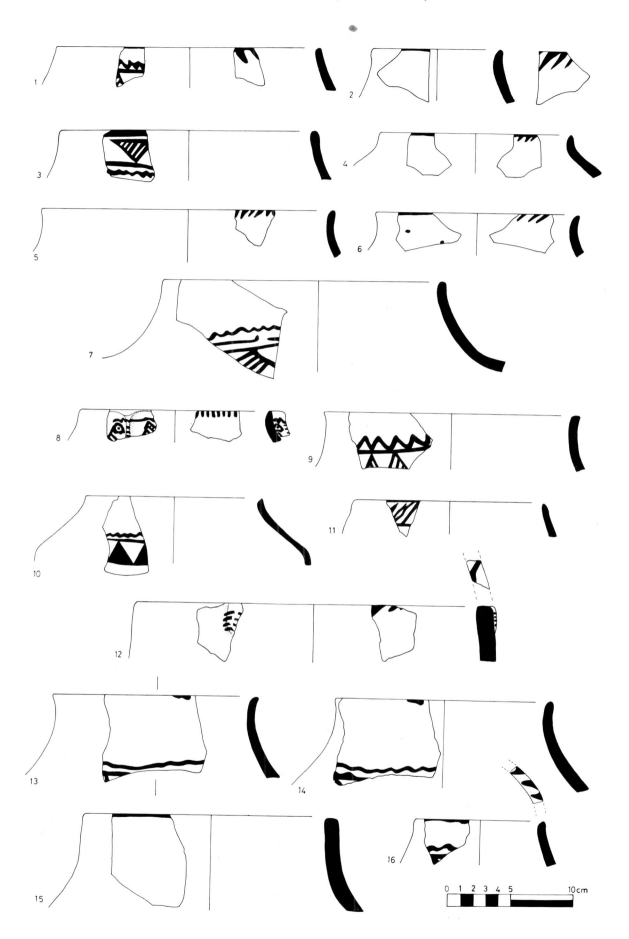

Fig. 120

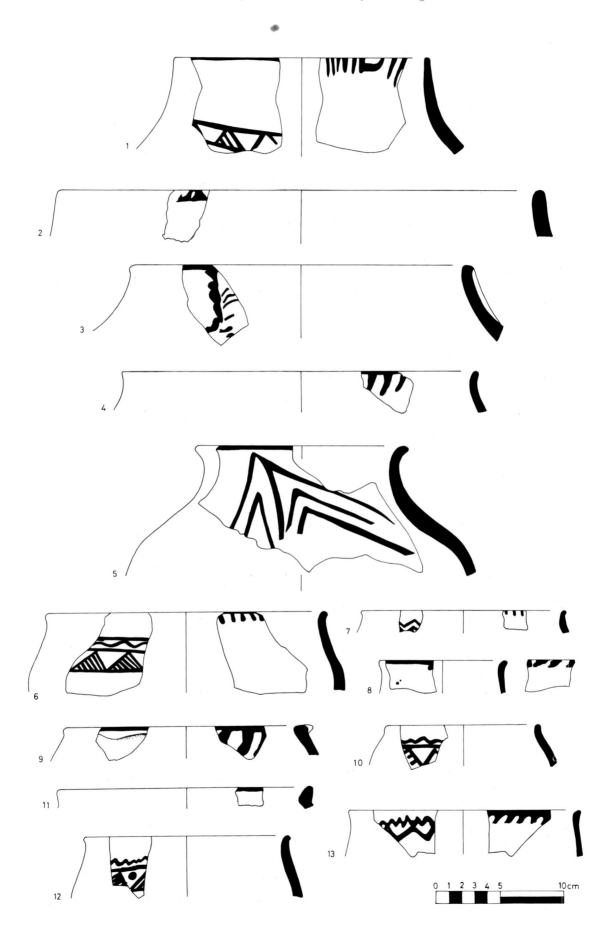

Fig. 121

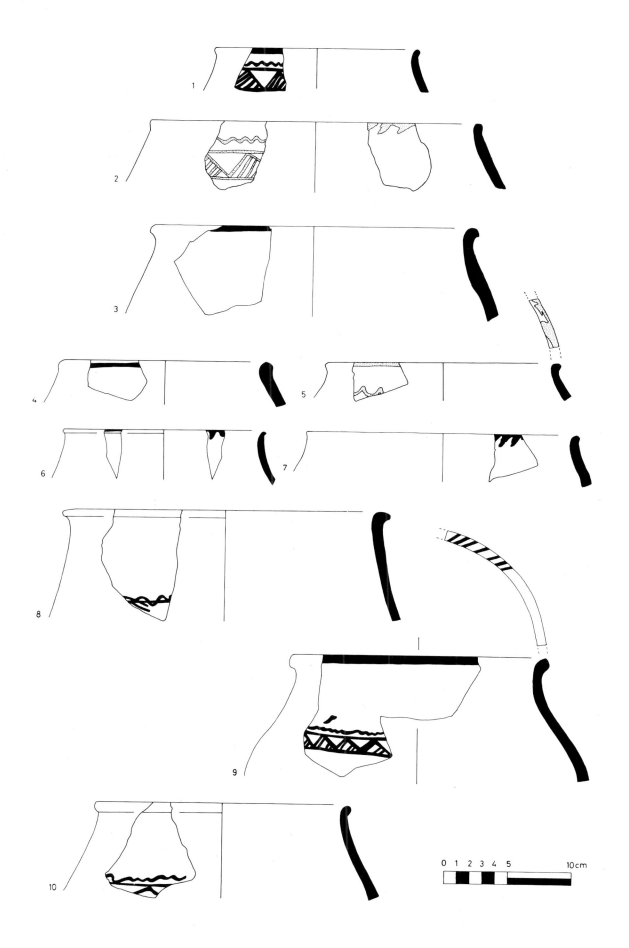

Fig. 122

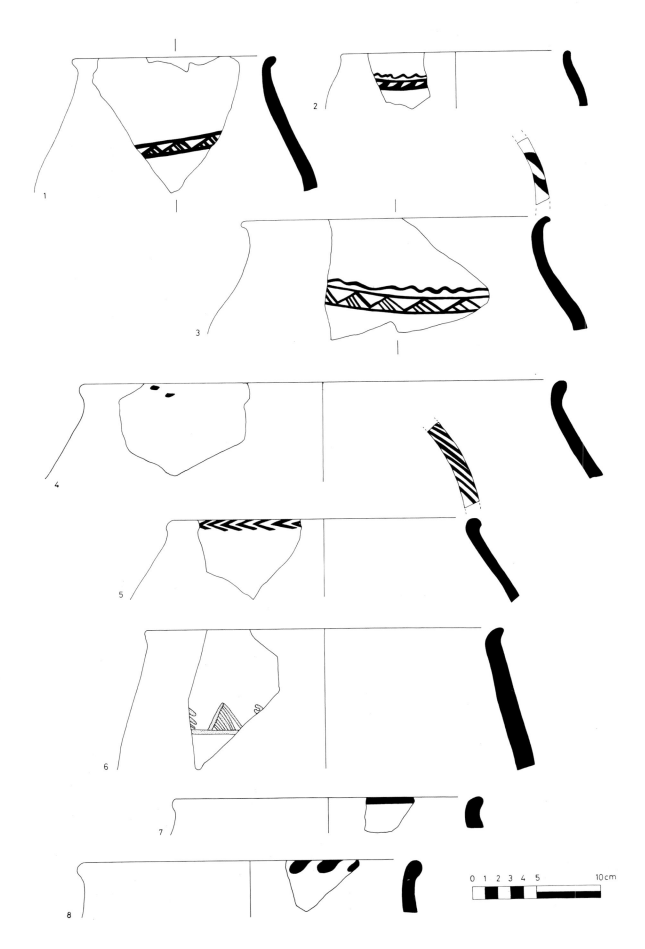

Fig. 123

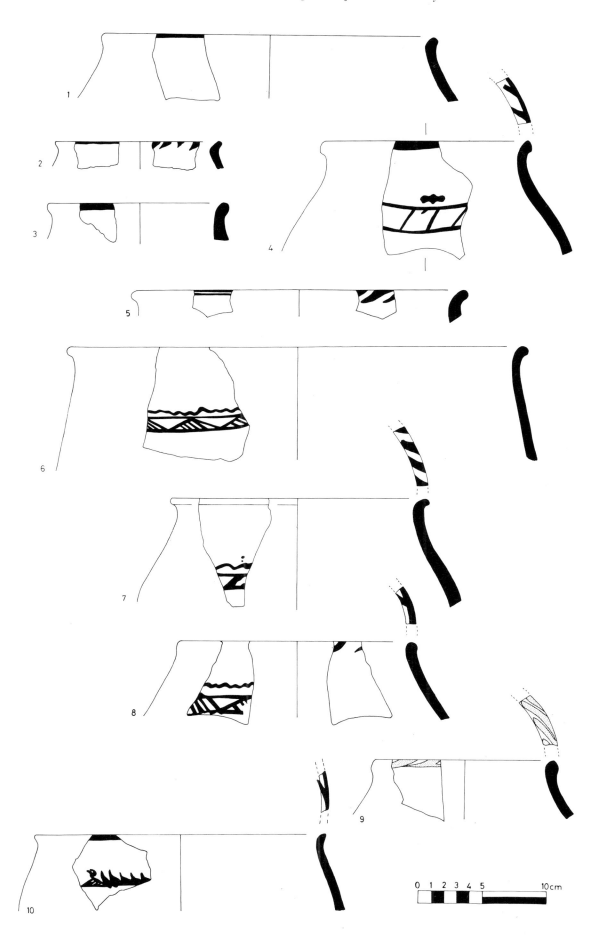

Fig. 124

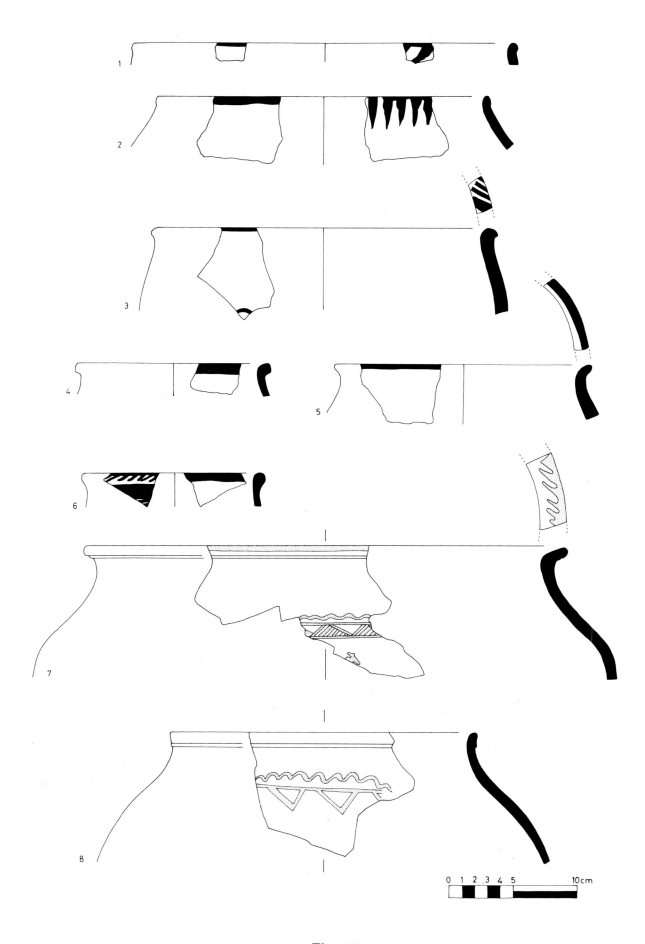

Fig. 125

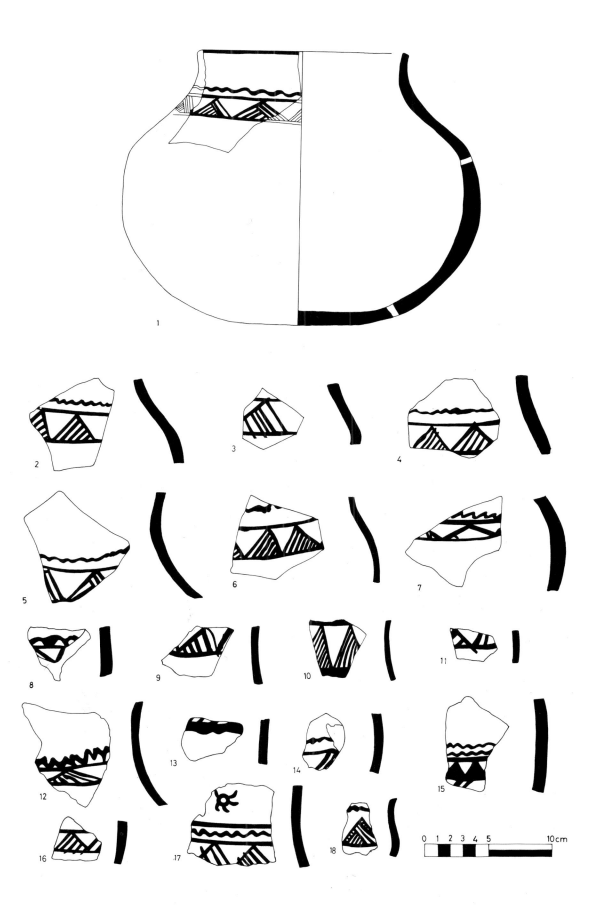

Fig. 126

Fig. 127

Fig. 128

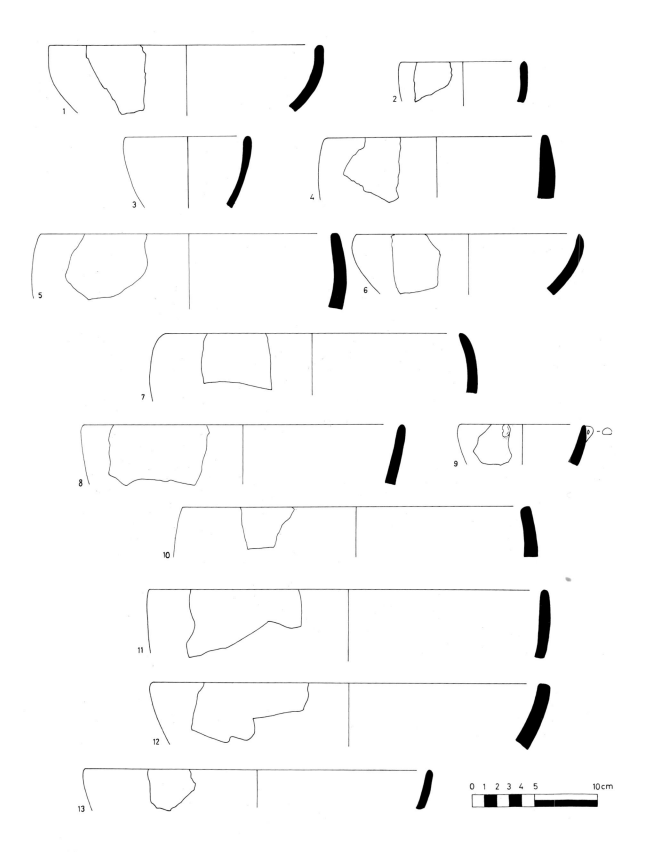

Fig. 129

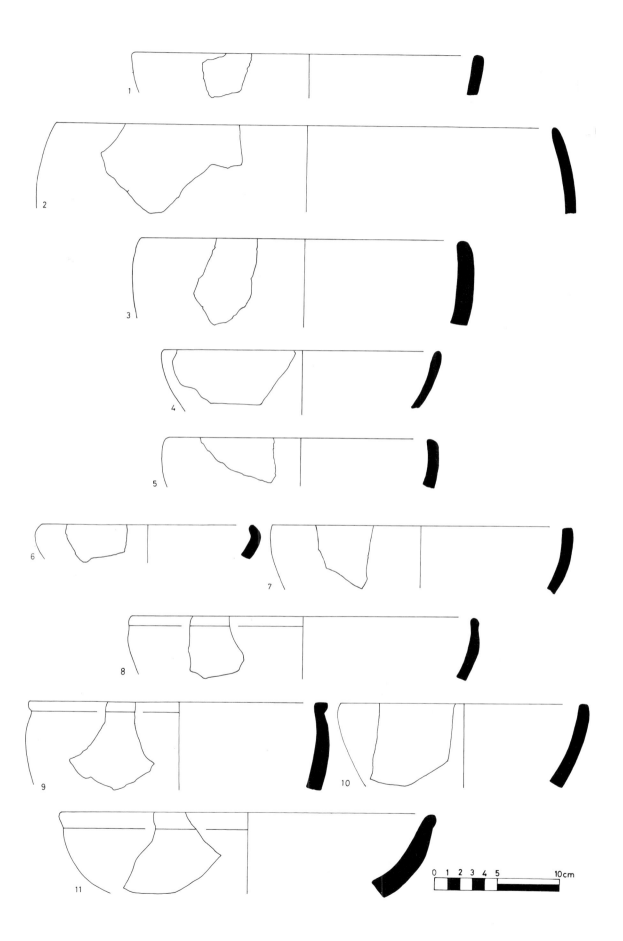

Fig. 130

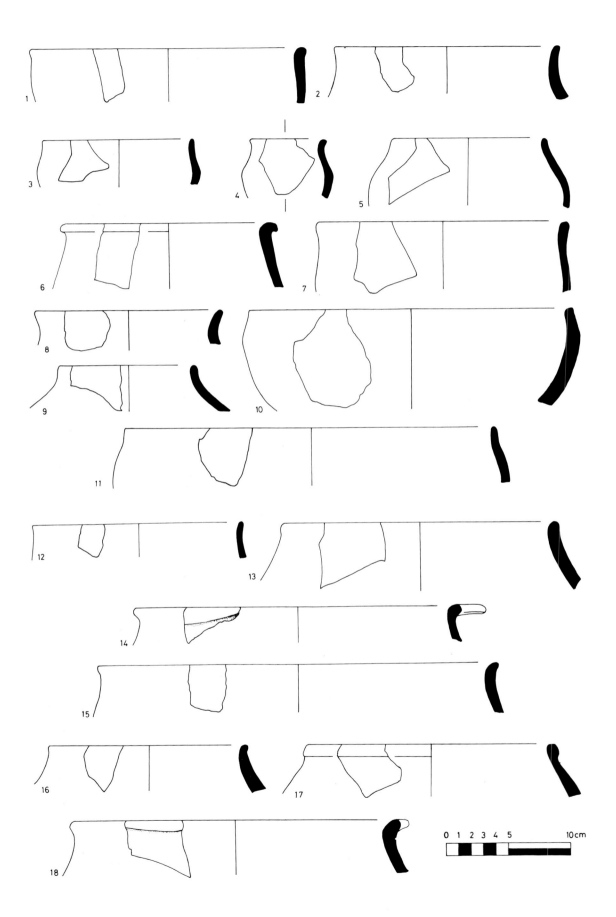

Fig. 131

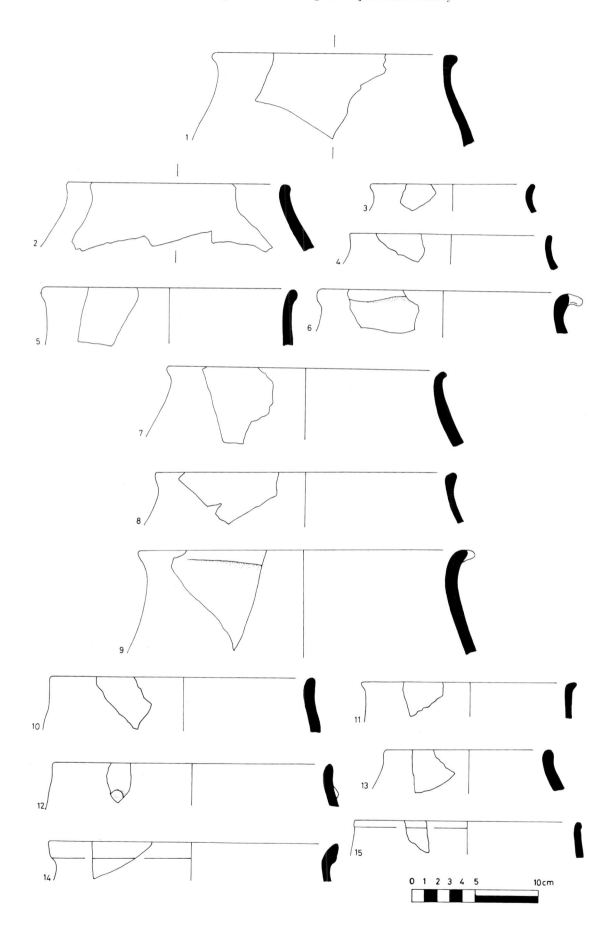

Fig. 132

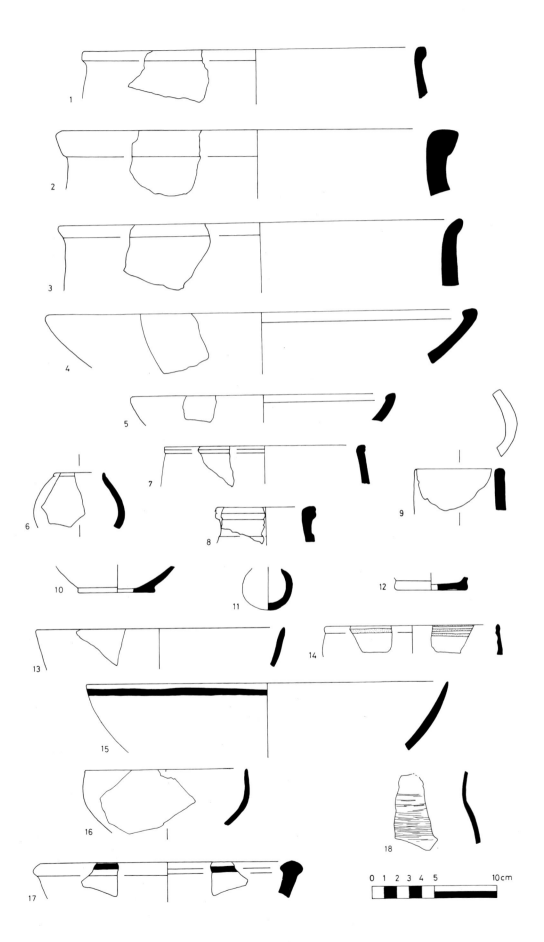

Fig. 133

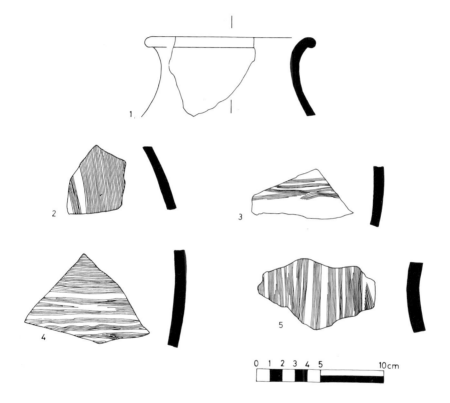

Fig. 134

CATALOGUE OF POTTERY FROM AŞVAN KALE

Fig. 72

1. G1b 1400.1
   HM, tempered with medium grit. Grey fabric, orange brown slipped exterior and interior, stroke smoothed in parts. RD 15, H (pres.) 3.6.
2. G1b 1401.11
   HM, tempered with chaff. Black throughout, burnished exterior and interior. RD 18, H (pres.) 3.3.
3. G1b 1401.9
   HM, tempered with medium grit, grey core. Brown burnished exterior and interior. RD 20, H (pres.) 3.3.
4. G1b 1401.5
   HM, fine fabric tempered with medium-fine grit. Reddish brown burnished interior, pale pinkish brown smoothed exterior. RD 18, H (pres.) 2.4.
5. G1d 1300.10
   HM, tempered with chaff and a little grit. Greyish brown throughout, plain interior and exterior. RD 27, H (pres.) 5.4.
6. G1d 1300.7
   HM, tempered with chaff, grey core. Pale greyish brown smoothed exterior and interior. RD 30, H (pres.) 5.4.
7. G1d 1302.2
   HM, tempered with medium grit. Black throughout, burnished exterior and interior. RD 12, H (pres.) 6.0.
8. G1d 1303.10
   HM, fine fabric tempered with medium-fine grit, pale brown core. Brown burnished exterior and interior. RD 16, H (pres.) 6.0.
9. G1d 1303.10
   HM, tempered with medium grit and chaff. Black burnished exterior except along the rim, which is brown burnished, brown smoothed interior. RD 20, H (pres.) 6.4.
10. G1d 1303.16
    HM, tempered with medium grit, dark grey core. Brown burnished exterior and interior. RD 17, H (pres.) 2.7.
11. G1d 1303.18
    HM, coarse fabric tempered with coarse grit and chaff. Greyish black slightly burnished exterior, pale brown smoothed interior. RD 20, H (pres.) 4.5.
12. G1d 1303.17
    HM, tempered with medium grit and chaff. Black throughout, burnished exterior and interior. RD 40, H (pres.) 5.1.
13. G1d 1303.18
    HM, tempered with chaff, dark grey core. Brown slipped exterior and interior, stroke smoothed in parts. RD 24, H (pres.) 3.9.
14. G1d 1303.18
    HM, tempered with chaff, traces of a dark grey core. Brown plain exterior and interior. RD 36, H (pres.) 7.3.
15. G1d 1303.18
    HM, coarse fabric tempered with coarse grit. Dark brown throughout, plain exterior and interior, smoke blackened in parts. RD 30, H (pres.) 7.0.

Fig. 73

1. G1d 1303.24
   HM, tempered with medium grit, dark grey core. Pale brown slipped exterior and interior, smoothed in parts. Horizontal lug handle set at the rim. RD 18, H (pres.) 6.9.
2. G1d 1303.28
   HM, tempered with chaff, dark grey core. Reddish brown smoothed exterior, grey smoothed interior. RD 26, H (pres.) 3.6.
3. G1d 1303.32
   HM, tempered with chaff and medium grit. Pale brown burnished exterior, smoke blackened in parts, reddish brown smoothed interior. RD 38, H (pres.) 7.9.
4. G1d 1303.7
   HM, tempered with chaff and medium grit, dark grey core. Brown slightly smoothed exterior, brown plain interior. RD 28, H (pres.) 3.9.
5. G1d 1303.7
   HM, tempered with medium grit. Black throughout, burnished exterior and interior. Horizontal lug set at the rim. RD 18, H (pres.) 2.0.
6. G1d 1304.11
   HM, tempered with chaff and medium grit. Black burnished exterior, dark brown burnished interior. RD 18, H (pres.) 4.7.
7. G1d 1303.7
   HM, tempered with medium grit. Brown throughout, plain exterior and interior. RD 16, H (pres.) 2.7.
8. G2b 1201.13
   HM, coarse fabric tempered with medium-coarse grit, grey core. Reddish brown burnished exterior, reddish brown smoothed interior. RD 36, H (pres.) 8.4.
9. G1d 1304.7
   HM, coarse fabric tempered with chaff and coarse grit, dark grey core. Black plain interior, pale brown plain exterior. RD 34, H (pres.) 6.0.
10. G2b 1203.3
    HM, coarse fabric tempered with medium-coarse grit and chaff, dark grey core. Reddish brown and black mottled exterior, patchily burnished, pale reddish brown smoothed interior. RD 22, H (pres.) 4.5.
11. G2b 1201.10
    HM, tempered with medium grit. Pale brown throughout, burnished exterior and interior. RD 16, H (pres.) 3.0.
12. G2b 1200.13
    HM, tempered with chaff and medium grit. Black burnished exterior, pinkish buff smoothed interior. RD 32, H (pres.) 4.5.

Fig. 74

1. G2b 1200.4
   HM, coarse fabric tempered with chaff and medium-coarse grit, dark grey core. Pale brown throughout, patchily burnished exterior, smoothed interior. RD 30, H (pres.) 5.4.
2. G2b 1200.4
   HM, tempered with chaff and medium grit, grey core. Pale brown throughout, burnished exterior and interior. RD 28, H (pres.) 5.7.
3. G2b 1200.4
   HM, tempered with medium grit. Pale greyish brown throughout, slightly burnished exterior, smoothed interior. RD 19, H (pres.) 4.5.

4. G2b 1201.10.7
HM, tempered with medium grit. Pale grey burnished exterior, black smoothed interior. RD 10, H (pres.) 3.6.

5. G2b 1210.10.7
HM, tempered with medium grit. Black burnished exterior, reddish brown smoothed interior. RD 30, H (pres.) 6.6.

6. G2b 1201.14
HM, tempered with medium-fine grit. Pale grey throughout, burnished exterior and interior. RD 22, H (pres.) 1.9.

7. G2d 1100.6
HM, tempered with chaff and a little medium grit, black core. Black burnished interior and exterior except along the rim, which is brown burnished. RD 15, H (pres.) 1.1.

8. G2b 1201.15
HM, coarse fabric tempered with chaff. Pale brown fabric mottled with black on the exterior, slightly burnished on both surfaces. RD 20, H (pres.) 6.9.

9. G2b 1201.16
HM, tempered with medium grit, grey core. Pale greyish brown smoothed exterior, pale reddish brown smoothed interior. RD 18, H (pres.) 4.2.

10. G2b 1201.16
HM, tempered with medium grit. Black burnished exterior, pale brown smoothed interior. RD 20, H (pres.) 3.3.

11. G2b 1211.16
HM, tempered with medium grit. Pale greyish brown smoothed exterior, pale reddish brown smoothed interior. RD 16, H (pres.) 2.7.

12. G2b 1201.16
HM, tempered with medium grit. Black throughout, burnished exterior, smoothed interior. RD (pres.) 14, H (pres.) 3.7.

13. G2b 1201.12
HM, tempered with medium grit. Dark grey throughout, plain exterior and interior. RD 18, H (pres.) 1.8.

14. G2b 1201.16
HM, tempered with medium-fine grit, grey core. Pale reddish brown exterior and interior, smoothed in parts. RD 14, H (pres.) 4.5. Previously published: French and (Helms 1973: Fig. 3 no. 1).

15. G2b 1201.16
HM, coarse fabric tempered with chaff, grey core. Pale reddish brown smoothed exterior, dirty brown plain interior. RD 28, H (pres.) 6.3.

Fig. 75

1. G2b 1201.18
HM, tempered with medium grit, grey core. Reddish brown stroke smoothed exterior, reddish brown plain interior. RD 36, H (pres.) 7.8.

2. G2b 1201.18
HM, tempered with medium grit and a little chaff. Pale greyish brown throughout, burnished exterior and interior. RD 26, H (pres.) 5.1. Previously published (French and Helms 1973: Fig. 3 no. 8).

3. G2b 1201.20
HM, tempered with chaff and medium grit. Black burnished exterior, dark brownish grey smoothed interior. Triangular lug set at the rim. RD 20, H (pres.) 6.0.

4. G2b 1201.19
HM, tempered with medium grit and a little chaff,

dark grey core. Pale greyish brown smoothed exterior and interior. RD 30, H (pres.) 6.5.

5. G2b 1201.24
HM, tempered with chaff and a little medium grit, grey core. Pale greyish brown burnished exterior and interior. RD 34, H (pres.) 3.9.

6. G2b 1201.26
HM, tempered with medium grit. Black throughout, burnished exterior and interior. RD 18, H (pres.) 3.3.

7. G2b 1201.26
HM, tempered with medium grit. Smoke blackened exterior, pale greyish brown smoothed interior. RD 18, H (pres.) 3.6.

8. G2b 1201.26
HM, tempered with chaff, dark grey core. Pale grey exterior and interior, both surfaces are plain. RD 24, H (pres.) 6.6.

9. G2b 1201.27
HM, tempered with medium grit. Pale greyish brown throughout, smoothed exterior and interior. RD 26, H (pres.) 3.0.

10. G2b 1201.32
HM, tempered with chaff and medium grit. Reddish pale brown smoothed exterior, pale greyish brown smoothed interior. RD 30, H (pres.) 1.4.

11. G2b 1201.30
HM, tempered with chaff and medium grit, dark grey core. Pale brown smoothed exterior and interior. RD 26, H (pres.) 6.6.

Fig. 76

1. G2b 1201.32
HM, tempered with chaff and medium grit. Greyish black smoothed exterior except along the rim, which is pale reddish brown smoothed, like the interior. RD 20, H (pres.) 4.5.

2. G2b 1201.4
HM, tempered with chaff and medium grit, grey core. Pale brown plain exterior and interior. RD 20, H (pres.) 6.0.

3. G2b 1201.35
HM, coarse fabric tempered with medium-coarse grit. Pale reddish brown throughout, burnished exterior and interior. RD 26, H (pres.) 1.7.

4. G2b 1201.40
HM, tempered with medium grit. Greyish brown throughout, burnished exterior and interior. RD 45, H (pres.) 1.9.

5. G2b 1201.4
HM, tempered with medium grit. Black throughout, burnished exterior and interior. RD 16, H 5.4. Previously published (French and Helms 1973: Fig. 2 no. 1).

6. G2b 1201.4
HM, tempered with medium grit, dark grey core. Brown and black mottled and patchily burnished exterior, red burnished interior. RD 14, H (pres.) 7.2. Previously published (French and Helms 1973: Fig. 3 no. 2).

7. G2b 1201.40
HM, tempered with chaff and medium grit, dark grey core. Reddish brown burnished exterior, pale brown smoothed interior. RD 36, H (pres.) 9.3.

8. G2b 1201.41
HM, tempered with chaff and medium grit. Black throughout, burnished exterior and interior. RD 17, H (pres.) 3.3.

9. G2b 1201.46
HM, tempered with chaff and medium grit, dark grey core. Greyish brown exterior and interior, both surfaces are plain. RD 14, H (pres.) 3.6.

10. G2b 1203.3
HM, tempered with chaff. Pale reddish brown throughout, slightly burnished exterior, smoothed interior. RD 35, H (pres.) 5.1.

11. G2b 1200.13
HM, tempered with medium grit. Black burnished exterior, pale reddish brown plain interior. RD 30, H (pres.) 2.7.

12. G2b 1203.8
HM, tempered with medium grit. Blackish brown burnished exterior, pale reddish brown smoothed interior. RD 35, H (pres.) 3.0.

13. G2b sieving
HM, tempered with chaff and medium grit, grey core. Reddish brown burnished exterior and interior. RD 24, H (pres.) 4.5.

Fig. 77

1. G2d 1102.16
HM, coarse fabric tempered with chaff, dark grey core. Pale reddish brown fabric, smoothed and grey mottled in parts. RD 27, H (pres.) 7.8.

2. G2b 1202.4
HM, tempered with chaff and medium grit. Black throughout, smoothed exterior, burnished interior. RD 14, H (pres.) 5.1.

3. G2d 1104.1
HM, tempered with chaff and medium grit. Black slightly burnished exterior except along the rim, which is pale brown smoothed like the interior. RD 18, H (pres.) 5.1.

4. G2d 1103.11
HM, tempered with chaff and a little medium grit, grey core. Pale reddish brown and grey mottled on both surfaces, smoothed exterior, plain interior. RD 27, H (pres.) 10.2.

5. G2d 1103.12
HM, tempered with chaff and a little medium grit, grey core. Pale greyish brown burnished exterior, pale reddish brown smoothed interior. RD 32, H (pres.) 4.2.

6. G3b 1009.4
HM, tempered with chaff and a little medium grit. Pale greyish brown throughout, slightly burnished exterior, smoothed interior. RD 22, H (pres.) 3.9.

7. G3b 1009.9
HM, tempered with medium-fine grit. Pale reddish buff throughout, smoothed exterior, plain interior. RD 15, H (pres.) 2.4.

8. G3b 1009.9
HM, tempered with chaff and a little medium grit, dark grey core. Reddish brown plain exterior and interior. RD 24, H (pres.) 3.6.

9. G3b 1013.1 HM, tempered with medium grit. Brown burnished exterior, except along the rim, which is greyish brown burnished like the interior. RD 15, H (pres.) 4.2.

10. G3b 1016.10
HM, tempered with chaff, grey core. Pale pinkish brown plain exterior, dirty pinkish brown interior. RD 19, H (pres.) 4.2.

11. G3b 1015.4
HM, tempered with chaff and medium grit, dark grey core. Black smoothed exterior, reddish brown smoothed interior. RD 20, H (pres.) 4.8.

12. G3d 509.7.
HM, tempered with medium grit. Pale greyish brown throughout, burnished exterior and interior. RD 28, H (pres.) 4.9.

Fig. 78

1. G2b 1202.13
HM, tempered with medium grit. Black burnished exterior, reddish brown smoothed interior. RD 26, H (pres.) 8.7.

2. G2b 1201.13
HM, tempered with medium grit. Black throughout, burnished exterior and interior. RD 22, H (pres.) 2.7.

3. G2b 1202.26
HM, tempered with medium grit. Black throughout, burnished exterior and interior. RD 18, H (pres.) 2.6.

4. G2b 1201.15
HM, tempered with medium grit. Black throughout, burnished exterior and interior. RD 14, H (pres.) 3.9. Previously published (French and Helms 1973: Fig. 2 no. 2).

5. G2b 1201.26
HM, tempered with medium grit. Blackened exterior, pale greyish brown smoothed interior. RD 25, H (pres.) 3.9.

6. G2d 1103.2
HM, tempered with chaff and medium grit. Black throughout, slightly burnished exterior, smoothed interior. RD 22, H (pres.) 3.3.

7. G3b (Pit 3)
HM, tempered with medium grit. Black throughout, burnished exterior and interior. RD 30, H (pres.) 0.9.

8. G3b (Pit 3)
HM, tempered with medium grit and a little chaff. Black throughout, burnished exterior and interior. RD 35, H (pres.) 3.9.

9. G3b (Pit 3)
HM, tempered with chaff and medium grit. Black throughout, burnished exterior and interior. RD 40, H (pres.) 6.1.

10. G3b 1004.7
HM, tempered with medium grit. Brown throughout, slightly burnished exterior and interior. RD 23, H (pres.) 5.1.

11. G3b 1009.4
HM, tempered with medium white grit. Black burnished exterior, pale greyish brown burnished interior. RD 28, H (pres.) 8.4.

12. G3b 1009.9 (Pit 3)
HM, coarse fabric tempered with medium-coarse grit, pale reddish brown core. Blackish brown burnished exterior, dark brown smoothed interior. RD 21, H (pres.) 4.8.

13. G3b 1009.8 (Pit 3)
HM, tempered with medium grit. Greyish black throughout, burnished exterior and interior. RD 20, H (pres.) 4.9.

Fig. 79

1. G3b 1009.9 (Pit 3)
HM, coarse fabric tempered with medium-coarse grit. Dark brown throughout, slightly burnished exterior and interior. RD 24, H (pres.) 8.7.

2. G3b 1009.9 (Pit 3)
HM, tempered with medium white grit. Black

burnished exterior, dark grey burnished interior. RD 21, H (pres.) 6.4.

3. G3b 1009.9 (Pit 3)
HM, tempered with medium grit. Black throughout, burnished exterior and interior. RD 20, H (pres.) 3.0.

4. G2d 1103.7
HM, tempered with chaff and medium grit. Black slightly burnished exterior, dark greyish brown smoothed interior. RD 19, H (pres.) 3.0.

5. G1d 1303.8.Pit 1
HM, tempered with chaff and medium grit. Black burnished exterior, pale greyish brown smoothed interior. RD 19, H (pres.) 3.6.

6. G2d 1103.12
HM, tempered with chaff and medium grit. Black throughout, burnished exterior and interior. RD 23, H (pres.) 3.3.

7. G2b 1200.13
HM, tempered with medium grit, dark grey core. Reddish brown burnished exterior and interior. RD 38, H (pres.) 6.6.

8. G1d 1303.22
HM, tempered with chaff and medium grit. Black slightly burnished exterior, black and brown smoothed interior. RD 32, H (pres.) 10.5.

9. G2d 1102.13
HM, tempered with medium grit. Pale grey brown throughout, burnished exterior, smoothed interior. RD 6, H (pres.) 4.5.

10. G1d 1303.34
HM, tempered with medium grit. Black throughout, burnished exterior and interior. RD 16, H (pres.) 3.3.

11. G1d 1304.14
HM, tempered with medium grit. Greyish black throughout, burnished exterior and interior. RD 13, H (pres.) 3.3.

12. G1d 1303.7
HM, tempered with chaff and medium grit. Black burnished exterior, reddish brown smoothed interior. Horizontal ledge handle set at the rim. RD 25, H (pres.) 6.0.

13. G1d 1304.13
HM, tempered with medium grit. Black throughout, burnished exterior and interior. RD 6, H (pres.) 1.3.

Fig. 80

1. G1d 1304.14
HM, tempered with medium grit. Black burnished exterior except below the rim, which is pale brown burnished like the interior. RD 14, H (pres.) 8.7.

2. G1d 1304.14
HM, tempered with medium white grit, grey core. Brown burnished exterior and interior, except round lower part of the exterior, which is black burnished. RD 13, H (pres.) 4.8.

3. G1d 1304.6
HM, tempered with medium grit. Black burnished exterior except along the rim, which is greyish brown smoothed like the interior. RD 20, H (pres.) 3.9.

4. G1d 1303.18
HM, fine fabric tempered with medium-fine grit. Black throughout, burnished exterior and interior. RD 18, H (pres.) 4.6.

5. G2b 1200.1
HM, tempered with medium grit, grey core.

Greyish brown plain exterior and interior. Small loop handle, grooved down the spine, set at the rim. RD 14, H (pres.) 4.0.

6. G2b 1200.4
HM, tempered with medium grit and a little chaff. Black burnished exterior except along the rim, which is pale greyish brown smoothed like the interior. RD 17, H (pres.) 3.6.

7. G2b 1201.26
HM, tempered with medium grit. Pale greyish brown throughout, slightly smoothed exterior, plain interior. Vertical lug handle pendent from the rim. RD 16, H (pres.) 6.0.

8. G2b 1201.16
HM, tempered with chaff and a little medium grit, dark grey core. Pale greyish brown smoothed exterior, reddish brown smoothed interior. RD 27, H (pres.) 5.8.

9. G2b 1201.29
HM, tempered with chaff and medium grit, pale grey core. Pale reddish brown plain exterior and interior. RD 10, H (pres.) 5.1.

10. G2b 1201.33
HM, tempered with medium grit. Pale greyish brown smoothed exterior and interior. RD 40, H (pres.) 4.9.

11. G2b 1201.8
HM, tempered with chaff and medium grit. Black burnished exterior, pale greyish brown smoothed interior. RD 17, H (pres.) 4.9.

12. G2b 1201.6
HM, tempered with medium grit. Pale brown throughout, smoothed exterior blackened in parts, plain interior. RD 18, H (pres.) 2.4.

13. G2b 1201.47
HM, tempered with chaff and medium grit. Black throughout, burnished exterior and interior. RD 10, H (pres.) 2.7.

14. G2b 1203.3
HM, tempered with chaff and medium grit. Black throughout, burnished exterior and interior. RD 16, H (pres.) 2.9.

15. G2b 1203.2
HM, tempered with chaff and medium grit. Black throughout, burnished exterior and interior. RD 13, H (pres.) 8.7.

16. G2b 1203.5
HM, coarse fabric tempered with chaff and medium-coarse grit. Pale reddish brown smoothed exterior, pale greyish plain interior. RD 34, H (pres.) 9.6.

Fig. 81

1. G2b 1203.5
HM, tempered with chaff and medium grit. Black burnished exterior except along the rim, which is greyish brown burnished like the interior. RD 28, H (pres.) 2.9.

2. G2b 1203.8
HM, tempered with medium grit and a little chaff. Black throughout, burnished exterior and interior. RD 23, H (pres.) 6.0.

3. G2b 1203.8
HM, coarse fabric tempered with medium-coarse grit. Smoothed exterior varying in colour from grey to greyish black, pale reddish brown plain interior. RD 26, H (pres.) 8.7.

4. G2d 1102.6
HM, tempered with chaff and a little medium grit,

grey core. Pale greyish brown burnished exterior and interior. RD 16, H (pres.) 4.5.

5. G2d 1103.12
HM, tempered with chaff and medium grit. Reddish brown throughout, burnished exterior, smoothed interior. RD 18, H (pres.) 4.8.

6. G2d 1103.12
HM, tempered with chaff and medium grit, grey core. Reddish brown burnished exterior, reddish brown smoothed interior. RD 23, H (pres.) 5.9.

7. G3b 1001.1
HM, tempered with chaff and medium grit. Slightly burnished exterior varies from grey to pale brown, smoothed interior varies from grey to reddish brown. Loop handle links rim to belly. RD 14, H (pres.) 10.4.

8. G3b 1001.3
HM, tempered with medium grit and a little chaff. Slightly burnished exterior varies from greyish black to pale brown, smoothed interior is pale brown. RD 14, H (pres.) 6.2.

9. G3b 1001.3
HM, tempered with medium grit. Pale greyish brown throughout, smoothed exterior and interior. RD 13, H (pres.) 6.3.

10. G3d 507.3.
HM, tempered with medium grit. Brown burnished exterior and interior except around rim, which is greyish black burnished. RD 21, H (pres.) 5.7.

11. G3d 508.1
HM, coarse fabric tempered with medium-coarse grit. Reddish brown throughout, smoothed exterior, plain interior. RD 21, H (pres.) 3.9.

Fig. 82

1. G1d 1300.7
HM, tempered with chaff and medium-fine grit. Black throughout, burnished exterior and interior. RD 11, H (pres.) 2.7.

2. G1d 1304.7
HM, tempered with chaff, grey core. Pale brown burnished exterior, pale brown smoothed interior. RD 12, H (pres.) 4.8.

3. G1d 1304.7
HM, tempered with medium grit. Black throughout, burnished exterior and interior. RD 12, H (pres.) 3.1.

4. G2b 1201.24
HM, tempered with medium grit. Pale grey slightly burnished exterior, brown smoothed interior. Small loop handle set at the rim. RD 15, H (pres.) 4.2.

5. G2b 1201.25
HM, tempered with medium grit. Pale greyish brown throughout, burnished exterior, smoothed interior. RD 16, H (pres.) 4.3.

6. G2b 1201.29
HM, tempered with chaff and a little grit. Pale greyish brown smoothed exterior, pale reddish brown smoothed interior. RD 18, H (pres.) 4.1.

7. G2b 1201.7
HM, tempered with medium white grit. Reddish brown throughout, burnished exterior and interior. RD 12, H (pres.) 4.8.

8. G2b 1210.10
HM, tempered with medium grit. Pale greyish brown throughout, plain exterior and interior. Smoke blackened around loop handle, which links rim to shoulder. RD 20, H (pres.) 5.1.

9. G2d 1103.16
HM, tempered with chaff and medium grit. Black burnished exterior, pale greyish brown smoothed interior. Solid lug handle, splayed at the bottom, set vertically at the rim. RD 14, H (pres.) 5.8.

10. G2d 1103.11
HM, tempered with chaff and a little grit. Black burnished exterior, greyish brown smoothed interior. Solid lug handle set vertically at the rim. RD 17, H (pres.) 5.0.

11. G3d 506.39
HM, tempered with medium grit. Greyish brown throughout, burnished exterior and interior. RD 18, H (pres.) 6.8.

12. G1d 1303.22
HM, tempered with medium-fine grit. Black throughout, burnished exterior and interior. RD 10, H (pres.) 3.1.

13. G1d 1300.8
HM, tempered with medium grit. Brown throughout, plain exterior smoke blackened patch, smoothed interior. RD 9, H (pres.) 3.3.

14. G1d 1304.7
HM, tempered with medium grit. Black burnished exterior, pale grey smoothed interior. RD 14, H (pres.) 6.1.

15. G1d 1303.18
HM, tempered with medium grit. Black burnished exterior, except along rim, which is pale brown burnished like interior. RD 30, H (pres.) 4.4.

16. G1d 1304.7
HM, tempered with chaff, grey core. Pale brown burnished exterior, pale brown smoothed interior. RD 10, H (pres.) 4.5.

17. G1d 1304.7
HM, tempered with medium grit. Brown throughout, smoothed exterior, plain interior. RD 10, H (pres.) 5.1.

18. G2b 1201.14
HM, tempered with medium grit. Black burnished exterior, pale grey smoothed interior. RD 14, H (pres.) 7.7.

19. G2b 1201.15
HM, tempered with chaff and medium grit, grey core. Reddish brown burnished exterior, pale brown smoothed interior. RD 20, H (pres.) 5.6.

Fig. 83

1. G2b 1201.14
HM, tempered with chaff. Reddish brown plain exterior, greyish black along the rim, grey smoothed interior. RD 28, H (pres.) 12.3. Previously published (French and Helms 1973: Fig. 4 no. 8).

2. G2b 1201.16
HM, tempered with chaff. Pinkish brown throughout, plain exterior and interior. RD 28, H (pres.) 7.1.

3. G2b 1201.26
HM, tempered with medium grit. Dark grey throughout, burnished exterior and interior. RD 9, H (pres.) 3.2.

4. G2b 1201.29
HM, tempered with chaff and medium grit. Black burnished exterior, greyish brown smoothed interior. RD 18, H (pres.) 4.3.

5. G2b 1201.32
HM, tempered with chaff and a little medium grit. Black burnished exterior, pale brown smoothed

interior, pale greyish brown burnished along rim. RD 21, H (pres.) 5.9.

6. G2b 1201.29
HM, tempered with chaff and a little medium grit. Pale greyish brown burnished exterior, brownish black smoothed interior. RD 28, H (pres.) 4.6.

7. G2b 1201.41
HM, tempered with medium grit, grey core. Black burnished exterior, dark brown burnished interior. RD 27, H (pres.) 6.7.

8. G2b 1201.42
HM, tempered with medium grit. Pale greyish brown burnished exterior, reddish brown plain interior. RD 28, H (pres.) 4.8.

9. G2b 1201.46
HM, tempered with medium grit. Black throughout, burnished exterior and interior. RD 22, H (pres.) 4.7.

10. G2d 1103.11
HM, coarse fabric tempered with medium-coarse grit. Reddish brown throughout, burnished exterior and interior. Small loop handle set at rim. RD 12, H (pres.) 3.9.

11. G2b 1201.47
HM, tempered with chaff and medium grit. Black burnished exterior, pale grey smoothed interior. RD 28, H (pres.) 6.2.

Fig. 84

1. G2b 1203.6
HM, tempered with medium grit. Black throughout, burnished exterior and interior. RD 27, H (pres.) 5.4.

2. G2d 1104.6
HM, tempered with chaff and a little grit. Pale greyish brown throughout, slightly burnished exterior, smoothed interior. RD 20, H (pres.) 5.9.

3. G2d 1100.6
HM, tempered with chaff and a little medium grit, grey core. RD 23, H (pres.) 7.1.

4. G3b 1015.4
HM, coarse fabric tempered with chaff and coarse grit, dark greyish black core. Brown slightly burnished exterior, brown smoothed interior. RD 23, H (pres.) 6.4.

5. G3b 1016.10
HM, tempered with chaff and medium grit. Black burnished exterior, brown burnished interior. RD 21, H (pres.) 5.5.

6. G3b 1017.2
HM, tempered with medium white grit. Brown throughout, burnished and smoke blackened exterior, burnished interior. RD 19, H (pres.) 5.5.

7. G2b 1201.16
HM, tempered with chaff. Pale greyish brown smoothed exterior, dark grey plain interior. RD 18, H (pres.) 8.8. Previously published (French and Helms 1973: Fig. 4 no. 7).

8. G2b 1201.28
HM, tempered with medium grit, grey core. Brown burnished exterior, reddish brown smoothed interior. RD 13, H (pres.) 6.4. Previously published (French and Helms 1973: Fig. 3 no. 5).

9. G1b 1401.11
HM, tempered with medium grit. Brown throughout, slightly burnished exterior, smoothed interior. RD 32, H (pres.) 6.2.

10. G2b 1201.26
HM, tempered with chaff and medium grit. Black burnished exterior, brown burnished interior. RD 25, H (pres.) 3.7.

11. G1d 1300.7
HM, tempered with medium white grit. Black burnished exterior, pale brown smoothed interior. RD 25, H (pres.) 4.5.

Fig. 85

1. G1d 1300.7
HM, coarse fabric tempered with medium-coarse grit, dark grey core. Pale brown plain exterior and interior. RD 24, H (pres.) 4.9.

2. G1d 1300.7
HM, tempered with medium grit. Pale greyish brown smoothed exterior and interior. Fugitive red paint on rim. RD 21, H (pres.) 2.9.

3. G1d 1300.7
HM, coarse fabric tempered with medium-coarse white grit. Greyish brown plain exterior, reddish buff plain interior. RD 22, H (pres.) 4.3.

4. G1d 1300.8
HM, coarse fabric tempered with chaff and coarse grit, grey core. Brown plain exterior and interior, smoke blackened exterior and along the rim. RD 34, H (pres.) 8.8.

5. G1d 1302.2
HM, coarse fabric tempered with coarse grit. Black and pale grey mottled exterior, pale greyish brown interior, both surfaces are plain except for parts of exterior which are smoothed. RD 30, H (pres.) 7.3.

6. G1d 1303.18
HM, coarse fabric tempered with medium-coarse grit, dark grey core. Grey smoothed exterior, pale reddish brown plain interior. Part of a triangular ledge handle set at the rim survives. RD 22, H (pres.) 4.0.

7. G1d 1303.18
HM, tempered with chaff, dark grey core. Pale brown slipped exterior and interior, burnished exterior, smoke blackened patches, smoothed interior. RD 24, H (pres.) 7.6.

8. G1d 1303.34
HM, tempered with medium grit. Black burnished exterior, brown plain interior. RD 39, H (pres.) 4.3.

9. G1d 1303.7
HM, tempered with chaff and medium grit. Pale brown throughout, patchily smoothed exterior, plain interior. RD 18, H (pres.) 5.4.

10. G1d 1303.17
HM, tempered with medium grit. Black burnished exterior, grey smoothed interior. RD 22, H (pres.) 4.6.

11. G1d 1303.17
HM, tempered with chaff. Black burnished exterior except along rim, which is brown burnished, pale brown smoothed interior. RD 18, H (pres.) 4.3.

Fig. 86

1. G2d 1102.16
HM, coarse fabric tempered with coarse white grit and chaff, black core. Exterior and interior vary from dirty greyish black to brown, both surfaces are plain. Triangular ledge handle set at rim. RD 23, H (pres.) 2.9.

2. G2d 1103.11
HM, tempered with chaff and medium grit, grey core. Reddish brown smoothed exterior and interior. RD 22, H (pres.) 6.4.

3. G2b 1200.4
HM, tempered with chaff and medium grit, grey core. Pale greyish brown patchily smoothed exterior and interior. RD 30, H (pres.) 4.5.

4. G2b 1200.4
HM, tempered with medium grit, grey core. Dirty pale brown and grey mottled exterior and interior, smoke-blackened from use over fire. RD 24, H (pres.) 3.4.

5. G2b 1200.4
HM, tempered with medium grit, dark grey core. Greyish black patchily smoothed exterior, greyish brown plain interior. RD 21, H (pres.) 4.1.

6. G2b 1200.4
HM, tempered with chaff, grey core. Pale greyish brown smoothed exterior, pale greyish brown plain interior. RD 15, H (pres.) 2.4.

7. G2b 1200.4
HM, tempered with medium grit, dark grey core. Reddish brown burnished exterior and interior. RD 30, H (pres.) 4.2.

8. G2b 1201.10
HM, tempered with medium grit, grey core. Reddish brown plain exterior and interior. RD 17, H (pres.) 4.0.

9. G2b 1201.10
HM, tempered with chaff and medium grit. Pale greyish brown plain exterior, dirty grey plain interior. RD 16, H (pres.) 3.6.

10. G2b 1201.10
HM, tempered with medium grit. Black burnished exterior except along the rim, which is reddish brown burnished like interior. RD 20, H (pres.) 4.0.

11. G2b 1201.12
HM, tempered with medium white grit. Brown throughout, slightly burnished exterior and interior. Smoke-blackened, triangular ledge handle set at rim. RD 20, H (pres.) 6.3.

12. G2b 1201.13
HM, tempered with chaff and medium grit, dark grey core. Dirty reddish brown exterior, reddish brown plain interior. RD 38, H (pres.) 5.2.

13. G2b 1200.13
HM, coarse fabric tempered with chaff and coarse grit. Black burnished exterior, dark brownish grey smoothed interior. RD 32, H (pres.) 6.1.

Fig. 87

1. G2b 1201.13
HM, tempered with medium grit, grey core. Dirty reddish brown exterior and interior, both surfaces are plain. RD 34, H (pres.) 8.0.

2. G2b 1201.15
HM, tempered with chaff, dark grey core. Pale grey smoothed exterior, pale grey plain interior. RD 32, H (pres.) 6.4.

3. G2b 1201.16
HM, tempered with chaff and a little medium grit, grey core. Pale greyish brown smoothed exterior, pale greyish brown plain interior. RD 20, H (pres.) 5.4.

4. G2b 1201.16
HM, tempered with chaff and medium grit, grey core. Brown slightly burnished exterior, brown smoothed interior. Triangular ledge handle set at rim. RD 18, H (pres.) 4.5.

5. G2b 1201.17
HM, tempered with medium grit. Black burnished exterior, pale grey smoothed interior. RD 18, H (pres.) 6.0.

6. G2b 1201.19
HM, coarse fabric tempered with medium-coarse grit. Black throughout, burnished exterior and interior. RD 22, H (pres.) 4.9.

7. G2b 1201.20
HM, tempered with medium grit. Plain greyish black throughout, reddish brown mottled patches on the exterior. Part of a triangular ledge handle set at the rim. RD 14, H (pres.) 4.2.

8. G1d 1300.7
HM, tempered with medium-coarse grit. Black slightly burnished exterior, pale brown smoothed interior. Part of a ledge handle set at the rim. RD 20, H (pres.) 3.3.

9. G2b 1201.24
HM, tempered with medium grit and a little chaff, grey core. Dirty greyish black and brown burnished exterior, pale brown smoothed interior. RD 20, H (pres.) 7.9. Previously published (French and Helms 1973: Fig. 3 no. 3).

10.
G2b 1201.24
HM, tempered with medium grit. Pale grey burnished exterior, pale brown smoothed interior. RD 22, H (pres.) 2.7.

11. G2b 1201.26
HM, tempered with chaff and a little grit. Black burnished exterior except along the rim, which is brown like the interior. RD 34, H (pres.) 5.5.

12. G2b 1201.26
HM, tempered with chaff and a little grit. Greyish black smoothed exterior, reddish brown smoothed interior. RD 30, H (pres.) 2.4.

Fig. 88

1. G2b 1201.31
HM, coarse fabric tempered with coarse white grit. Greyish black plain exterior, pale reddish brown smoothed interior. Triangular ledge handle set at rim. RD 34, H (pres.) 6.0.

2. G2b 1201.32
HM, coarse fabric tempered with medium-coarse grit. Black burnished exterior, pale brown smoothed interior. Triangular ledge handle set on rim. RD 34, H (pres.) 9.4.

3. G2b 1201.33
HM, tempered with chaff and medium grit. Black burnished exterior, reddish brown plain interior. Triangular ledge handle set on rim. RD 30, H (pres.) 8.2.

4. G2b 1201.33
HM, tempered with chaff and medium grit. Pale greyish brown throughout, burnished exterior and interior. RD 23, H (pres.) 3.4.

5. G2b 1201.26
HM, coarse fabric tempered with medium-coarse grit. Black burnished exterior, dark greyish brown smoothed interior. RD 20, H (pres.) 6.4.

6. G2b 1201.41
HM, tempered with chaff and medium white grit, dark grey core. Plain reddish brown throughout, smoke blackened in parts. Triangular ledge handle set at the rim. RD 27, H pres 4.2.

7. G2b 1201.41
HM, tempered with chaff and medium grit. Black burnished exterior, plain pale brown interior. RD 42, H (pres.) 5.2.

8. G2b 1201.41
HM, tempered with chaff and a little grit, grey core. Pale greyish brown throughout, burnished exterior, smoothed interior. RD 30, H (pres.) 3.1.

9. G2b 1201.47
HM, tempered with chaff and a little grit. Black burnished exterior, smoothed greyish brown interior. RD 26, H (pres.) 8.2. Previously published (French and Helms 1973: Fig. 2 no. 6).

10. G2b 1200.4
HM, tempered with medium grit. Black burnished exterior, smoothed greyish brown interior. Ledge handle set at the rim. RD 24, H (pres.) 2.9.

Fig. 89

1. G2b 1201.5
HM, tempered with medium white grit. Black smoothed exterior except around the neck, which is plain pale grey, interior is smoothed, reddish brown. Ledge handle set at the rim. RD 26, H (pres.) 12.6.

2. G2b 1202.11
HM, tempered with chaff. Black burnished exterior, pale brown smoothed interior. RD 15, H (pres.) 3.3.

3. G2b 1202.11
HM, tempered with medium grit. Greyish black smoothed exterior. RD 26, H (pres.) 4.3.

4. G2b 1202.13
HM, coarse fabric tempered with medium-coarse grit. Black burnished exterior, dark brown burnished interior. RD 14, H (pres.) 5.4.

5. G2b 1202.2
HM, coarse fabric tempered with chaff and medium-coarse grit, grey core. Brown burnished exterior and interior. RD 19, H (pres.) 7.8.

6. G2b 1202.2
HM, coarse fabric tempered with medium grit and a little coarse grit. Pale reddish brown plain exterior and interior. RD 36, H (pres.) 8.4.

7. G2b 1202.9
HM, tempered with chaff and medium grit. Black burnished exterior, grey smoothed interior. RD 17, H (pres.) 3.3.

8. G2b 1203.3
HM, tempered with medium grit. Pale grey burnished exterior and interior. RD 20, H (pres.) 4.5.

9. G2b 1203.5
HM, tempered with chaff. Black burnished exterior, pale brown smoothed interior. Triangular ledge handle set at the rim. RD 26, H (pres.) 5.4.

10. G2b 1203.8
HM, tempered with medium grit. Pale grey burnished exterior, pale greyish brown burnished interior. RD 32, H (pres.) 3.6.

11. G2b 1203.8
HM, coarse fabric tempered with medium-coarse white grit, grey core. Pale greyish brown slightly burnished exterior, pale greyish brown smoothed interior. RD 28, H (pres.) 3.4.

Fig. 90

1. G2b 1203.8
HM, tempered with medium-coarse grit. Dirty greyish black exterior, pale brown plain interior. Triangular ledge handle set at the rim. RD 30, H (pres.) 4.5.

2. G2b 1203.3
HM, coarse fabric tempered with medium-coarse grit. Black burnished exterior except along the rim, which is pale grey burnished, dirty pale greyish brown interior. RD 30, H (pres.) 7.3.

3. G2d 1002.2
HM, tempered with medium grit. Dark grey burnished exterior, pale grey burnished interior. RD 20, H (pres.) 4.3.

4. G2d 1103.6
HM, tempered with medium grit. Greyish black smoothed exterior, pale brown smoothed interior. Triangular ledge handle set at the rim. RD 15, H (pres.) 5.2.

5. G2d 1104.4
HM, tempered with chaff and a little coarse grit. Colour varies from pale reddish brown to pale grey throughout, slightly burnished exterior, smoothed interior. RD 22, H (pres.) 6.0.

6. G3b 1001.3
HM, tempered with medium grit, dark grey core. Dirty grey exterior and interior. RD 19, H (pres.) 2.1.

7. G3b 1001.8
HM, tempered with medium grit. Grey smoothed exterior and interior. RD 16, H (pres.) 3.0.

8. G3b 1001.2
HM, tempered with medium-fine grit, pale brown core. Black burnished exterior and interior. RD 6, H (pres.) 1.9.

9. G3b 1017.2
HM, tempered with chaff. Black burnished exterior except along the rim, which is reddish brown burnished, interior is smoothed and reddish brown. RD 22, H (pres.) 4.6.

10. G3b 1002.9
HM, tempered with medium grit, grey core. Pale reddish brown plain exterior and interior. RD 11, H (pres.) 4.5.

11. G3b 1004.2
HM, tempered with medium white grit. Grey burnished exterior. RD 23, H (pres.) 3.4.

12. G3b 1009.6
HM, coarse fabric tempered with chaff and medium-coarse grit. Pale greyish brown burnished exterior, pale greyish brown patchily smoothed interior. RD 26, H (pres.) 6.3.

13. G3b 1011.19
HM, tempered with medium grit. Colour varies from black, through dirty grey to brown, smoothed exterior and interior. RD 15, H (pres.) 6.2.

14. G3d 507.3
HM, tempered with medium grit. Reddish brown plain exterior and interior, blackened along the rim. RD 22, H (pres.) 4.2.

15. G3b (Pit 3)
    HM, tempered with medium white grit. Black burnished exterior, grey smoothed interior. RD 27, H (pres.) 5.5.
16. G3b (Pit 3)
    HM, tempered with medium grit, grey core. Pale grey smoothed exterior and interior. Part of a ledge handle set at the rim. RD 15, H (pres.) 4.2.
17. G3b (Pit 3)
    HM, tempered with medium grit. Greyish black burnished exterior and interior. Triangular ledge handle set at the rim. RD 17, H (pres.) 2.2.

Fig. 91

1. G1d 1302.1
   HM, tempered with chaff. Black throughout, burnished exterior, smoothed interior. RD 26, H (pres.) 9.4.
2. G1d 1303.7
   HM, tempered with medium grit. Black burnished exterior and interior. RD 12, H (pres.) 5.2.
3. G1d 1304.10
   HM, coarse fabric temperd with medium-coarse grit. Black burnished exterior, greyish brown smoothed interior. RD 22, H (pres.) 3.0.
4. G2b 1200.13
   HM, tempered with medium grit. Black burnished exterior, brown slightly burnished interior. RD 30, H (pres.) 5.5.
5. G2b 1200.4
   HM, tempered with medium grit. Dirty pale brown throughout, burnished exterior, smoothed interior. RD 19, H (pres.) 5.4.
6. G2b 1200.4
   HM, tempered with medium-fine grit. Pale brown slightly burnished exterior and interior. RD 17, H (pres.) 3.0.
7. G2b 1201.32
   HM, tempered with smedium grit. Black throughout, burnished exterior and interior. RD 28, H (pres.) 7.3. Previously published (French and Helms 1973: Fig. 2 no. 7).
8. G2b 1200.4
   HM, tempered with chaff and medium grit. Dirty pale greyish brown throughout, patchily smoothed exterior, plain interior. RD 11, H (pres.) 4.3.
9. G2b 1201.37
   HM, tempered with medium-coarse fabric, dark grey core. Pale greyish brown smoothed exterior and interior. RD 18, H (pres.) 3.0.
10. G2b 1201.6
    HM, coarse fabric tempered with medium-coarse grit. Reddish brown throughout, burnished exterior and interior. RD 13, H (pres.) 4.0. Previously published (French and Helms 1973: Fig. 3 no. 4).
11. G2b 1201.43.
    HM, tempered with medium-fine grit. Black throughout, burnished exterior and interior. RD 13, H (pres.) 4.1. Previously published (French and Helms 1973: Fig. 2 no. 3).
12. G2b 1202.2
    HM, tempered with medium grit. Black burnished exterior, dirty pale brown plain interior. RD 20, H (pres.) 7.4.
13. G2b 1202.5
    HM, tempered with medium grit. Pale grey burnished exterior, pale brown smoothed interior. Part of a small pellet set on the shoulder. RD 20, H (pres.) 4.8.

Fig. 92

1. G2b 1203.5
   HM, tempered with medium grit. Black burnished exterior, pale reddish brown smoothed interior. RD 20, H (pres.) 7.5. Previously published (French and Helms 1973: Fig. 2 no. 9).
2. G2b 1203.8
   HM, tempered with medium-coarse grit. Greyish black to pale grey plain exterior, pale reddish brown interior. Triangular ledge handle set at the rim. RD 28, H (pres.) 12.7.
3. G2b 1201.10
   HM, tempered with medium grit. Pale greyish brown throughout, plain exterior and interior. RD 10, H (pres.) 3.0.
4. G2b 1202.4
   HM, tempered with medium grit. Pale greyish brown throughout, smoothed exterior and interior. Small vertical lug handle pendent to the rim. RD 12, H (pres.) 6.0.
5. G2d 1102.16
   HM, tempered with chaff, dark grey core. Pale reddish brown throughout, smoothed exterior and interior. RD 18, H (pres.) 4.8.
6. G2b 1201.4
   HM, tempered with chaff and medium grit. Pale brown throughout, burnished exterior, smoothed interior. RD 14, H (pres.) 5.7.
7. G2d 1104.9
   HM, tempered with chaff and medium-coarse grit, dark grey core. Pale greyish brown throughout, slightly burnished exterior, smoothed interior. RD 21, H (pres.) 5.7.
8. G3d 507.4
   HM, tempered with chaff and medium grit. Plain greyish black throughout. Rough exterior and interior. RD 28, H (pres.) 6.3.
9. G3d 506.52
   HM, tempered with medium grit. Pale greyish brown and black mottled exterior and interior, stroke smoothed in parts. RD 18, H (pres.) 3.3.
10. G3d 506.52
    HM, tempered with medium grit. Black throughout, burnished exterior and interior. RD 14, H (pres.) 3.3.
11. G1b 1401.11
    HM, tempered with chaff and medium grit, grey core. Brown burnished exterior, brown smoothed interior. RD 34, H (pres.) 3.1.
12. G1b 1401.5
    HM, tempered with chaff and medium grit. Plain black exterior except along the rim, which is pale greyish brown. Pale reddish brown interior. RD 33, H (pres.) 6.2.
13. G1b 1401.4
    HM, tempered with medium grit. Pale grey throughout, burnished exterior and interior. RD 21, H (pres.) 3.2.

Fig. 93

1. G1b 1400.1.
   HM, tempered with medium grit. Black burnished exterior, pale brown plain interior. RD 25, H (pres.) 3.3.
2. G1d 1303.24
   HM, tempered with medium grit. Brown throughout, burnished exterior, smoothed interior. RD 20, H (pres.) 5.1.

3. G1d 1303.15
HM, coarse fabric tempered with coarse grit, dark grey core. Pale brown smoothed exterior blackened in patches, pale brown plain interior. RD 18, H (pres.) 5.2.

4. G1d 1304.14
HM, tempered with medium grit. Black throughout, burnished exterior and interior. Triangular ledge handle set at the rim. RD 22, H (pres.) 3.3.

5. G1d 1304.14
HM, tempered with chaff and a little medium grit. Black burnished exterior, reddish buff smoothed interior. RD 28, H (pres.) 3.6.

6. G1d 1300.3
HM, tempered with chaff and medium grit. Black patchily smoothed exterior except along rim, which is plain pale brown, interior is plain reddish brown. RD 28, H (pres.) 4.9.

7. G1d 1303.6
HM, tempered with medium grit. Black burnished exterior, pale brown smoothed interior. RD 22, H (pres.) 6.0.

8. G1d 1304.7
HM, tempered with medium grit, dark grey core. Brown plain interior and exterior. RD 20, H (pres.) 2.2.

9. G1d 1303.34
HM, tempered with medium grit. Black throughout, burnished exterior, smoothed interior. Vertical lug handle pendent to rim. RD 23, H (pres.) 3.3.

10. G1d 1303.28
HM, tempered with chaff and a little medium grit, grey core. Pale brown burnished exterior, pale brown smoothed interior. RD 23, H (pres.) 4.2.

11. G1d 1300.7
HM, tempered with medium grit and a little chaff. Black throughout, burnished exterior and interior. RD 16, H (pres.) 5.2.

12. G1d 1300.6
HM, tempered with medium grit and a little chaff. Black throughout, burnished exterior, smoothed interior. Solid tab handle vertically pendent to rim. RD 16, H (pres.) 4.3.

13. G1d 1302.2
HM, coarse fabric tempered with medium-coarse grit. Dirty greyish brown burnished exterior, reddish buff plain interior. Part of a ledge handle set at the rim. RD 33, H (pres.) 8.2.

Fig. 94

1. G1d 1300.6
HM, tempered with chaff, grey core. Reddish brown burnished exterior, reddish brown smoothed interior. RD 40, H (pres.) 5.9.

2. G1d 1300.7
HM, tempered with chaff and medium grit. Black throughout, burnished exterior and interior. RD 27, H (pres.) 4.0.

3. G1d 1300.7
HM, tempered with medium grit. Black burnished exterior, brown slightly burnished interior. RD 17, H (pres.) 7.5.

4. G1d 1300.7
HM, tempered with chaff and a little medium grit. Black throughout, burnished exterior and interior. RD 18, H (pres.) 4.8.

5. G1d 1303.16
HM, tempered with medium grit. Black slightly burnished exterior, dark brown to black smoothed interior. Part of a ledge handle set at the rim. RD 11, H (pres.) 3.9.

6. G1d 1303.15
HM, tempered with medium grit. Black burnished exterior except along rim, which is pale brown smoothed, like the interior. RD 21, H (pres.) 3.6.

7. G1d 1303.17
HM, tempered with medium grit. Black burnished exterior, pale brown smoothed interior. RD 18, H (pres.) 6.0.

8. G1d 1303.18
HM, tempered with chaff. Black burnished exterior except along the rim which is brown burnished, like the interior. RD 24, H (pres.) 5.2.

9. G1d 1303.20
HM, coarse fabric tempered with chaff and coarse grit. Black burnished exterior, pale reddish brown smoothed interior. RD 28, H (pres.) 6.0.

10. G1d 1303.31
HM, tempered with medium grit. Black burnished exterior, dirty pale brown smoothed interior. Triangular ledge handle set at the rim. RD 20, H (pres.) 3.2.

11. G1d 1304.7
HM, tempered with chaff and medium grit, grey core. Black burnished exterior, reddish brown smoothed interior. RD 36, H (pres.) 9.4.

Fig. 95

1. G2b 1200.4
HM, tempered with chaff and medium grit. Black burnished exterior, pale brown smoothed interior. RD 29, H (pres.) 8.7.

2. G2b 1200.4
HM, tempered with medium grit. Black burnished exterior, pale brown smoothed interior. RD 22, H (pres.) 8.7.

3. G2b 1200.4
HM, tempered with medium grit. Pale greyish brown burnished exterior, pale brown smoothed interior. RD 24, H (pres.) 8.9.

4. G2b 1200.7
HM, tempered with chaff, dark grey core. Pale brown smoothed exterior, reddish brown slightly burnished interior. RD 32, H (pres.) 9.0.

5. G2b 1201.10
HM, coarse fabric tempered with chaff and medium-coarse grit. Black burnished exterior except along rim, which is plain buff, like interior. RD 18, H (pres.) 4.2.

6. G2b 1200.4
HM, tempered with medium grit. Black burnished exterior, reddish brown slightly burnished interior. RD 22, H (pres.) 3.6.

7. G2b 1201.10
HM, tempered with medium white grit. Brown throughout, burnished exterior and interior. RD 25, H (pres.) 6.2.

8. G2b 1201.10
HM, tempered with medium grit, pale brown core. Pale pinkish brown plain exterior and interior. RD 22, H (pres.) 3.6.

9. G2b 1201.12
HM, coarse fabric tempered with medium-coarse grit. Black throughout, burnished exterior and interior. RD 30, H (pres.) 4.5.

10. G2b 1201.10
HM, tempered with medium grit, pale grey core. Pinkish red plain exterior and interior. RD 20, H (pres.) 6.4.

Fig. 96

1. G2b 1201.13
HM, tempered with medium grit, dark grey core fired to pale brown. Dark grey burnished exterior, dark brown slightly burnished interior. RD 30, H (pres.) 6.4.
2. G2b 1201.13
HM, tempered with chaff. Black burnished exterior, pale brown smoothed interior. RD 24, H (pres.) 2.5.
3. G2b 1201.15
HM, tempered with chaff and medium-coarse grit. Black burnished exterior, pale brown smoothed interior. RD 36, H (pres.) 5.8.
4. G2b 1201.16
HM, coarse fabric tempered with chaff and medium-coarse grit, dark grey core. Dirty pale grey burnished exterior, smoothed reddish brown interior. RD 30, H (pres.) 5.2.
5. G2b 1201.17
HM, tempered with chaff and medium-coarse grit. Brown throughout, smoothed exterior, rough interior. RD 36, H (pres.) 7.9.
6. G2b 1201.18
HM, tempered with chaff and medium grit. Pale brown throughout, burnished exterior, smoothed interior. RD 47, H (pres.) 7.2.
7. G2b 1201.18
HM, tempered with medium grit, pale brown core. Reddish brown burnished exterior and interior, grey patch on the exterior. Part of a triangular ledge handle set at the rim. RD 38, H (pres.) 7.9.
8. G2b 1201.18
HM, tempered with medium grit. Pale greyish brown throughout, smoke blackened patch on the exterior, burnished exterior, smoothed interior. RD 20, H (pres.) 4.6.
9. G2b 1201.32
HM, bempered with chaff and a little medium grit, grey core. Pale greyish brown smoothed exterior and interior. RD 15, H (pres.) ;2.7.
10. G2b 1201.19
HM, tempered with chaff and a little medium grit, grey core. Reddish brown burnished exterior, smoothed brown interior. RD 26, H (pres.) 8.7.

Fig. 97

1. G2b 1201.18
HM, tempered with chaff, grey core. Red and pale brown mottled throughout, plain on both surfaces. Black patch from firing on exterior. Previously published (French and Helms 1973: Fig. 3 no. 6). RD rim 16, H 15.4.
2. G2b 1201.22
HM, tempered with medium grit, grey core. Dirty pale greyish brown plain exterior, grey plain interior. RD 26, H (pres.) 4.8.
3. G2b 1201.24
HM, tempered with medium grit. Pale grey burnished exterior, brown slightly smoothed interior. Part of a ledge handle set at the rim. RD 36, H (pres.) 4.9.

4. G2b 1201.24
HM, tempered with chaff, dark grey core. Reddish brown burnished exterior except along the rim, which is black burnished like the interior. RD 20, H (pres.) 5.4.
5. G2b 1201.24
HM, tempered with chaff and a little grit. Black burnished exterior, smoothed dark brown interior. RD 12, H (pres.) 3.7.
6. G2b 1201.24
HM, tempered with chaff. Black burnished exterior, pale smoothed brown interior. RD 22, H (pres.) 5.4.
7. G2b 1201.25
HM, tempered with medium grit. Dirty greyish black throughout, plain interior except along the rim, which is slightly burnished like the exterior. RD 30, H (pres.) 7.2.
8. G2b 1201.25
HM, tempered with chaff, grey core. Pale greyish brown smoothed exterior and interior. RD 28, H (pres.) 11.4.
9. G2b 1201.25
HM, tempered with chaff and a little grit. Black burnished exterior, greyish black smoothed interior. RD 26, H (pres.) 6.5.

Fig. 98

1. G2b 1201.25
HM, tempered with medium grit, pale brown core. Black burnished exterior, pinkish pale brown smoothed interior. RD 34, H (pres.) 8.2.
2. G2b 1201.26
HM, tempered with chaff and a little medium grit. Dark grey slightly burnished exterior, pale brown smoothed interior. RD 40, H (pres.) 3.8.
3. G2b 1201.10
HM, tempered with medium-coarse white grit, dark grey core. Reddish brown plain exterior and interior. Part of a triangular ledge handle set at the rim. RD 32, H (pres.) 3.7.
4. G2b 1201.26
HM, tempered with medium grit, dark grey core. Pale brown smoothed exterior, reddish brown plain interior. RD 18, H (pres.) 6.0.
5. G2b 1201.26
HM, tempered with chaff and a little grit. Black burnished exterior, dark brown smoothed interior. RD 28, H (pres.) 7.2.
6. G2b 1201.27
HM, tempered with chaff and medium grit. Pale brown smoothed interior except along the inside of rim, which is black burnished like the exterior. Part of a grooved geometric pattern survives. RD 25, H (pres.) 6.6.
7. G2b 1201.28
HM, tempered with chaff and a little grit, dark grey core. Pale grey burnished exterior, grey rough interior. RD 22, H (pres.) 5.4.
8. G2b 1201.30
HM, tempered with chaff and medium grit. Pale greyish brown throughout, burnished exterior, smoothed interior. RD 26, H (pres.) 3.8.
9. G2b 1201.28
HM, tempered with chaff and medium-coarse grit, dark grey core. Pale reddish brown smoothed exterior and interior. RD 18, H (pres.) 6.4.

Fig. 99

1. G2b 1201.31
   HM, tempered with chaff and medium grit. Black burnished exterior, pale greyish brown smoothed interior. RD 24, H (pres.) 3.9.
2. G2b 1201.36
   HM, tempered with medium grit. Dirty dark brown throughout, plain exterior and interior. RD 28, H (pres.) 4.4.
3. G2b 1201.4.1
   HM, tempered with medium grit. Black burnished exterior except along the rim, which is pale brown, reddish brown smoothed interior. RD 20, H (pres.) 4.8.
4. G2b 1201.40
   HM, tempered with chaff and a little medium grit. Black burnished exterior, black and grey mottled and smoothed interior. RD 22, H (pres.) 4.9.
5. G1b 1304.5
   HM, tempered with medium grit, black burnished exterior, pale greyish brown smoothed interior. RD 19, H (pres.) 2.7.
6. G2b 1201.40
   HM, tempered with chaff and a little medium grit. Black and pale greyish brown mottled and smoothed exterior, pale reddish brown plain interior. RD 17, H (pres.) 3.3.
7. G2b 1201.40
   HM, tempered with chaff and a little medium grit. Greyish black burnished exterior, pale reddish brown smoothed interior. RD 35, H (pres.) 5.4.
8. G2b 1201.41
   HM, tempered with chaff. Pale greyish brown throughout, smoothed exterior and interior. RD 30, H (pres.) 4.2.
9. G2b 1201.41
   HM, tempered with chaff and medium grit. Pale brown throughout, burnished exterior and interior. RD 50, H (pres.) 6.9.
10. G2b 1201.41
    HM, tempered with chaff, grey core. Pale brown throughout, burnished exterior, smoothed interior. RD 38, H (pres.) 8.0.
11. G2b 1201.41
    HM, tempered with chaff and medium grit. Pale brown and black mottled and burnished exterior, pale brown smoothed interior. RD 26, H (pres.) 4.9.
12. G2b 1201.42
    HM, tempered with medium grit. Pale greyish brown throughout, burnished exterior and interior. RD 32, H (pres.) 1.9.
13. G2b 1201.41
    HM, tempered with chaff and medium grit. Black burnished exterior, pale brown smoothed interior. RD 22, H (pres.) 2.7.

Fig. 100

1. G2b 1201.41
   HM, tempered with medium-fine grit. Pale pinkish brown throughout, plain exterior and interior. RD 12, H (pres.) 5.4.
2. G2b 1201.47
   HM, tempered with medium grit. Greyish black plain exterior, brown plain interior. RD 14, H (pres.) 4.5.
3. G2b 1201.94
   HM, tempered with medium-coarse grit. Greyish black burnished exterior, pale brown smoothed interior. RD 30, H (pres.) 5.4.
4. G2b 1201.6
   HM, tempered with medium-coarse white grit. Reddish brown burnished exterior and interior. RD 18, H (pres.) 5.2.
5. G2b 1203.2
   HM, tempered with medium grit. Pale grey slightly smoothed exterior, grey plain interior. RD 20, H (pres.) 3.3.
6. G2b 1201.6
   HM, tempered with medium white grit, dark grey core. Pale brown plain exterior and interior. RD 30, H (pres.) 6.9.
7. G2b 1202.11
   HM, tempered with chaff and coarse grit, grey core. Greyish brown slightly smoothed exterior, greyish brown plain interior. RD 38, H (pres.) 7.9.
8. G2b 1202.11
   HM, coarse fabric tempered with chaff and a little coarse grit. Black burnished exterior, brown slightly burnished interior. RD 30, H (pres.) 6.1.
9. G2b 1202.11
   HM, tempered with chaff and medium grit. Black burnished exterior, pale grey smoothed interior. RD 34, H (pres.) 6.9.
10. G2b 1202.13
    HM, tempered with medium grit. Black burnished exterior, pale brown plain interior. RD 26, H (pres.) 7.0.
11. G2b 1202.2.33
    HM, tempered with chaff. Reddish buff throughout, plain interior and exterior. RD 26, H (pres.) 6.9.

Fig. 101

1. G2b 1202.4
   HM, tempered with chaff and medium grit. Pale greyish brown throughout, slightly burnished exterior, smoothed interior. RD 26, H (pres.) 5.4.
2. G2b 1202.5
   HM, tempered with chaff and a little medium grit. Black burnished exterior, pale greyish buff smoothed interior. RD 16, H (pres.) 7.3.
3. G2b 1202.13
   HM, tempered with chaff and a little medium grit. Black slightly burnished exterior, reddish smoothed interior. RD 24, H (pres.) 6.2.
4. G2b 1202.9
   HM, tempered with chaff and medium grit. Greyish black plain exterior except along the rim, which is pale greyish brown like the interior. RD 36, H (pres.) 4.6.
5. G2b 1202.9
   HM, tempered with chaff and medium grit. Pale grey burnished exterior, pale brown smoothed interior. RD 34, H (pres.) 4.5.
6. G2b 1203.2
   HM, tempered with chaff and medium grit. Black burnished exterior, reddish brown smoothed interior. RD 26, H (pres.) 4.6.
7. G2b 1203.2
   HM, coarse fabric tempered with chaff and medium-coarse grit. Black burnished exterior, reddish brown plain interior. RD 26, H (pres.) 6.4. Previously published (French and Helms 1973: Fig. 2 no. 8).
8. G2d 1100.6
   HM, tempered with chaff and a little medium grit. Pale reddish brown throughout, plain exterior and

interior. RD 24, H (pres.) 6.6.

9. G2d 1100.6
HM, tempered with chaff and medium grit, dark grey core. Pale grey plain exterior and interior. RD 28, H (pres.) 3.6.

10. G2d 1100.6
HM, tempered with medium white grit. Pale reddish brown throughout, smoothed exterior, plain interior. RD 21, H (pres.) 4.3.

Fig. 102

1. G2d 1102.16
HM, tempered with chaff and a little medium grit. Black burnished exterior, pale reddish brown smoothed interior. RD 28, H (pres.) 15.3.

2. G2d 1102.16
HM, coarse fabric tempered with chaff and a little coarse white grit, black core. Dirty greyish brown exterior and interior. Part of a triangular ledge handle set at the rim. RD 25, H (pres.) 4.5.

3. G2d 1102.16
HM, coarse fabric tempered with chaff and medium-coarse grit. Brown throughout, smoothed exterior, slightly smoothed interior. RD 21, H (pres.) 5.2.

4. G2d 1102.16
HM, tempered with chaff and medium grit, grey core. Brown smoothed exterior and interior. RD 21, H (pres.) 2.5.

5. G2d 1102.16
HM, tempered with chaff and coarse white grit, black core. Dirty greyish black to brown exterior and interior, both surfaces are plain. Triangular ledge handle set at the rim. RD 24, H (pres.) 7.6.

6. G2d 1104.1
HM, coarse fabric tempered with coarse white grit, black core. Dirty pale grey plain exterior, reddish brown plain interior. Triangular ledge handle set at the rim. RD 30, H (pres.) 4.8.

7. G2d 1102.9
HM, tempered with chaff, dark grey core. Reddish brown burnished exterior and interior. RD 40, H (pres.) 4.9.

8. G2f 1103.12
HM, tempered with chaff, grey core. Pale reddish brown burnished exterior, pale reddish brown smoothed interior. RD 28, H (pres.) 5.4.

9. G2d 1103.6
HM, tempered with medium grit, grey core. Pale greyish brown plain exterior and interior. RD 19, H (pres.) 5.2.

Fig. 103

1. G2d 1104.4
HM, tempered with chaff and medium-coarse grit, dark grey core. Brown to pale brown burnished exterior, brown to pale brown smoothed interior. RD 26, H (pres.) 3.0.

2. G2d 1104.1
HM, tempered with chaff and medium grit, black core. Dirty grey to reddish brown slightly burnished exterior, pale reddish brown plain interior. RD 30, H (pres.) 3.9.

3. G2d 1104.2
HM, tempered with chaff and a little medium grit, dark grey core. Pale reddish brown smoothed exterior and interior. RD 10, H (pres.) 2.6.

4. G2d 1104.4
HM, tempered with chaff and a little medium grit, dark grey core. Pale reddish brown smoothed exterior and interior. RD 15, H (pres.) 3.8.

5. G2d 1100.7
HM, tempered with chaff and medium white grit. Pale brown throughout, burnished exterior and interior. RD 18, H (pres.) 3.6.

6. G3b 1000.2
HM, tempered with medium grit, grey core. Brown burnished exterior and interior. RD 34, H (pres.) 4.1.

7. G3b 1000.10
HM, tempered with chaff and medium grit. Black burnished exterior, reddish brown burnished interior. RD 31, H (pres.) 7.0.

8. G3b 1008.1
HM, tempered with medium grit. Reddish brown throughout, burnished exterior, smoothed interior, smoke blackened arounRD. RD 19, H (pres.) 4.8.

9. G3b 1002.5
HM, tempered with chaff. Dirty grey throughout, plain exterior and interior. RD 21, H (pres.) 7.4.

10. G3b 1005.5
HM, tempered with medium grit. Greyish brown throughout, burnished exterior and interior. RD 27, H (pres.) 3.6.

11. G3b 1008.5
HM, tempered with medium grit. Black throughout, burnished exterior and interior. RD 19, H (pres.) 2.7.

12. G3b 1009.2
HM, tempered with chaff and medium white grit, dark grey core. Reddish brown slightly burnished exterior and interior. RD 34, H (pres.) 3.3.

13. G3b 1011.13
HM, tempered with chaff and medium grit. Pale greyish brown throughout, burnished exterior and interior. RD 33, H (pres.) 3.1.

Fig. 104

1. G3b 1000.2
HM, tempered with medium grit. Grey throughout, burnished exterior and interior. RD 35, H (pres.) 3.5.

2. G3d 507.3
HM, tempered with medium grit, buff core. Greyish black burnished exterior and interior. RD 16, H (pres.) 3.5.

3. G3d 507
HM, tempered with medium grit. Black throughout, burnished exterior and interior. RD 28, H (pres.) 2.7.

4. G3d 507.3
HM, tempered with medium grit, reddish brown core. Black burnished exterior, greyish black smoothed interior. RD 30, H (pres.) 11.3.

5. G3d 507.3
HM, tempered with medium grit. Grey throughout, burnished exterior and interior. RD 29, H (pres.) 3.4.

6. G3d 507.3
HM, tempered with medium grit. Black burnished exterior, grey burnished interior. RD 29, H (pres.) 3.5.

7. G3d 507.3
HM, tempered with medium grit. Grey throughout, burnished exterior and interior. RD 26, H (pres.) 3.0.

8. G3d 507.3
   HM, tempered with medium grit. Black burnished exterior, pale grey burnished interior. RD 28, H (pres.) 3.0.
9. G3d 507.3
   HM, tempered with medium grit. Black throughout, burnished exterior and interior. RD 36, H (pres.) 6.4.
10. G3d 507.3
    HM, tempered with medium grit. Greyish black burnished exterior, black burnished interior. RD 25, H (pres.) 3.9.
11. G3d 507.3
    HM, tempered with medium grit, pale brown core. Black burnished exterior and interior. RD 22, H (pres.) 3.0.
12. G3d 507.3
    HM, tempered with medium grit, pale brown core. Black burnished exterior and interior. RD 24, H (pres.) 3.0.

Fig. 105

1. G3d 507.3
   HM, tempered with medium grit, pale brown core. Black burnished exterior and interior. RD 28, H (pres.) 3.0.
2. G3d 507.3
   HM, tempered with medium grit. Grey burnished exterior and interior. RD 34, H (pres.) 3.3.
3. G3d 507.3
   HM, tempered with medium grit. Grey burnished exterior and interior. RD 27, H (pres.) 4.5.
4. G3d 507.3
   HM, tempered with medium grit. Greyish black burnished exterior and interior, brown along the rim. RD 27, H (pres.) 3.6.
5. G3d 507.3
   HM, tempered with medium grit. Grey throughout, burnished exterior and interior. RD 23, H (pres.) 2.7.
6. G3d 507.3
   HM, tempered with medium white grit. Black throughout, burnished exterior and interior. RD 27, H (pres.) 2.7.
7. G3d 507.3
   HM, tempered with medium grit. Black throughout, burnished exterior and interior. RD 17, H (pres.) 1.4.
8. G3d 507.4
   HM, tempered with medium grit. Black throughout, burnished exterior and interior. RD 17, H (pres.) 3.9.
9. G3d 507.4
   HM, tempered with medium white grit. Black throughout, burnished exterior and interior. RD 28, H (pres.) 4.2.
10. G3d 507.4
    HM, tempered with medium grit. Grey burnished exterior, pale greyish brown burnished along the rim, black burnished interior. RD 21, H (pres.) 2.6.
11. G3d 507.6
    HM, tempered with medium grit. Greyish black throughout, burnished exterior and interior. RD 26, H (pres.) 2.7.
12. G3d 507.6
    HM, tempered with medium-fine grit. Greyish black throughout, burnished exterior and interior. RD 25, H (pres.) 4.5.

13. G3d 507.8
    HM, tempered with medium-fine grit. Greyish black throughout, burnished exterior and interior. RD 20, H (pres.) 3.9.
14. G3d 509.7
    HM, tempered with medium grit. Greyish black throughout, burnished exterior and interior. RD 23, H (pres.) 3.3.

Fig. 106

1. G3d 509.14
   HM, tempered with medium grit. Grey throughout, burnished exterior and interior. RD 20, H (pres.) 4.8.
2. G3b 1000.2
   HM, tempered with medium white grit. Grey throughout, burnished exterior, smoothed interior. RD 27, H (pres.) 4.9.
3. G3b 1000.2
   HM, tempered with medium white grit, grey inner core. Brown burnished exterior and interior. RD 28, H (pres.) 4.2.
4. G3b 1001.9
   HM, tempered with medium-fine grit. Pale greyish brown throughout, burnished exterior and interior. RD 26, H (pres.) 3.3.
5. G3b 1005.6
   HM, tempered with chaff and medium white grit. Brown throughout, plain exterior and interior, except along the top of rim, which is burnished. RD 21, H (pres.) 3.1.
6. G3b 1008.6
   HM, tempered with medium-coarse white grit, grey core. Dirty black to brown, smoothed exterior except along the rim, which is black burnished, brown smoothed interior. RD 22, H (pres.) 2.5.
7. G3b 1008.5
   HM, tempered with medium-coarse white grit. Dirty greyish brown throughout, burnished exterior and interior. RD 21, H (pres.) 3.6.
8. G2b 1200.4
   HM, tempered with chaff and medium grit. Black burnished exterior, dark grey slightly smoothed interior. BD 8, H (pres.) 1.5.
9. G2b 1201.27
   HM, tempered with chaff and a little grit. Dark brown to black burnished exterior, black smoothed interior. BD 14, H (pres.) 3.1.
10. G2b 1201.41
    HM, tempered with chaff and medium grit, dark grey core. Pale brown burnished exterior and interior. BD 20, H (pres.) 2.1.
11. G2b 1201.74
    HM, coarse fabric tempered with chaff and medium-coarse grit. Manufactured in two layers. Pale brown throughout, plain exterior and interior. Smoke blackened around the base. BD 14, H (pres.) 7.2.
12. G2b 1203.2
    HM, coarse fabric tempered with chaff. Black throughout, burnished exterior, plain interior. BD 18, H (pres.) 5.4.
13. G2d 1103.12
    HM, tempered with chaff and a little medium grit. Reddish brown smoothed exterior, dirty greyish brown smoothed interior. BD 18, H (pres.) 3.0.

Fig. 107
1. G2d 1102.9
   HM, tempered with chaff and a little medium grit, grey core. Reddish brown and grey mottled and smoothed exterior, greyish black plain interior. BD 24, H (pres.) 9.4.
2. G2d 1104.4
   HM, tempered with chaff, dark grey core. Pale reddish brown smoothed exterior and interior. BD 30, H (pres.) 2.7.
3. G3b 1001.3
   HM, tempered with medium grit. Reddish brown throughout, burnished exterior, smoothed interior. BD 24, H (pres.) 3.1.
4. G3b 1002.7
   HM, tempered with medium grit. Dirty reddish brown throughout, plain exterior and interior, smoke blackened in parts. BD 30, H (pres.) 2.7.
5. G3b 1001.3
   HM, tempered with medium grit and a little chaff. Brown throughout, plain exterior and interior. BD 14, H (pres.) 2.4.
6. G2b 1201.18
   HM, coarse fabric tempered with chaff and medium-coarse grit. Pale greyish brown throughout, plain smoke blackened exterior, plain interior. BD 15, H (pres.) 3.6.
7. G2b 1201.20
   HM, tempered with chaff and medium grit, grey core. Black and reddish brown mottled exterior and interior, burnished exterior, smoothed interior. BD 18, H (pres.) 3.3.
8. G2b 1201.24
   HM, tempered with chaff and a little coarse grit. Pale grey burnished exterior, grey burnished interior. BD 22, H (pres.) 4.8.
9. G2b 1201.24
   HM, coarse fabric tempered with coarse grit. Black burnished exterior, pale brown rough interior. BD 26, H (pres.) 4.2.
10. G2b 1203.3
    HM, tempered with chaff and a little coarse grit, grey core. Pale reddish brown to grey exterior and interior, plain to slightly smoothed on both surfaces. BD 20, H (pres.) 4.4.
11. G2b 1201.22
    HM, tempered with medium grit. Pale greyish brown throughout, burnished exterior, smoothed interior. BD 26, H (pres.) 3.9.
12. G2b 1201.42
    HM, coarse fabric tempered with coarse grit. Black throughout, burnished exterior, rough interior. BD 25, H (pres.) 5.4.

Fig. 108
1. G2b 1201.43
   HM, coarse black fabric tempered with coarse grit. Black burnished exterior, reddish brown plain interior. BD 15.5, H (pres.) 3.3.
2. G3b 1001.1
   HM, coarse fabric tempered with chaff and coarse grit. Black burnished exterior, pale reddish brown plain interior. BD 24, H (pres.) 5.8.
3. G3b 1013.4
   HM, coarse fabric tempered with chaff and coarse white grit, dark grey core. Dirty greyish brown exterior and interior, plain on both surfaces. BD 22, H (pres.) 4.2.

4. G3b 1018.5
   HM, coarse fabric tempered with chaff. Dirty brown to pale brown exterior, brownish black rough interior. BD 22, H (pres.) 5.9.
5. G2b 1200.4
   HM, tempered with chaff and medium grit. Black burnished exterior and underneath the base, pale greyish brown plain interior. Decorated around the exterior with broad horizontal flutes. D (max.) 16, H 13.6. Previously published (French and Helms 1973: Fig. 2 no. 11).
6. G2b 1201.14
   HM, tempered with chaff and medium grit. Black burnished exterior, pale brown plain interior. Decorated with deep horizontal flutes around the middle. RD 20, H (pres.) 12.9.
7. G2b 1201.24
   HM, tempered with chaff. Black burnished exterior, pale pinkish brown plain interior except along the edge, which is grey. Horizontally grooved exterior. RD 26, H (pres.) 6.5.
8. G2b 1200.4
   HM, tempered with chaff and medium grit. Black throughout, burnished exterior, smoothed interior. RD 12, H (pres.) 3.6.
9. G2b 1202.8
   HM, tempered with chaff and medium grit. Black burnished exterior, pale brown plain interior. Decorated around the exterior with broad horizontal flutes. D (max.) 20, H 13.1.
10. G2b 1202.4
    HM, tempered with chaff and a little medium grit. Black burnished exterior, pale greyish brown smoothed interior. Decorated round the exterior with broad horizontal flutes. RD 18, H (pres.) 6.0.

Fig. 109
1. G2b 1202.5
   HM, tempered with medium grit, pinkish cream throughout, smoothed exterior and interior. BD 10, H (pres.) 3.0.
2. G2b 1201.16
   HM, tempered with chaff and a little medium grit, dark grey core. Pale greyish brown throughout, rough interior, plain exterior. BD 10, H (pres.) 2.9.
3. G2b 1201.39
   HM, tempered with medium grit and a little chaff, greyish cream throughout, smoothed exterior and interior. BD 10, H (pres.) 2.7.
4. G2b 1202.8
   HM, tempered with medium grit, pinkish cream throughout, smoothed exterior, plain interior. Smoke blackened in parts on the exterior. BD 10, H (pres.) 2.7.
5. G3b 1005.4
   HM, tempered with medium grit, pale creamy brown throughout. Plain exterior and interior. BD 20, H (pres.) 8.3.
6. G2b 1201.15
   HM, tempered with medium-coarse grit, grey core. Pale creamy brown fabric, plain exterior and interior. BD 16, H (pres.) 2.7.

Fig. 110

1. G2b 1203.8
   HM, tempered with medium grit, dark grey core. Pale pinkish brown exterior and interior, smoothed exterior, plain interior. RD 50, H (pres.) 8.8.
2. G1b 1401.5
   HM, coarse fabric tempered with chaff and some grit, dark grey core. Brown burnished exterior, brown smoothed interior. RD 36, H (pres.) 5.1.
3. G1d 1303.18
   HM, tempered with chaff and a little medium grit, dark grey core. Reddish brown slightly burnished exterior, reddish brown smoothed interior. RD 46, H (pres.) 6.4.
4. G1d 1303.8
   HM, tempered with chaff. Black burnished exterior, pale reddish brown smoothed interior. RD 40, H (pres.) 6.3.
5. G2b 1200.4
   HM, tempered with chaff and medium-coarse grit. Black burnished exterior, pale brown smoothed interior. RD 40, H (pres.) 4.4.
6. G2b 1200.4
   HM, tempered with chaff and a little medium grit. Black throughout, slightly burnished exterior and interior. RD 50, H (pres.) 6.0.
7. G2b 1201.10
   HM, coarse fabric tempered with chaff and medium-coarse grit, grey core. Pale brown plain exterior and interior. RD 50, H (pres.) 8.0.
8. G2b 1201.16
   HM, tempered with chaff and a little medium grit. Pale greyish brown throughout, slightly burnished exterior and interior. RD 44, H (pres.) 10.7.
9. G2b 1201.16
   HM, tempered with chaff. Black burnished exterior, reddish brown smoothed interior. RD 34, H (pres.) 8.0.
10. G2b 1201.17
    HM, tempered with medium-coarse grit. Greyish black slightly burnished exterior, reddish brown smoothed interior. RD 40, H (pres.) 5.6.

Fig. 111

1. G2b 1202.11
   HM, coarse fabric tempered with chaff and medium-coarse grit. Pale reddish brown and black mottled and smoothed interior except along the rim, which is black burnished like the exterior. RD 45, H (pres.) 17.5.
2. G2d 1103.6
   HM, tempered with chaff, grey core. Reddish brown smoothed interior and exterior. RD 40, H (pres.) 7.2.
3. G2d 1103.12
   HM, tempered with medium-coarse grit, dark grey core. Reddish brown slightly burnished exterior, reddish brown smoothed interior. RD 40, H (pres.) 6.4.
4. G2d 1003.12
   HM, tempered with chaff and medium to coarse grit, dark grey core. Pale reddish brown burnished exterior, pale reddish brown smoothed interior. RD 40, H (pres.) 6.8.
5. G2d 1103.3
   HM, tempered with chaff and medium grit, dark grey core. Reddish brown slightly burnished exterior, reddish brown smoothed interior. RD 32, H (pres.) 6.4.

6. G2d 1104.6
   HM, tempered with medium-coarse grit, pale brown core. Brown burnished exterior and interior. RD 36, H (pres.) 5.5.
7. G3d 507.4
   HM, tempered with chaff and medium grit, greyish brown core. Brown plain exterior and interior. RD 42, H (pres.) 6.3.
8. G2b 1201.24
   HM, tempered with chaff and medium grit. Black burnished exterior, pale pinkish brown smoothed interior. Decorated with a series of horizontal grooves. RD 52, H (pres.) 9.1.

Fig. 112

1. G2b 1201.18
   HM, tempered with chaff and medium grit. Black throughout, burnished exterior and interior. RD 40, H (pres.) 8.0.
2. G2b 1201.18
   HM, coarse fabric tempered with chaff. Black and pale brown mottled throughout, burnished exterior, slightly burnished interior. RD 40, H (pres.) 6.4.
3. G2b 1201.24
   HM, tempered with chaff and medium grit, dark grey core. Pale greyish brown exterior and interior, burnished exterior, smoothed interior. RD 50, H (pres.) 7.9.
4. G2b 1201.24
   HM, coarse fabric tempered with chaff and a little medium-coarse grit. Pale greyish brown throughout, burnished exterior, smoothed interior. RD 42, H (pres.) 7.2.
5. G2b 1201.24
   HM, tempered with chaff and a little medium grit, dark grey core. Pale grey brown burnished exterior, pale brown smoothed interior. RD 44, H (pres.) 12.4.
6. G2b 1201.24
   HM, tempered with chaff, grey core. Pale greyish brown exterior and interior, smoothed exterior, rough interior. RD 38, H (pres.) 15.2. Previously published (French and Helms 1973: Fig. 3 no. 10).
7. G2b 1201.24
   HM, tempered with chaff and a little medium grit. Black burnished exterior, pale pinkish brown smoothed interior. RD 40, H (pres.) 4.8.
8. G2b 1201.32
   HM, tempered with chaff and medium grit, grey core. Pale greyish brown smoothed exterior and interior. RD 40, H (pres.) 4.7.
9. G2b 1201.17
   HM, tempered with chaff and a little medium-coarse grit. Pale brown to black smoothed exterior, pale brown slightly smoothed interior. RD 42, H (pres.) 5.6.

Fig. 113

1. G2b 1201.24
   HM, coarse fabric tempered with chaff and medium-coarse grit. Pale greyish brown throughout, burnished exterior, smoothed interior. RD 60, H (pres.) 23.4.
2. G2b 1201.24
   HM, tempered with chaff. Black burnished exterior, pale brown smoothed interior. RD 60, H (pres.) 22.8.

3. G2b 1202.13
   HM, tempered with medium-coarse grit. Pale brown burnished exterior, reddish brown smoothed interior. Part of a grooved pattern survives. H (pres.) 6.3.
4. G2b 1202.13
   HM, tempered with medium-coarse grit. Pale brown throughout, burnished exterior and interior. Part of a grooved and impressed pattern survives. H (pres.) 5.4.
5. G1d 1303.18
   HM, tempered with chaff and medium grit, cream core. Black burnished exterior, pale brown plain interior. Part of a grooved design survives. H (pres.) 7.1.
6. G1d 1303.6
   HM, tempered with chaff, grey core. Black burnished exterior, brown plain interior. Part of a grooved design survives. H (pres.) 10.4.
7. G1d 1303.16
   HM, tempered with medium grit. Black burnished exterior, pale brown interior. Part of a relief pattern survives. H (pres.) 7.4.

Fig. 114

1. G1d 1300.7
   HM, tempered with chaff and medium grit. Black burnished top, pale brown smoothed bottom. D 21, Th (max. pres.) 1.8.
2. G2b 1201.20
   HM, tempered with chaff. Pale greyish brown throughout, plain top and bottom. D 18, Th (max. pres.) 2.1.
3. G1d 1303.10
   HM, coarse black fabric tempered with coarse grit. Black slightly smoothed top, pale brown plain bottom. Part of a grooved pattern survives. D 28, Th (max. pres.) 1.4.
4. G1d 1303.8
   HM, tempered chaff. Black plain top, pale brown slightly burnished bottom. D 26, Th (max. pres.) 1.6.
5. G2b 1201.26
   HM, tempered with medium grit. Pale brown to cream throughout, plain on both surfaces. Part of a grooved pattern survives. D 22, Th (max. pres.) 1.4.

Fig. 115

1. G2d 1103.11
   HM, tempered with chaff and a little medium grit, grey core. Pale greyish brown slightly smoothed top, dirty greyish brown plain bottom. Decorated with a grooved design along the top edge. D 29, Th (max. pres.) 2.7.
2. G2b 1201.35
   HM, tempered with medium-coarse grit. Pale brown throughout, plain top and bottom. D 28, Th (max. pres.) 1.9.
3. G2b 1201.26
   HM, tempered with chaff, dark grey core. Pale greyish brown top and bottom, mostly plain with an occassional smoothed patch. D 26, Th (max. pres.) 2.0.
4. G2b 1201.27
   HM, tempered with chaff. Pale greyish brown throughout, slightly smoothed top, plain bottom.

Part of a grooved pattern on the top surface survives. D 14, Th (max. pres.) 1.3.

Fig. 116

1. G1d 1300.6
   HM, plain cream fabric tempered with medium grit. Exterior decoration, in reddish brown, consists of a linear design, possibly part of a row of hatched triangles. RD 15, H (pres.) 3.6.
2. G1d 1300.7
   HM, plain cream fabric tempered with medium grit. A spot of reddish brown paint on the interior. RD 11, H (pres.) 2.7.
3. G1d 1303.15
   HM, plain cream fabric tempered with medium grit. Interior decoration, in reddish brown, consists of a row of oblique strokes pendent to the rim. RD 13, H (pres.) 4.3.
4. G1d 1304.7
   HM, plain cream fabric tempered with medium grit. Exterior decoration, in reddish brown, consists of a wavy line and zig-zags(?). RD 16, H (pres.) 2.8.
5. G1d 1303.7
   HM, plain cream fabric tempered with medium grit. Decoration, in reddish brown, consists of a solid band on top of the rim. RD 30, H (pres.) 3.1.
6. G2b 1201.24
   HM, greyish cream fabric tempered with medium grit, smoothed on both surfaces. Interior decoration, in pinkish buff, consists of solid oblique lozenges pendent to the rim. RD 26, H (pres.) 3.0.
7. G2b 1201.41
   HM, plain cream fabric tempered with medium grit. Fugitive red painted design. RD 40, H (pres.) 7.3.
8. G2b 1201.6
   HM, plain cream fabric tempered with medium grit. Decoration, in brown, consists of a row of haphazardly painted oblique lines round the rim. RD 19, H (pres.) 2.8.
9. G2b 1201.28
   HM, plain cream fabric tempered with medium grit. Decoration, in red, consists of band round the exterior edge of the rim and short, oblique bands on the top of rim. RD 20, H (pres.) 3.5.
10. G1d 1303.5
    HM, tempered with medium grit. Cream smoothed exterior, plain reddish brown interior. Decoration, in brown, consists of a haphazardly painted wavy and horizontal lines on the exterior, and broad oblique strokes pendent to the interior rim. RD 34, H (pres.) 7.2.
11. G1d 1304.7
    HM, plain cream fabric tempered with medium grit. Interior decoration, in red, consists of oblique strokes pendent to the rim. RD 24, H (pres.) 3.1.
12. G2b 1202.5
    HM, plain cream fabric tempered with medium grit. Decoration, in brown, consists of a solid thin band on edge of exterior rim, and oblique strokes pendent to the interior rim. RD 26, H (pres.) 3.0.

Fig. 117

1. G1d 1303.7
   HM, plain cream fabric tempered with medium grit. Interior decoration, in reddish brown, consists

of a pair of solid elongated, inverted triangles pendent to the rim. RD 20, H (pres.) 7.0.

2. G1b 1401.9
HM, plain cream fabric tempered with medium grit. Exterior decoration, in dark brown, consists of a row of framed hatched triangles, interior decoration, in red, consists of oblique strokes pendent to the rim. RD 9, H (pres.) 4.9.

3. G2b 1201.35
HM, plain cream fabric tempered with medium grit. Exterior decoration, in reddish brown, consists of geometric pattern and a solid band on the top of rim. RD 20, H (pres.) 4.6.

4. G1d 1300.2
HM, plain cream fabric tempered with medium grit. Decoration, in reddish brown, consists of part of a wavy line above a hatched triangle on the exterior, and oblique strokes pendent to the interior rim. RD 9, H (pres.) 3.5.

5. G2b 1202.4
HM, pale pinkish brown fabric tempered with chaff and a little medium grit. Smoothed on both surfaces. Solid brown band painted on the top of rim. RD 24, H (pres.) 5.1.

6. G1d 1300.6
HM, plain cream fabric tempered with medium grit. Exterior decoration, in reddish brown, consists of a horizontal and wavy line, above a row of hatched triangles, and a solid band on the exterior rim edge. RD 13, H (pres.) 4.0.

7. G2b 1201.47.65
HM, plain cream fabric tempered with medium grit. Exterior decoration, in reddish brown, consists of horizontals above a row of hatched triangles. RD 20, H (pres.) 6.1.

8. G1d 1303.9
HM, plain cream fabric tempered with medium grit. Exterior decoration, in reddish brown, consists of a wavy line above a row of framed triangles each filled with a line. RD 10, H (pres.) 6.2.

9. G2b 1203.7
HM, creamy pink smoothed fabric tempered with medium grit. Exterior decoration, in reddish brown, consists of two horizontals. RD 22, H (pres.) 2.6.

10. G1d 1303.7
HM, plain cream fabric tempered with medium grit. Exterior decoration, in fugitive reddish brown, consists of horizontals and a wavy line. RD 14, H (pres.) 5.2.

11. G1d 1301.1
HM, tempered with medium grit. Pale pinkish brown throughout, smoothed exterior and interior. Exterior decoration, in reddish brown, consists of a linear design. RD 18, H (pres.) 5.3.

12. G1d 1301.1
HM, plain cream fabric tempered with medium grit. Exterior decoration, in reddish brown, consists of a linear design. RD 25, H (pres.) 3.6.

13. G1d 1303.40
HM, plain cream fabric tempered with medium grit. Decoration, in orange brown, consists of a row of hatched triangles on the exterior, and a series of strokes over the rim. RD 16, H (pres.) 6.4.

14. G1d 1304.5
HM, plain cream fabric tempered with medium grit. Exterior decoration, in red, consists of a wavy line above a row of hatched triangles. RD 24, H (pres.) 5.2.

Fig. 118

1. G2b 1200.1
HM, plain cream fabric tempered with medium grit. Exterior decoration, in reddish brown, consists of a row of hatched triangles, with three lines pendent to its base. RD 16, H (pres.) 6.1.

2. G2b 1201.40
HM, tempered with medium-fine grit. Pale creamy brown smoothed exterior, smoke blackened interior. Exterior decoration, in brown, consists of a horizontal and wavy line, above a framed row of hatched triangles. RD 8, H (pres.) 3.7. Previously published (French and Helms 1973: Fig. 5 no. 3).

3. G2b 1201.47
HM, tempered with medium grit. Cream throughout, smoothed exterior and interior. Exterior decoration, in tan, consists of a horizontal and wavy line, above a row of hatched triangles. Interior decoration, in fugitive tan, consists of elongated solid triangles set obliquely pendent to the rim. RD 30, H (pres.) 5.9.

4. G2b 1201.26
HM, tempered with medium grit. Cream throughout, smoothed exterior, plain interior. Exterior decoration, in orange cream, consists of carelessly painted horizontal and wavy lines, and a row of hatched triangles, top of the rim is decorated with short oblique strokes. RD 8, H (pres.) 4.3.

5. G2b 1201.26
HM, tempered with medium grit. Cream throughout, smoothed exterior and interior. Exterior decoration, in brownish cream, consists of a row of oblique lines round the belly. RD 12, H (pres.) 6.1.

6. G2b 1201.32
HM, tempered with medium grit. Cream fabric fired to greenish tinge, smoothed exterior, plain interior. Decoration, in black, consists of a row of framed oblique lines. RD 7, H 5.9. Previously published (French and Helms 1973: Fig. 5 no. 2).

7. G2b 1202.5
HM, plain cream fabric tempered with medium grit. Solid, double-notched lug set vertically at the rim. Exterior decoration, in red, consists of a horizontal and wavy line, above a parade of carelessly painted solid triangles. Top of rim has a series of oblique strokes, one of which continues down the back of lug. RD 18, H (pres.) 5.2.

8. G2b 1202.4
HM, tempered with medium grit. Cream exterior, pale brown interior, smoothed on both surfaces. Exterior decoration, in reddish brown, consists of a horizontal and wavy line, above a row of hatched triangles, and a band on the exterior rim edge. RD 19, H (pres.) 5.1.

9. G2b 1201.46
HM, plain cream fabric tempered with medium grit. Decoration, in brown, consists of a horizontal and wavy line, above a row of framed, hatched triangles on exterior, and oblique strokes pendent to the interior of rim. RD 21, H (pres.) 3.9.

10. G3b 1009.10
HM, tempered with medium-fine grit. Pale brown throughout, smoothed exterior and interior. Decoration, in fugitive black, consists of a linear design. RD 16, H (pres.) 5.9.

11. G2b 1203.3
    HM, tempered with medium grit. Pinkish cream throughout, smoothed on both surfaces. Exterior decoration, in reddish brown, consists of a row of framed, hatched triangles. RD 20, H (pres.) 5.2.
12. G1b 1304.5
    HM, plain cream fabric tempered with medium grit. Exterior decoration, in reddish brown, consists of a wavy and horizontal line. RD 19, H (pres.) 2.6.
13. G1b 1304.5
    HM, plain cream fabric tempered with medium grit. Interior decoration, in reddish brown, consists of oblique strokes pendent to the rim. RD 10, H (pres.) 3.6.
14. G1d 1303.18
    HM, plain cream fabric tempered with medium grit. Decoration, in red, consists of a carelessly painted wavy line on exterior, and broad, oblique strokes pendent to the rim. RD 20, H (pres.) 4.1.
15. G1d 1303.2
    HM, plain cream fabric tempered with medium grit. Decoration, in reddish brown, consists of part of a hatched triangle on exterior, and short strokes pendent to the interior of rim. RD 20, H (pres.) 2.4.
16. G1d 1303.7
    HM, plain cream fabric tempered with medium grit. Interior decoration, in reddish brown, consists of oblique strokes pendent to the rim. RD 24, H (pres.) 2.1.

Fig. 119

1. G1d 1303.18
   HM, plain cream fabric tempered with medium grit. Decoration, in reddish brown, consists of a series of oblique strokes pendent to the interior of rim, and a band on the exterior rim edge. RD 24, H (pres.) 2.5.
2. G2b 1201.15. HM or SW, fine fabric tempered with medium-fine grit. Pinkish cream throughout, smoothed interior and exterior. Decoration, in red, consists of a series of oblique strokes on the rim, and a band on the exterior rim edge. RD 42, H (pres.) 5.2.
3. G2b 1201.28
   HM, tempered with medium grit. Pale brown to grey smoothed exterior, pinkish buff plain interior. Decoration, in fugitive off-white, consists of oblique strokes pendent to the interior and exterior of rim. RD 18, H (pres.) 3.1.
4. G2b 1201.25
   HM, fine fabric tempered with medium-fine grit. Pinkish cream smoothed exterior, plain cream interior. Fugitive brown along the interior of rim. RD 10, H (pres.) 3.2.
5. G2b 1201.43
   HM, plain cream fabric tempered with medium grit. Decoration, in reddish brown, consists of oblique strokes pendent to the interior of rim. RD 18, H (pres.) 2.6.
6. G2b 1201.26.24
   HM, plain cream fabric tempered with medium grit. Traces of orange cream band on the top of rim. RD 39, H (pres.) 3.2.
7. G2b 1201.42
   HM, plain cream fabric tempered with medium grit. Decoration, in plum brown, consists of wavy and horizontal lines, and oblique strokes pendent to the rim on the exterior and interior. RD 16, H (pres.) 3.1.
8. G2b 1201.44
   HM, plain cream fabric tempered with medium grit. Traces of reddish brown linear design survives. RD 12, H (pres.) 3.0.
9. G2b 1201.32
   HM, tempered with medium grit. Light cream throughout, smoothed exterior and interior. Traces of brown oblique strokes pendent to interior rim. RD 18, H (pres.) 3.5.
10. G2b 1202.5
    HM, plain cream fabric tempered with medium grit. Decoration, in brown, consists of oblique strokes pendent to the interior of rim, and a band along the exterior rim edge. RD 20, H (pres.) 2.4.
11. G2b 1201.24
    HM, plain creamy grey fabric tempered with medium grit. Decoration, in brown, consists of oblique strokes pendent to the interior of rim, and a band along the exterior rim edge. RD 25, H (pres.) 2.9.
12. G2b 1203.3
    HM, tempered with medium grit. Pale tan burnished exterior, cream smoothed interior. Decoration, in reddish brown, consists of elongated solid triangles pendent to the interior of rim, and a band on the exterior rim edge. RD 28, H (pres.) 8.5.
13. G2b 1203.6
    HM, tempered with medium grit. Cream throughout, smoothed exterior and interior. Decoration, in reddish brown, consists of oblique solid triangles on the top of rim, and a band on the exterior rim edge. RD 32, H (pres.) 5.4.
14. G2b 1203.3
    HM, plain cream fabric tempered with medium grit. Decoration, in reddish brown, consists of a series of strokes pendent to the interior and exterior of rim. RD 24, H (pres.) 3.6.
15. G2b 1203.3
    HM, tempered with medium grit. Pinkish cream throughout, smoothed on both surfaces. Decoration, in red, consists of solid triangles obliquely pendent to the interior rim, and a band on the exterior rim edge. RD 30, H (pres.) 1.5.

Fig. 120.

1. G1d 1300.7
   HM, tempered with medium grit. Greyish cream throughout, smoothed exterior, plain interior. Exterior decoration, in brown, consists of a wavy and horizontal line above part of a hatched triangle, interior decoration consists of oblique strokes pendent to the rim. RD 21, H (pres.) 3.1.
2. G1d 1303.21
   HM, plain cream fabric tempered with medium grit. Decoration, in dark red, consists of elongated solid triangles obliquely pendent to the interior rim, and a band along the exterior rim edge. RD 10, H (pres.) 4.3.
3. G1b 1401.2
   HM, plain cream fabric tempered with medium grit. Decoration, in reddish brown, consists of a wavy and horizontal line below an inverted hatched triangle, and a band along the exterior rim edge. RD 20, H (pres.) 4.2.
4. G1d 1304.2
   HM, plain cream fabric tempered with medium grit. Decoration, in brown, consists of oblique

strokes pendent to the interior rim, and a band along the exterior rim edge. RD 15, H (pres.) 3.3.

5. G1d 1300.7
HM, tempered with medium grit. Cream throughout, smoothed exterior and interior. Interior decoration, in reddish brown, consists of oblique strokes pendent to the rim. RD 23, H (pres.) 3.0.

6. G1d 1304.2
HM, plain cream fabric tempered with medium grit. Decoration, in red, consists of oblique strokes pendent to the interior rim, and a horizontal and two dots on the exterior. RD 16, H (pres.) 3.0.

7. G1d 1304.8
HM, plain cream hard fabric tempered with medium grit. Exterior decoration, in red, consists of a wavy and horizontal line, above part of a framed, hatched triangle. RD 22, H (pres.) 7.9.

8. G1d 1304.5
HM, tempered with medium grit. Cream throughout, smoothed, patchily burnished exterior and interior. Vertical lug handle set at the rim. Decoration, in brown, consists of vertical strokes pendent to the interior rim, and part of a geometric design incorporating the lug. RD 15, H (pres.) 2.5.

9. G1d 1304.5
HM, plain cream fabric tempered with medium grit. Exterior decoration, in red, consists of a horizontal and wavy line above a row of hatched triangles. RD 20, H (pres.) 4.8.

10. G2b 1200.4
HM, plain cream fabric tempered with medium grit. Exterior decoration, in reddish brown, consists of a wavy and horizontal line, above a row of solid triangles. RD 12, H (pres.) 6.4.

11. G2b 1201.6
HM, plain cream fabric tempered with medium grit. Smoothed exterior, plain interior. Exterior decoration, in brown, consists of a row of haphazardly painted oblique lines. RD 15, H (pres.) 2.9.

12. G2b 1201.41
HM, plain cream fabric tempered with medium grit. Vertical lug handle set at rim. Exterior decoration, in brown, consists of short horizontals down both sides of the lug, interior decoration, in red, consists of oblique strokes pendent to the rim. RD 36, H (pres.) 4.6.

13. G2b 1201.47
HM, plain cream ware tempered with medium grit. Exterior decoration, in reddish brown, consists of a wavy line, part of a linear design, and a stroke on the rim. RD 16, H (pres.) 6.9.

14. G2b 1201.47
HM, tempered with medium grit. Cream fabric smoothed on exterior and interior. Decoration, in reddish brown, consists of wavy lines, and a stroke on the rim. RD 17, H (pres.) 6.8.

15. G2b 1201.25
HM, tempered with medium grit and a little chaff. Cream throughout, smoothed on both surfaces. A red band along the exterior rim edge. RD 20, H (pres.) 7.6.

16. G2b 1202.13
HM, plain cream fabric tempered with medium grit. Exterior decoration, in red, consists of a horizontal and wavy line, and oblique strokes on top of the rim. RD 10, H (pres.) 3.6.

Fig. 121

1. G2b 1302.13
HM, plain cream fabric tempered with medium grit. Decoration, in brown, consists of horizontals and a row of hatched triangles on the exterior, and vertical strokes pendent from the interior rim. RD 20, H (pres.) 7.8.

2. G2b 1202.13
HM, plain cream fabric tempered with medium grit. Traces of reddish brown decoration on the exterior rim. RD 38, H (pres.) 4.2.

3. G2b 1202.5
HM, plain cream fabric tempered with medium grit. Elongated vertical lug handle linking the rim to the base of neck. Decoration, in reddish brown, consists of a linear pattern carelessly painted on the lug. RD 26, H (pres.) 6.5.

4. G2b 1203.3
HM, plain cream fabric tempered with medium grit. Interior decoration, in reddish brown, consists of oblique strokes pendent to the rim. RD 28, H (pres.) 3.4.

5. G2b 1203.3
HM, tempered with medium grit. Cream throughout, smoothed exterior, plain interior. Exterior decoration, in reddish brown, consists of a bold linear design. RD 16, H (pres.) 10.3.

6. G1d 1300.7
HM, plain cream fabric tempered with medium grit. Decoration, in reddish brown, consists of a horizontal and wavy line, above a row of hatched triangles on the exterior, and a series of vertical strokes pendent to the interior rim. RD 22, H (pres.) 6.7.

7. G1d 1303.32
HM, plain cream fabric tempered with medium grit. Exterior decoration, in brown, consists of a part of a zig-zag and triangle(?) design, interior decoration, in orange buff, consists of vertical strokes pendent to the rim. RD 16, H (pres.) 1.6.

8. G1b 1303.29
HM, plain greyish cream fabric tempered with medium grit. Decoration, in dark red, consists of a horizontal and a pair of dots on the exterior, and oblique strokes pendent to the interior rim. RD 10, H (pres.) 2.6.

9. G1d 1303.7
HM, plain cream fabric tempered with medium grit. Horizontal ledge handle set at the rim. Decoration, in red, consists of broad strokes pendent to the interior rim, and a band along the exterior rim edge. RD 18, H (pres.) 2.7.

10. G1d 1303.20
HM, plain cream fabric tempered with medium grit. Exterior decoration, in reddish brown, consists of a horizontal and wavy line, above part of a series of hatched triangles. RD 12, H (pres.) 3.6.

11. G1d 1303.6
HM, fine fabric tempered with medium-fine grit. Cream throughout, smoothed exterior and interior. Red band on the interior rim. RD 20, H (pres.) 1.5.

12. G1d 1304.2
HM, plain cream fabric tempered with medium grit. Exterior decoration, in red, consists of a horizontal and wavy line, above a solid dot and part of a series of hatched triangles. RD 16, H (pres.) 4.9.

13. G1d 1303.18
HM, plain cream fabric tempered with medium

grit. Decoration, in reddish brown, consists of a wavy line and zig-zag on the exterior, and a frill design pendent to the interior rim. RD 18, H (pres.) 3.7.

Fig. 122

1. G1d 1304.2
HM, plain cream fabric tempered with medium grit. Exterior decoration, in red, consists of a horizontal and wavy line above a row of hatched triangles and a horizontal along the exterior rim edge. RD 16, H (pres.) 3.4.
2. G2b (sieving)
HM, plain cream fabric tempered with medium grit. Decoration in orange buff, consists of a wavy line above a row of hatched triangles on the exterior, and oblique strokes pendent to the interior rim. RD 26, H (pres.) 5.4.
3. G2b 1200.4
HM, plain cream fabric tempered with medium grit. A band, in fugitive reddish brown, along the exterior rim. RD 25, H (pres.) 7.2.
4. G2b 1201.25
HM, tempered with medium grit. Pinkish cream throughout, smoothed exterior, plain interior. A band, in fugitive reddish brown, along the exterior rim. RD 16, H (pres.) 3.3.
5. G2b 1201.16
HM, tempered with medium grit. Cream throughout, slipped exterior, smoothed interior. Exterior decoration, in orange, consists of a horizontal and wavy line, and oblique strokes pendent to the interior rim. RD 18, H (pres.) 3.1.
6. G2b 1201.19
HM, plain pinkish cream fabric tempered with medium grit. Decoration, in dark red, consists of strokes pendent to the interior rim. RD 16, H (pres.) 3.9.
7. G2b 1201.43
HM, tempered with medium grit. Cream throughout, smoothed on both surfaces. Interior decoration, in brown, consists of oblique strokes pendent to the interior rim. RD 21, H (pres.) 3.9.
8. G2b 1201.24
HM, plain cream fabric tempered with medium grit. Exterior decoration, in fugitive reddish brown, consists of a horizontal and wavy line. RD 26, H (pres.) 9.0. Previously published (French and Helms 1973: Fig. 5 no. 5).
9. G2b 1201.27
HM, tempered with medium grit. Greyish buff throughout, burnished exterior, smoothed interior. Exterior decoration, in reddish brown, consists of a horizontal and wavy line above a row of hatched triangles. Top of rim has a series of oblique strokes, and its exterior edge is highlighted by a solid band. D (pres.) 20, H (pres.) 9.6. Previously published (French and Helms 1973: Fig. 5 no. 4).
10. G2b 1201.32
HM, plain cream fabric tempered with medium grit. Exterior decoration, in brown, consists of a horizontal and wavy line above part of a row of triangles. RD 20, H (pres.) 7.8.

Fig. 123

1. G2b 1201.32
HM, tempered with medium grit. Cream throughout, smoothed exterior, plain interior.

Exterior decoration, in black, consists of a row of hatched triangles set between horizontal lines. RD 16, H (pres.) 11.1.
2. G2b 1201.41
HM, plain pale pinkish brown fabric tempered with medium grit. Exterior decoration, in fugitive red, consists of a horizontal and wavy line above a parade of sloping, solid triangles. RD 18, H (pres.) 4.6.
3. G2b 1201.21
HM, tempered with medium grit and a little chaff. Greyish cream smoothed exterior, plain pinkish buff interior. Exterior decoration, in brown, consists of a horizontal and wavy line above a row of hatched triangles. Top of rim is ornamented with oblique strokes. RD 24, H (pres.) 9.9.
4. G2b 1201.13
HM, plain cream fabric tempered with medium grit. Traces of reddish orange paint along the rim. RD 38, H (pres.) 7.6.
5. G2b 1201.26
HM, plain cream fabric tempered with medium grit. Decoration, in reddish brown, consists of a row of chevrons along the exterior rim and extending over its top. RD 24, H (pres.) 6.7.
6. G2b 1201.41
HM, tempered with medium grit. Pale grey throughout, burnished exterior, smoothed interior. Exterior decoration, in white, consists of a row of hatched triangles. RD 28, H (pres.) 11.4.
7. G2b 1201.15
HM, tempered with medium grit, grey core. Pale brown slightly burnished exterior, pale brown plain interior. Reddish brown band along the interior rim. RD 24, H (pres.) 3.0.
8. G2b 1201.19
HM, tempered with medium grit. Greyish cream throughout, smoothed on both surfaces. Decoration, in brown, consists of broad oblique strokes pendent to the interior rim. RD 15, H (pres.) 4.3.

Fig. 124

1. G2b 1201.24
HM, tempered with medium grit. Pinkish cream throughout, smoothed exterior, plain interior. Solid red band along the exterior rim. RD 26, H (pres.) 5.5.
2. G2b 1201.24
HM, plain cream fabric tempered with medium grit. Decoration, in orange buff, consists of a band along the exterior rim, and oblique strokes pendent to the interior rim. RD 13, H (pres.) 2.2.
3. G2b 1202.11
HM, plain cream fabric tempered with medium grit. Traces of a red band along the exterior rim. RD 14, H (pres.) 3.1.
4. G2b 1201.41
HM, tempered with medium grit. Pinkish cream throughout, smoothed exterior, plain interior. Exterior decoration, in red, consists of a geometric design, including a horizontal band of oblique lines round the shoulder. RD 16, H (pres.) 9.7. Previously published (French and Helms 1973: Fig. 4 no. 10).
5. G2b 1201.16
HM, plain pale creamy brown fabric tempered with medium grit. Exterior decoration, in brown, consists of a pair of horizontals along the rim.

10. G2b 1201.26
   HM, tempered with chaff and medium grit, cream throughout, smoothed exterior, plain interior. RD 28, H (pres.) 3.2.
11. G2b 1201.27
   HM, tempered with chaff and medium grit. Pinkish cream throughout, smoothed exterior and interior, grey streaks on the interior. RD 32, H (pres.) 5.6.
12. G2b 1201.31
   HM, tempered with chaff. Cream throughout, smoothed exterior and interior. RD 32, H (pres.) 4.8.
13. G2b 1201.33
   HM, tempered with medium grit, grey core. Cream throughout, cream slurry finish on the exterior and interior. RD 28, H (pres.) 3.3.

Fig. 130
1. G2b 1201.36
   HM, tempered with medium grit. Cream throughout, plain exterior and interior. RD 28, H (pres.) 3.6.
2. G2b 1201.39
   HM, coarse fabric tempered with chaff, grey core. Cream smoothed exterior, pinkish cream plain interior. RD 40, H (pres.) 7.2.
3. G2b 1201.43
   HM, tempered with medium grit. Cream throughout, smoothed exterior, plain interior. RD 26, H (pres.) 6.9.
4. G2b 1201.30
   HM, tempered with chaff and medium grit, grey core. Pinkish cream plain exterior and interior. RD 22, H (pres.) 4.6.
5. G2d 1100.6
   HM, tempered with chaff and medium grit, grey core. Pale pinkish brown throughout, smoothed exterior, plain interior. RD 21, H (pres.) 3.6.
6. G1b 1401.6
   HM, tempered with chaff and medium grit, dark grey core. Pale greyish cream plain exterior and interior. RD 17, H (pres.) 3.0.
7. G2b 1201.1.29
   HM, tempered with medium grit. Pinkish creamy throughout, smoothed exterior and interior. RD 24, H (pres.) 5.2.
8. G2b 1201.20
   HM, tempered with medium grit. Cream throughout, smoothed exterior and interior. RD 28, H (pres.) 5.1.
9. G2d 1100.6
   HM, tempered with chaff and a little medium grit, grey core. Pinkish cream smoothed exterior, pinkish cream plain interior. RD 23, H (pres.) 6.9.
10. G2b 1202.14
   HM, tempered with medium grit. Cream throughout, smoothed exterior and interior. RD 20, H (pres.) 6.6.
11. G2b 1201.9
   HM, tempered with chaff. Pale brown throughout, plain exterior and interior. RD 30, H (pres.) 6.7.

Fig. 131
1. G2b 1201.28
   HM, tempered with medium grit. Cream throughout, smoothed exterior and interior. RD 22, H (pres.) 4.4.

2. G2b 1201.46
   HM, tempered with medium grit. Pale cream throughout, smoothed exterior, plain interior. RD 18, H (pres.) 3.6.
3. G1d 1303.18
   Made on slow wheel, tempered with medium grit. Pinkish cream throughout, smoothed exterior and interior. RD 12, H (pres.) 3.3.
4. G2b 1201.13
   HM, tempered with medium grit. Cream throughout, smoothed exterior and interior. RD 6, H (pres.) 4.5.
5. G2b 1201.9
   HM, tempered with medium grit. Cream throughout, smoothed exterior, plain interior. RD 12, H (pres.) 5.2.
6. G2b 1201.24
   HM, tempered with medium grit, pinkish cream core. Plain cream exterior and interior. RD 16, H (pres.) 5.3.
7. G2b 1201.15
   HM, tempered with medium grit. Pinkish cream throughout, smoothed exterior and interior. RD 20, H (pres.) 5.9.
8. G1d 1300.10. WM, tempered with medium grit. Pale brownish cream throughout, plain exterior and interior. RD 15, H (pres.) 3.1.
9. G1d 1300.7
   HM, tempered with medium grit. Pinkish cream throughout, smoothed exterior, plain interior. RD 11, H (pres.) 3.6.
10. G3d 505.12
   HM, tempered with chaff. Pale brownish cream throughout, patchily smoothed exterior, plain interior. RD 26, H (pres.) 7.9.
11. G1d 1300.17
   HM, tempered with medium grit. Cream throughout, plain exterior and interior. RD 30, H (pres.) 4.6.
12. G1d 1303.18
   HM, tempered with medium grit. Cream throughout, plain exterior and interior. RD 17, H (pres.) 2.7.
13. G1d 1304.2
   HM, tempered with medium grit. Grey fabric, cream slipped exterior and interior. Both surfaces are plain. RD 22, H (pres.) 5.4.
14. G1d 1303.34
   HM, tempered with medium grit. Cream throughout, plain exterior and interior. Triangular ledge handle set at the rim. RD 26, H (pres.) 2.9.
15. G2b 1200.2
   HM, tempered with medium grit. Greyish cream throughout, smoothed exterior and interior. RD 32, H (pres.) 3.6.
16. G2b 1201.26
   HM, tempered with medium grit, grey core. Creamy buff exterior and interior, both surfaces are plain. RD 20, H (pres.) 3.6.
17. G2b 1202.14
   HM, tempered with medium grit. Cream throughout, smoothed exterior, plain interior. RD 16, H (pres.) 4.2.
18. G2b 1201.20
   HM, tempered with medium grit. Cream throughout, smoothed exterior, plain interior. Triangular ledge handle set at the rim. RD 26, H (pres.) 4.5.

Fig. 132

1. G2b 1201.21
   HM, fine fabric tempered with medium-fine grit. Pale pinkish cream, smoothed exterior, plain interior. RD 19, H (pres.) 6.9.
2. G2b 1201.24
   HM, tempered with chaff and medium grit. Cream throughout, plain exterior and interior. RD 18, H (pres.) 5.7.
3. G2b 1200.4
   HM, tempered with medium grit. Cream throughout, smoothed exterior, plain interior. RD 13, H (pres.) 2.1.
4. G2b 1201.24
   HM, tempered with medium grit. Cream throughout, smoothed exterior and interior. RD 16, H (pres.) 2.4.
5. G2b 1201.26
   HM, fine fabric tempered with medium-fine grit. Cream throughout, smoothed exterior, plain interior. RD 20, H (pres.) 4.8.
6. G2b 1201.70
   HM, tempered with medium grit. Cream throughout, smoothed exterior and interior. Triangular ledge handle set at the rim. RD 20, H (pres.) 3.6.
7. G2b 1201.32
   HM, tempered with medium grit. Cream throughout, smoothed exterior and interior. RD 22, H (pres.) 6.1.
8. G2b 1201.12
   HM, tempered with medium grit. Pinkish cream throughout, smoothed exterior, plain interior. RD 24, H (pres.) 4.3.
9. G2b 1202.5
   HM, tempered with medium grit. Cream throughout, smoothed exterior, plain interior. Triangular ledge handle set at the rim. RD 26, H (pres.) 8.1.
10. G2d 1102.4
    HM, tempered with chaff and medium grit. Pale pinkish brown throughout, smoothed exterior and interior. RD 21, H (pres.) 4.4.
11. G2d 1102.8
    HM, tempered with medium grit. Pale greyish cream throughout, smoothed exterior, plain interior. RD 17, H (pres.) 2.7.
12. G3b 1001.2
    HM, tempered with medium grit. Pale greyish cream throughout, plain exterior and interior. Solid knob below the rim. RD 22, H (pres.) 3.0.
13. G3b 1015.4
    HM, tempered with medium grit. Cream throughout, smoothed exterior and interior. RD 13, H (pres.) 3.3.
14. G1d 1303.20
    HM, tempered with medium grit. Cream throughout, smoothed exterior, plain interior. RD 23, H (pres.) 3.0.
15. G1d 1304.1
    HM, tempered with medium grit, grey core. Pale creamy brown, plain exterior and interior. RD 18, H (pres.) 2.6.

Fig. 133

1. G2b 1200.4
   HM, tempered with chaff and medium grit. Creamy brown plain exterior and interior. RD 27, H (pres.) 4.2.

2. G2b 1201.19
   HM, tempered with chaff and medium grit, grey core. Pale creamy brown smoothed exterior and interior. RD 32, H (pres.) 5.2.
3. G2b 1201.41
   HM, tempered with medium-fine grit. Pale greyish cream throughout, burnished exterior, smoothed interior. RD 39, H (pres.) 5.3.
4. G3d 507.3
   WM, tempered with medium grit. Pale pinkish brown throughout, smoothed exterior, plain interior. RD 34, H (pres.) 4.8.
5. G3b 1009.10
   WM, tempered with medium grit, pale pinkish brown throughout. RD 21, H (pres.) 2.1.
6. G2b 1201.4
   HM, tempered with medium-fine grit. Pale creamy brown throughout, smoothed exterior, plain interior. RD 4, H (pres.) 4.5.
7. G1b 1401.9
   WM, tempered with medium-fine grit, pinkish red throughout. RD 16, H (pres.) 3.3.
8. G1d 1303.10
   HM, tempered with medium-fine grit, cream throughout. RD 8, H (pres.) 3.0.
9. G2d 1102.9
   HM, tempered with medium grit, pinkish cream throughout. RD 7, H (pres.) 3.3.
10. G2d 1100.6
    WM, fine fabric tempered with fine grit, pale creamy brown throughout. BD 6, H (pres.) 2.4.
11. G2d 1104.1
    Hand moulded, tempered with medium grit, pale greyish brown throughout. W (max.) 41, H (pres.) 3.3.
12. G3b 1000.44
    HM, tempered with medium grit. Creamy brown throughout, smothed exterior and interior. BD 5.5., H (pres.)
13. G3d 506.40
    WM, fine fabric tempered with fine grit, pale creamy brown throughout. RD 20, H (pres.) 1.2.
14. G1d 1304.2
    WM, very fine hard fabric tempered with very fine grit, brown throughout. Decoration, in grey, consists of horizontals below the rim on the exterior and interior. Marked wheel striations on the interior. RD 14, H (pres.) 2.4.
15. G3b 1001.3
    WM, fine hard fabric tempered with fine grit. Pale orange brown throughout, burnished exterior and interior. A brown horizontal band below the rim decorates the exterior. RD 29, H (pres.) 5.7.
16. G3d 508.16
    WM, tempered with medium-fine grit, pale orange brown throughout. RD 13, H (pres.) 5.1.
17. G1d 1303.7
    WM, very fine hard fabric tempered with very fine grit, grey core. Reddish brown burnished exterior and interior. Dark brown horizontal bands decorate the edge of the exterior and interior rim. RD 20, H pres 2.8.
18. G2b 1201.37
    WM, very fine hard fabric tempered with very fine grit. Pale orange brown fabric washed in dark grey on the exterior. H (pres.) 6.3.

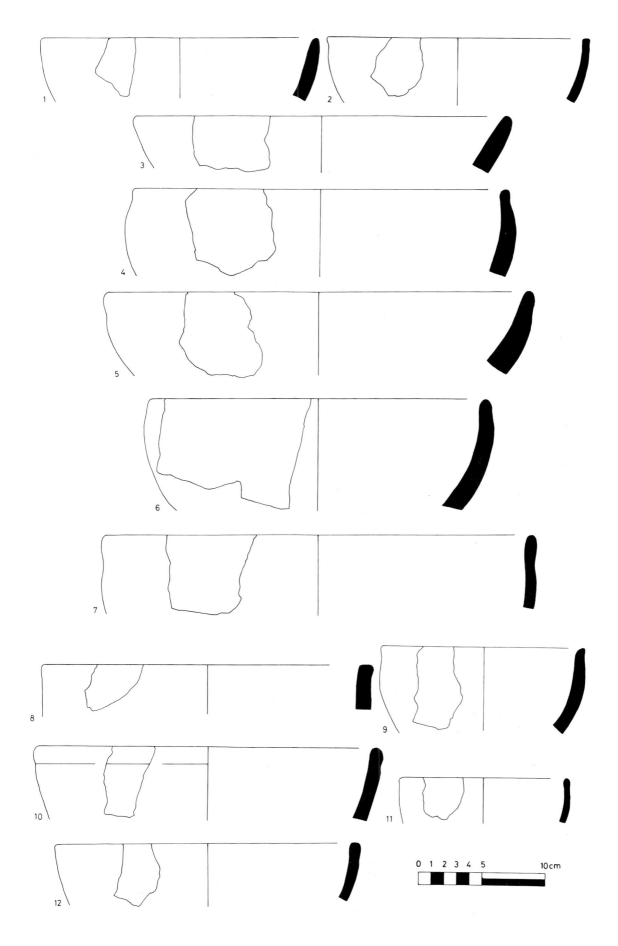

Fig. 139

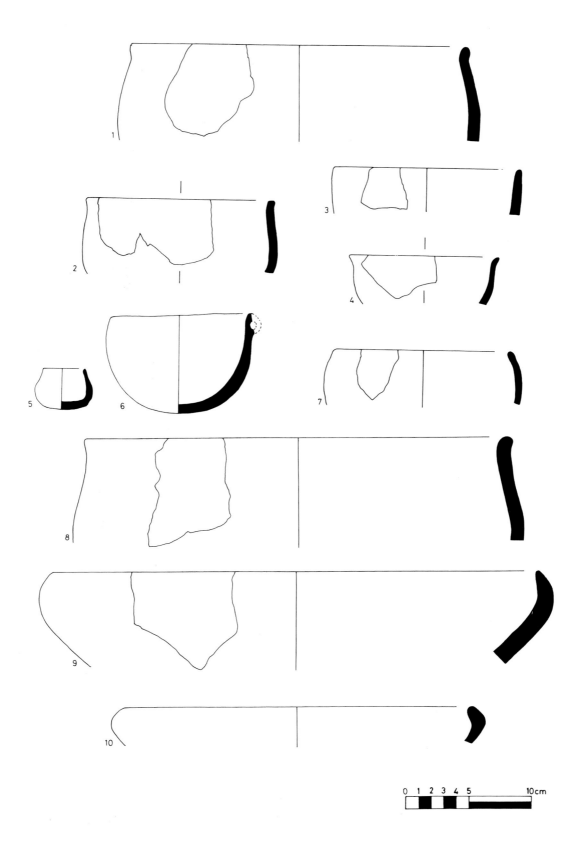

Fig. 140

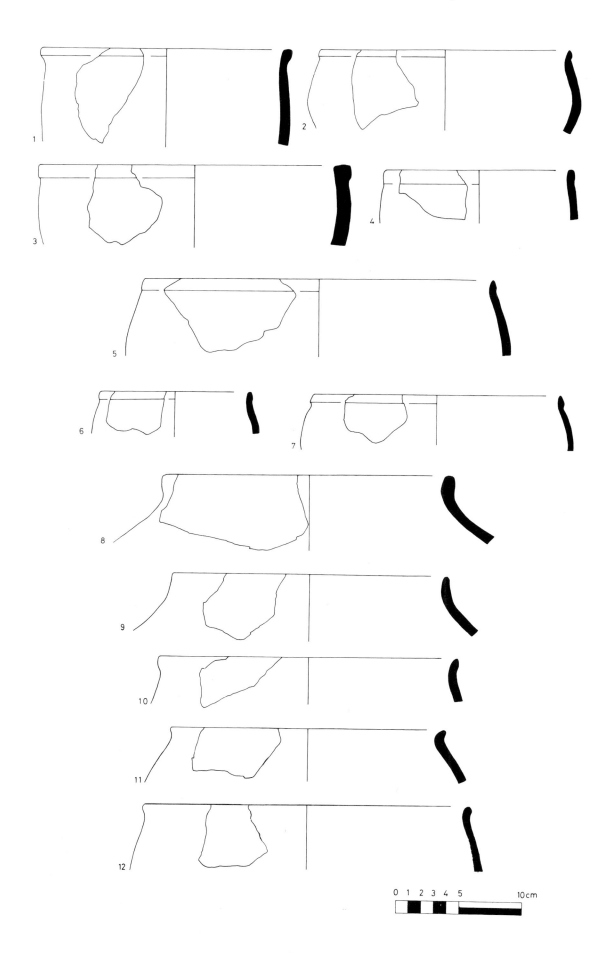

Fig. 141

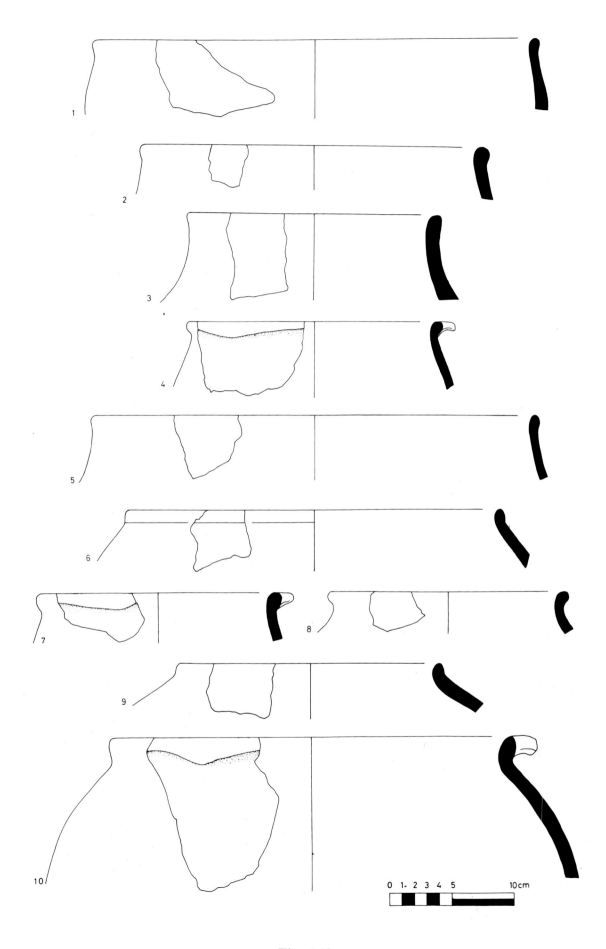

Fig. 142

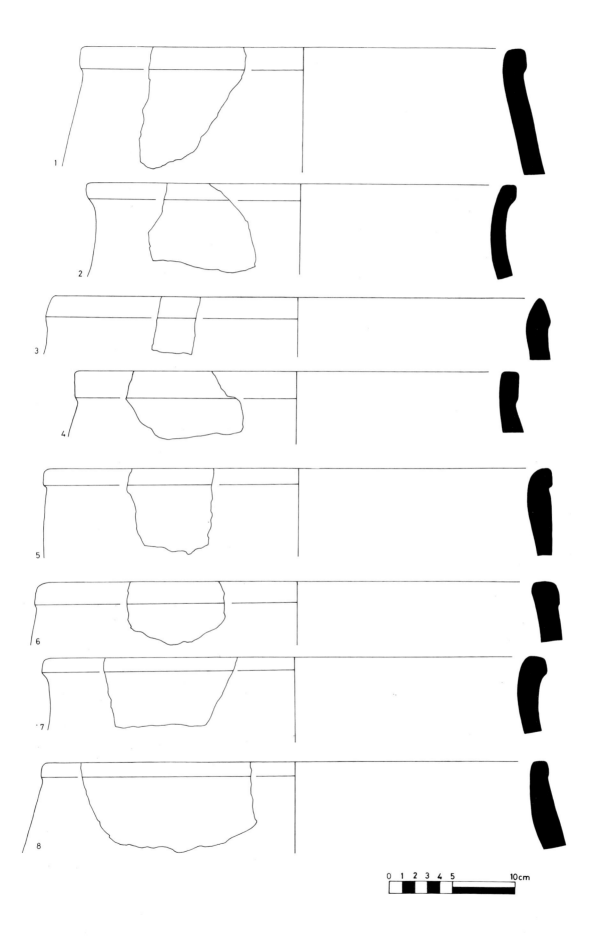

Fig. 151

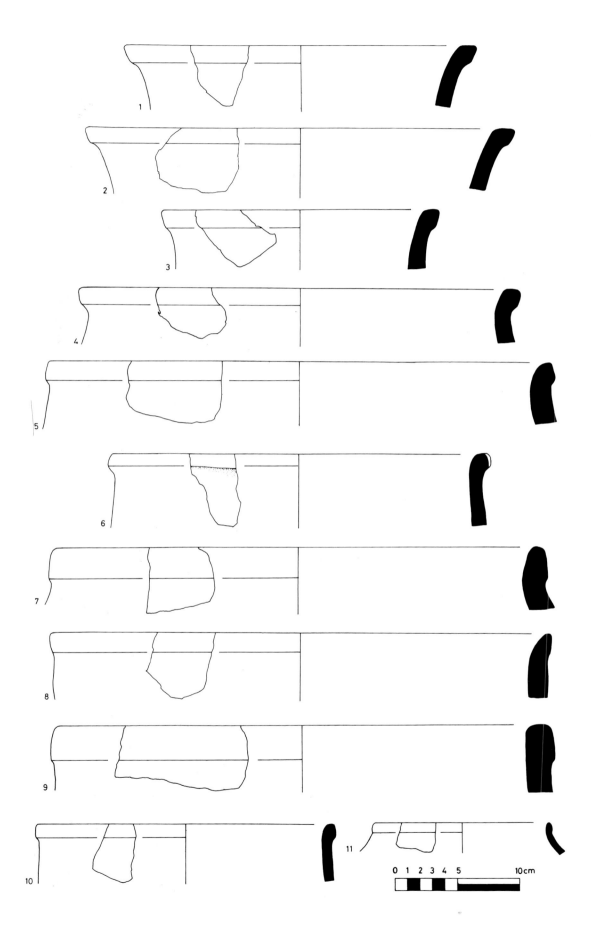

Fig. 152

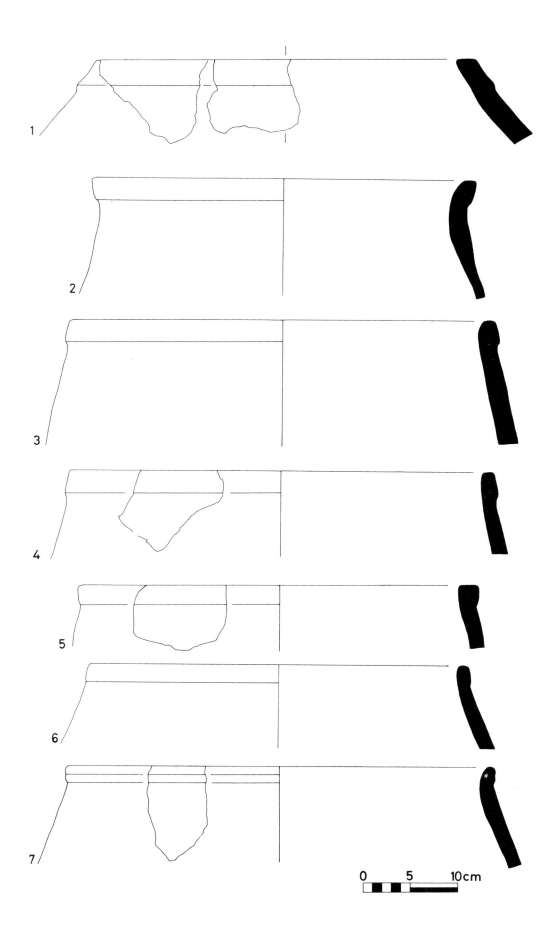

Fig. 153

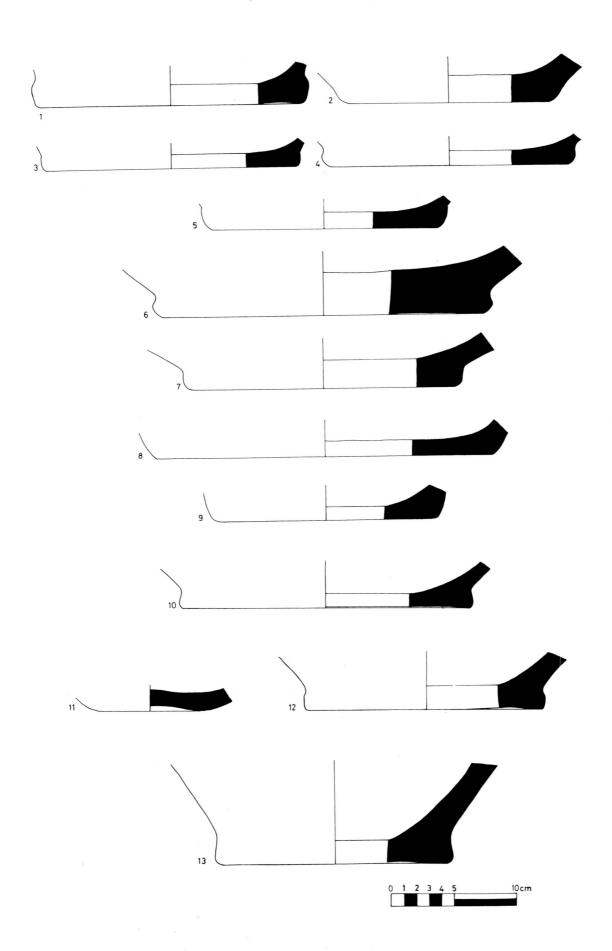

Fig. 154

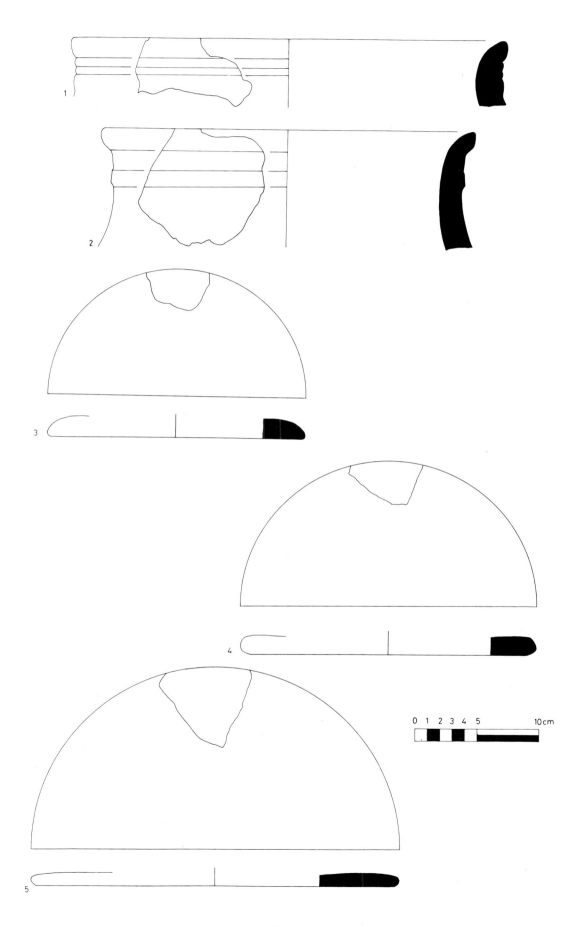

Fig. 155

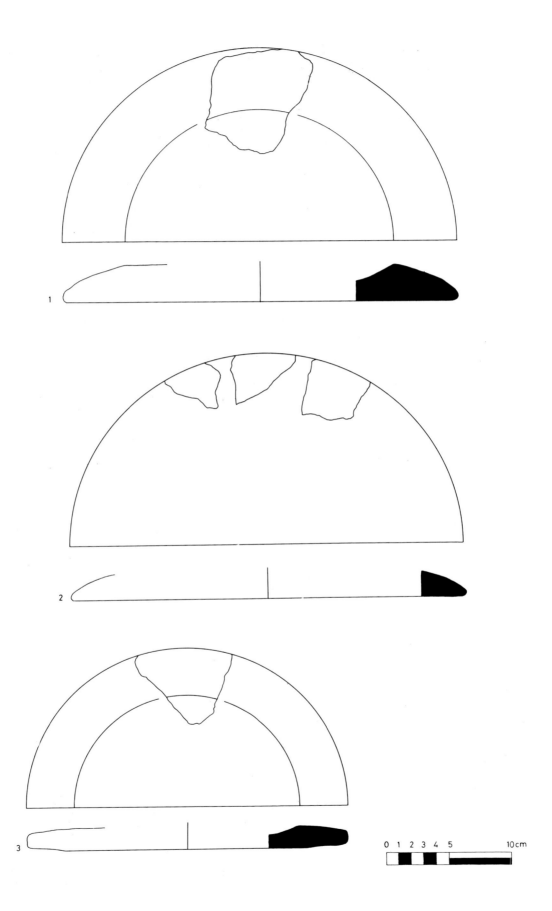

Fig. 156

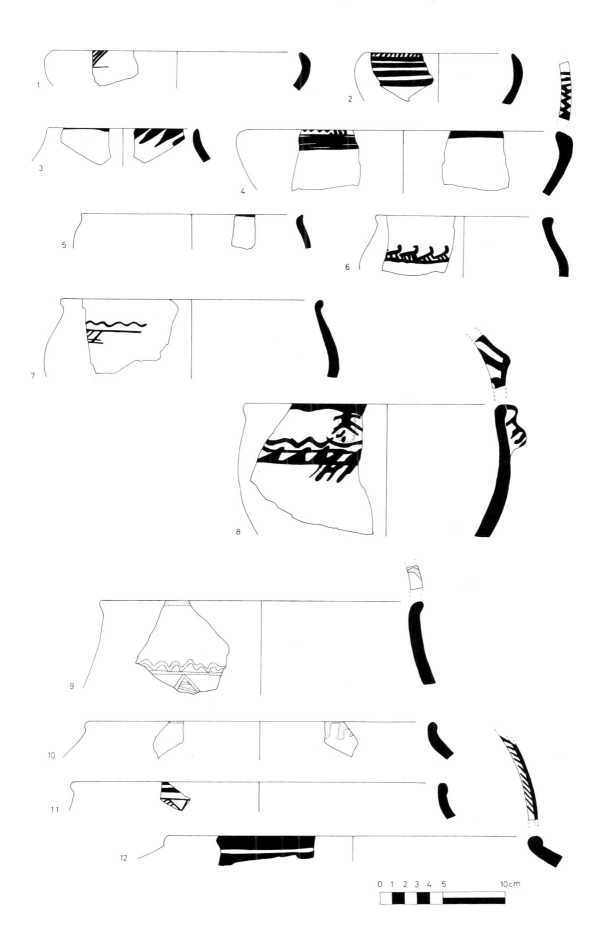

Fig. 157

Fig. 158

CATALOGUE OF OBJECTS FROM TAŞKUN KALE

Fig. 160

1. S9 1106.12

Bronze chisel in excellent condition. A square haft, an octagonal shaft, and a flattened and flaring chisel edge. L 16.1, W chisel edge 1.6, Th (max.) 1.3.

2. R10 1302.12

Flint projectile point in excellent condition with two wings and a shaft butt. Bifacially worked with fine flaking. L 3.1, W 2.5, Th (max.) 0.3.

TABLES

QUANTITY OF DIAGNOSTICS PER AREA

Type	TAŞKUN MEVKİİ							AŞVAN KALE								TAŞKUN KALE							
	J11	K10c	K10d	K11	L10c/d	Total	%	G1b	G1d	G2b	G2d	G3b	G3d	Total	%	R11	R12	S8	S9	S11	S12	Total	%
1	288	258	23	355	37	961	30.5	3	10	36	1	2	2	54	4.3	0	0	0	12	4	0	16	6.1
2	53	71	2	33	5	164	5.2	1	51	76	10	9	2	149	11.8	0	0	0	14	1	2	17	6.5
3	20	34	0	11	4	69	2.1	0	8	21	1	2	1	33	2.6	0	0	3	0	0	0	3	1.1
4	0	0	0	0	0	0	0	0	1	0	0	9	0	10	0.8	0	0	0	3	0	0	3	1.1
5	0	1	0	1	0	2	0	0	9	23	4	5	0	41	3.3	0	0	0	3	0	1	4	1.5
6	76	51	1	32	0	160	5	3	41	124	10	15	4	197	15.7	0	2	2	32	14	9	57	21.8
7	4	0	0	2	1	7	0.2	0	4	5	0	0	0	9	0.7	0	0	0	1	0	0	1	0.4
8	41	46	2	12	0	101	3.2	1	20	42	9	12	5	89	7	0	0	0	9	0	0	9	3.4
9	0	0	0	0	0	0	0	0	1	4	0	0	1	6	0.5	0	0	0	1	0	0	1	0.4
10	135	227	17	256	21	656	20.8	1	17	57	0	5	1	81	6.4	0	0	0	17	0	0	17	6.5
11	213	208	22	194	43	680	21.5	1	14	83	6	12	0	116	9.2	0	0	0	4	0	0	4	1.5
12	0	0	0	0	0	0	0	0	0	1	0	2	28	31	2.5	0	0	0	0	0	0	0	0
13	9	14	0	2	1	26	0.8	0	0	0	0	0	0	0	0	0	0	0	0	0	0	0	0
14	0	0	0	0	0	0	0	5	57	240	21	16	2	341	27.1	0	3	2	72	11	16	104	39.7
15	0	0	0	0	0	0	0	0	2	4	0	0	0	6	0.5	0	0	0	0	0	0	0	0
16	23	35	1	25	1	85	2.6	0	1	20	0	4	0	25	2	0	0	0	3	0	0	3	1.1
17	0	0	0	0	0	0	0	0	1	18	0	4	0	23	1.8	0	0	0	10	0	0	10	3.8
18	14	13	0	14	6	47	1.4	0	1	2	0	0	0	3	0.2	0	0	0	1	0	0	1	0.4
19	0	0	0	0	0	0	0	0	0	0	0	0	0	0	0	0	0	0	0	0	0	0	0
20	0	0	0	0	0	0	0	0	0	9	0	0	0	9	0.7	0	0	0	0	0	0	0	0
21	61	47	1	42	17	168	5.3	0	12	4	0	0	0	16	1.3	0	0	1	0	2	1	4	1.5
22	15	0	0	7	0	22	0.6	0	2	2	0	0	0	4	0.3	0	0	0	0	0	0	0	0
23	0	0	0	0	0	0	0	0	4	12	1	0	0	17	1.3	0	0	1	3	3	0	7	2.7
24	2	0	0	0	0	2	0	0	0	0	0	0	0	0	0	0	0	0	0	0	0	0	0
					Total:	3150							Total:	5							Total:	262	

TABLE 1
RED-BLACK BURNISHED WARE

QUANTITY OF DIAGNOSTICS PER AREA

Type	TAŞKUN MEVKİİ							AŞVAN KALE				TAŞKUN KALE		
	J11	K10c	K10d	K11	L10c/d	Total	%	Glb	Gld	Total	%	S9	Total	%
1	12	6	1	15	0	34	5.2	0	0	0	0	0	0	0
2	14	12	1	20	5	52	7.9	0	0	0	0	0	0	0
3	0	18	0	0	0	18	2.8	0	0	0	0	0	0	0
4	5	23	0	2	0	30	4.6	0	0	0	0	0	0	0
5	4	7	0	17	0	28	4.2	0	0	0	0	0	0	0
6	2	3	0	3	0	8	1.2	0	2	2	40	0	0	0
7	10	5	0	13	1	29	4.4	0	0	0	0	0	0	0
8	80	67	2	55	4	208	31.9	0	0	0	0	0	0	0
9	2	14	1	20	0	37	5.6	0	0	0	0	0	0	0
10	3	1	0	4	0	8	1.2	2	0	2	40	0	0	0
11	1	8	0	3	0	12	1.8	0	0	0	0	0	0	0
12	22	22	4	37	2	87	13.3	0	0	0	0	0	0	0
13	2	0	0	0	1	3	0.4	0	0	0	0	0	0	0
14	1	0	0	3	0	4	0.6	0	0	0	0	0	0	0
15	7	1	0	1	0	9	1.3	0	0	0	0	0	0	0
16	0	1	0	1	0	2	0.3	0	0	0	0	0	0	0
17	20	18	3	29	0	70	10.7	0	0	0	0	1	1	100
18	6	1	0	0	1	8	1.2	0	1	1	20	0	0	0
19	3	0	0	2	0	5	0.7	0	0	0	0	0	0	0
						Total: 652				Total: 5			Total: 6	

TABLE 2
PLAIN SIMPLE WARE

QUANTITY OF DIAGNOSTICS PER AREA

	TAŞKUN MEVKİİ						
Type	J11	K10c	K10d	K11	L10c/d	Total	%
1	0	5	0	2	0	7	43.7
2	3	2	0	4	0	9	56.2
					Total:	16	

TABLE 3
RESERVED SLIP WARE

	TAŞKUN MEVKİİ			AŞVAN KALE							
Type	K11	Total	%	Glb	Gld	G2b	G2d	G3b	G3d	Total	%
1	1	1	100	0	0	0	0	0	0	1	12.5
2	0	0	0	0	1	0	0	0	0	1	12.5
3	0	0	0	0	0	0	0	1	0	1	12.5
4	0	0	0	0	0	1	0	0	0	1	12.5
5	0	0	0	1	0	0	0	0	0	1	12.5
6	0	0	0	1	0	0	0	0	0	1	12.5
7	0	0	0	0	0	0	0	1	1	2	25
	Total:	1							Total:	8	

TABLE 4
SIMPLE AND PAINTED SIMPLE WARE

	TAŞKUN MEVKİİ						
Type	J11	K10c	K10d	K11	L10c/d	Total	%
	0	0	0	7	0	7	100
					Total:	7	

TABLE 5
PAINTED BEIGE-BROWN WARE

QUANTITY OF DIAGNOSTICS PER AREA

	TAŞKUN MEVKİİ						
Type	J11	K10c	K10d	K11	L10c/d	Total	%
1	0	1	0	1	0	2	6.4
2	2	0	0	1	0	3	9.6
3	0	2	0	5	0	7	22.5
4	2	0	0	4	0	6	19.3
5	1	0	0	3	0	4	12.9
6	4	0	0	0	0	4	12.9
7	1	0	0	1	0	1	3.2
8	0	0	0	1	0	1	3.2
9	1	0	0	0	0	1	3.2
10	1	0	0	1	0	1	3.2
11	1	0	0	0	0	1	3.2
					Total:	31	

TABLE 6
PERIPHERAL NINEVITE 5

	AŞVAN KALE								TAŞKUN KALE					
Type	G1b	G1d	G2b	G2d	G3b	G3d	Total	%	S8	S9	S11	S12	Total	%
1	0	3	15	0	0	0	18	10.9	0	0	0	0	0	0
2	0	1	0	0	0	0	1	0.6	0	0	0	0	0	0
3	0	4	9	0	0	0	13	7.8	0	0	0	0	0	0
4	0	0	0	0	0	0	0	0	1	2	0	0	3	23
5	1	3	4	0	0	0	8	4.8	0	1	0	1	2	15.4
6	2	4	5	0	0	0	11	6.7	0	0	0	0	0	0
7	0	13	13	0	0	0	26	15.8	1	3	0	0	4	30.8
8	2	11	12	0	0	0	25	15.2	0	0	0	0	0	0
9	0	19	43	0	1	0	63	38.2	0	3	0	1	4	30.8
					Total	165						Total	13	

TABLE 7
MALATYA-ELAZIG PAINTED WARE

QUANTITY OF DIAGNOSTICS PER AREA

	AŞVAN KALE								TAŞKUN KALE			
Type	G1b	G1d	G2b	G2d	G3b	G3d	Total	%	S9	S11	Total	%
1	0	3	17	0	0	0	20	16.5	1	0	1	16.7
2	0	0	14	0	0	0	14	11.6	0	0	0	0
3	0	0	1	0	0	0	1	0.8	0	0	0	0
4	0	0	2	0	0	0	2	1.6	1	0	1	16.7
5	0	0	6	0	0	0	6	5	0	0	0	0
6	0	6	15	0	0	0	21	17.4	0	0	0	0
7	0	6	33	0	0	0	39	32.2	3	0	3	50
8	0	2	8	0	0	0	10	8.3	1	0	1	16.7
9	0	2	0	0	0	0	2	1.6	0	0	0	0
10	0	1	4	0	1	0	6	5	0	0	0	0
						Total:	121			Total:	6	

TABLE 8
PLAIN CREAM WARE

Malatya		Murat basin					Norşuntepe	Altınova plain			Karababa	
Arslantepe	Gelincik-tepe	Taşkun Mevkii	Aşvan Kale	Taşkun Kale	Pulur	Han İbrahim Şah	Norşuntepe	Korucutepe	Tepecik	Değirmentepe	Hassek Höyük	Kurban Höyük
VID			Trench G3b	Trenches S9 and	?	V VII	EB III 7 'EB II' 13	F E	EB III Trenches 10-12, Levels 2-5			
VIC (pits)	Painted Ware		G2b	S11	I VIII	VIII X	14 22 23	D	EB II Trenches 14 I-K	I II		IV
VIB2		1	?	?	IX	XI	24	C		III	1	V
VIB1 post structures		4			X1	XIV	26		EB I	IV	4	
VIA Uruk-related Pottery							Hiatus		Late Chalc. Trenches 14-17, Buildings 1-2		C 5 A	VI

TABLE 9

CHRONOLOGICAL CORRELATIONS OF SITES IN THE TURKISH EUPHRATES BASIN